EFFECTIVE DATA VISUALIZATION

SAGE was founded in 1965 by Sara Miller McCune to support the dissemination of usable knowledge by publishing innovative and high-quality research and teaching content. Today, we publish over 900 journals, including those of more than 400 learned societies, more than 800 new books per year, and a growing range of library products including archives, data, case studies, reports, and video. SAGE remains majority-owned by our founder, and after Sara's lifetime will become owned by a charitable trust that secures our continued independence.

Los Angeles | London | New Delhi | Singapore | Washington DC | Melbourne

EFFECTIVE DATA VISUALIZATION

THE RIGHT CHART FOR THE RIGHT DATA

Stephanie D. H. Evergreen

Evergreen Data & Evaluation, LLC

Los Angeles | London | New Delhi
Singapore | Washington DC | Melbourne

FOR INFORMATION:

SAGE Publications, Inc.
2455 Teller Road
Thousand Oaks, California 91320
E-mail: order@sagepub.com

SAGE Publications Ltd.
1 Oliver's Yard
55 City Road
London EC1Y 1SP
United Kingdom

SAGE Publications India Pvt. Ltd.
B 1/I 1 Mohan Cooperative Industrial Area
Mathura Road, New Delhi 110 044
India

SAGE Publications Asia-Pacific Pte. Ltd.
3 Church Street
#10-04 Samsung Hub
Singapore 049483

Acquisitions Editor: Helen Salmon
Editorial Assistants: Anna Villarruel and Nicole
                                   Wineman
Production Editor: Veronica Stapleton Hooper
Copy Editor: Janet Ford
Typesetter: C&M Digitals (P) Ltd.
Proofreader: Dennis W. Webb
Indexer: Jean Casalegno
Cover Designer: Rose Storey
Marketing Manager: Susannah Goldes
eLearning Editor: John Scappini

Printed in the United States of America

Library of Congress Cataloging-in-Publication Data

Names: Evergreen, Stephanie D. H., author.

Title: Effective data visualization : the right chart for the right data / Stephanie D.H. Evergreen, Evergreen Data & Evaluation, LLC.

Description: Los Angeles : SAGE, [2017] | Includes bibliographical references and index.

Identifiers: LCCN 2015045992 | ISBN 9781506303055 (pbk. : alk. paper)

Subjects: LCSH: Visual communication. | Charts, diagrams, etc. | Presentation graphics software. | Graphic design (Typography) | Information visualization.

Classification: LCC P93.5 E937 2017 | DDC 302.2/22—dc23
LC record available at http://lccn.loc.gov/2015045992

This book is printed on acid-free paper.

Certified Chain of Custody
SUSTAINABLE FORESTRY INITIATIVE
Promoting Sustainable Forestry
www.sfiprogram.org
SFI-01268
SFI label applies to text stock

17 18 19 20 10 9 8 7 6 5 4 3

• BRIEF CONTENTS •

• DETAILED CONTENTS •

• ACKNOWLEDGMENTS •

When I wrote my first book, I holed myself away at a silent retreat center with no Internet or phone access. I was incredibly productive in that space. This time around, due to the success of the first book, I no longer have a few free days in a row where I can afford to isolate myself. With this book, I've had to write it on airplanes, in airport lounges, at coffee shops in new cities, and in hotel rooms. In each of those places, I had massive support from the people in the service industry who so often go underappreciated, but who did so much to make sure my needs were taken care of and I could just write. This book is for the airline stewards, bartenders, baristas, bed and breakfast managers, servers, and cabbies who made my life easier. They are probably the last people who would use anything I have written in these pages. Similarly, this book is for my parents and friends and family who have cooked meals and taken wonderful care of my son and generally made it possible for me to squirrel away in a room with my laptop and some data.

As always, I'm ever grateful to the support of my colleagues at SAGE, Anna Villarruel and Helen Salmon, as well as the input from generous peer reviewers:

David Boyns, California State University at Northridge

Thomas Cappaert, Rocky Mountain University of Health Professions

Michael G. Elasmar, Boston University

John O. Elliott, The Ohio State University and Ohio Health Research Institute

Brian Frederick, Bridgewater State University

David Han, University of Texas at San Antonio

Daniel Hawes, Kent State University

Mindy Hightower King, Indiana University

Kamir Kouzekanani, Texas A&M University–Corpus Christi

Jodi F. Paroff, NYU Robert F. Wagner Graduate School of Public Service

Shun-Yung Kevin Wang, University of South Florida—St. Petersburg

Jenny Lyons and Dan Kalleward are two of the best assistants anyone could want. Awesome people like Andy Cotgreave, Stuart Henderson, Stephen Few, Danyel Fisher, Viki Lorraine, Gavin McMahon, Patricia Rogers, Eric Walker, and Carl Westine gave input on sections of this book and invariably made it better. Finally, my stellar clients and colleagues contributed their own (often bad—but then improved!) work for public scrutiny and that is hard and brave and I'm grateful.

• ABOUT THE AUTHOR •

 **Dr. Stephanie D. H. Evergreen** is a sought-after speaker, designer, and researcher. She is best known for bringing a research-based approach to helping others better communicate their work through more effective graphs, slides, and reports. She holds a PhD from Western Michigan University in interdisciplinary research, which included a dissertation on the extent of graphic design use in written data reporting. Dr. Evergreen has trained audiences worldwide through keynote presentations and workshops for clients, such as Verizon, Head Start, American Institutes for Research, Brookings Institute, the Ad Council, Boys and Girls Club of America, and the United Nations. She led the first known attempt to revamp the quality of presentations for an entire association: the Potent Presentations Initiative for the American Evaluation Association (AEA). She is the 2015 recipient of the AEA's Marcia Guttentag Promising New Evaluator Award, which recognizes early notable and substantial accomplishments in the field. Dr. Evergreen is coeditor and coauthor of two issues of *New Directions for Evaluation* on data visualization. She writes a popular blog on data presentation at StephanieEvergreen.com. Her book, *Presenting Data Effectively: Communicating Your Findings for Maximum Impact,* was published by SAGE in Fall 2013 and was listed as number one in Social Science Research on Amazon in the United States and United Kingdom for several weeks.

1

OUR BACKBONE

WHY WE VISUALIZE

This chapter contains our justification for spending our time, energy, and resources on fiddling with our graphs. We address the very foundation of data visualization and the choices we need to make about the best chart type to use, and when to use it. This is the backbone of our work to visualize data, the reasoning we need to deliver to our boss when she or he asks why we are still dabbling in Excel when the report is due.

WHY WE VISUALIZE

What's your point?

Seriously, that's the most important question to ask when creating a data visualization. It's the first thing I ask a client who sends me data for redesign. And it's the primary reason we visualize: Because we have a point to communicate to the world. We have a compelling finding to share, a big idea revealed in our analysis that we need to say to people. A point.

Articulating the point generates an answer which drives nearly everything about visualizing that data. Here's how the conversation often goes:

Client: "Thanks for working with us, Stephanie. We have these data from parents and students and right now they are in a bar graph and we are certain it could be displayed better, we just aren't sure how" (see Figure 1.1).

Me: "I can help with that, Client! What's your point?"

Client: "Excuse me?"

Me: "What's the point of showing this data about parent and student perspectives? Right now, it looks like you want people to compare parents and students. Is that your point?"

Client: "Actually, no. And that's the most clarifying question you could have asked. Our point is that generally we expect students to report higher than parents on all of these questions, but our data showed that the students' expectations to go to college were way lower than their parents' expectations. That set off some alarm bells for us."

And this is when I silently pump my fist in the air because the client answered the most important question and now I know how to better display this data.

FIGURE 1.1   Traditional clustered bar graphs can cloud the point.

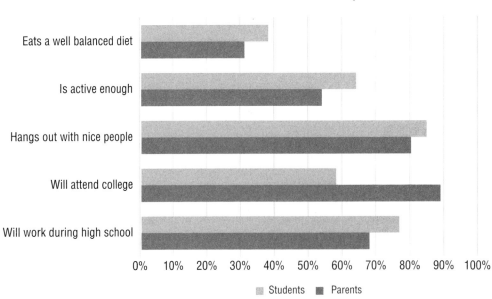

Parent v. Student Perspectives

Me (after I catch my breath from all that fist pumping):	"The first thing we are going to do, then, is take what you just said, and make it the headline of the graph. We are going to replace this generic title with your main point. The next thing we will do is swap out a different graph type, maybe something like a slopegraph since those are pretty good at highlighting when one thing is decreasing a lot and the rest are going up. Give me a day to play with some ideas and let's talk tomorrow."

The Next Day

Me:	"Good morning, Client! What did you think of that slopegraph I sent you (see Figure 1.2)?"
Client:	"It really does say exactly what we originally thought we needed to show. But, I talked to my colleagues after our call yesterday and asked them 'What's the point?' We decided that the real bottom-line point was that so few students have expectations to go to college. Forget the

FIGURE 1.2   Slopegraphs are one way to compare two groups on multiple variables.

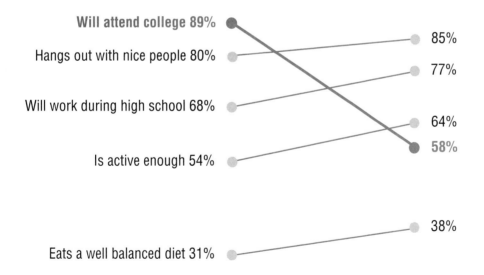

Surprisingly, students have lower expectations to go to college than their parents.

parents—that's a secondary issue right now. 'What's the point?' really helped us hone our thinking."

Me: "Ah well in that case, you have other options for showing that point." (Telepathically sends new visual possibilities a la Figure 1.3) "Maybe one of these?"

Client: "These are both right to the point. We will choose one today."

FIGURE 1.3   A single large number or a simple pie chart are two possible ways to help readers remember one important number.

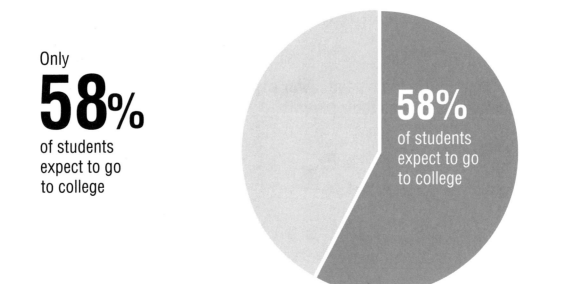

Only

58%

of students
expect to go
to college

58%
of students
expect to go
to college

Figuring out your point sharpens the thinking and the messaging surrounding the data, and in doing so reveals the best way to visualize the data. When you get stuck with your graph, keep asking "What's the point?" If you find you don't have a point, you probably shouldn't bother with graphing the data. We visualize to communicate a point.

We also visualize to add legitimacy or credibility. People are persuaded by numbers and stories (de Graaf & Hustinx, 2011; Kosara & Mackinlay, 2013). When we can combine those things and tell stories with numbers, we have a communication powerhouse.

The research tells us that data are more persuasive when shown in graphs. Pandey, Manivannan, Nov, Satterthwaite, and Bertini (2014) presented mildly controversial topics to study participants. Some of the topic narrative contained simple column graphs, and some contained the same information in tables. The participants who saw it in graph format showed greater attitude change, particularly those who didn't have strong beliefs about the controversy beforehand. In other words, people are more persuaded when they see data visually represented. In a super cool related study on political beliefs, Nyhan and Reifler (2013) found that misperception decreases when people are presented with (accurate) graphic representations of political information. One factor may be that we are primarily visual beings and that most of us, most of the time, are skimming the narrative for things that pop out at us and catch our attention (Evergreen, 2013). Data visualization does just that—it provides the pop.

Graphs and formulas seem to add credibility to data, even if they don't contain any new insights beyond what already exists in the narrative. Tal and Wansink (2014) experimented by including a graph (or a scientific formula) in materials about medication efficacy. They found that people who read the study materials believed the medications were more effective when the materials included a graph—even if the graph didn't contain substantial or additional information.

Of course, we use this power for good—to give more support and add credibility to our carefully researched points. But, the same tools can be used to deceive.

WHEN VISUALIZATION IS HARMFUL

At best, data visualization errors are unintentional mistakes that lead to misinformation. At worst, they are purposeful manipulations designed to influence the story a graph can tell. Elements like the scale of the axis or the size and shape of the graph can distort data and produce interpretation errors.

For example, take the advertisement in Figure 1.4, which arrived in my mail one day. Note how the y-axis begins at $5.50. This truncated axis cuts off most of the length of the columns so that it appears that the difference between Consumers and IGS Energy is greater than it really is. These errors create situations where data visualization is deceptive.

FIGURE 1.4   In a column graph, the axis should always start at 0. Otherwise the length of the bars sends a distorted message.

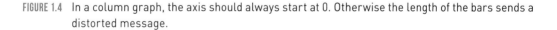

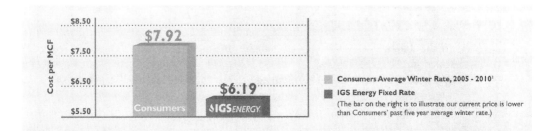

Changing aspects of the graph can lead to deception, whether intentional or benign. Pandey, Rall, Satterthwaite, Nov, and Bertini (2015) ran a study that included regular and distorted data visualizations. They manipulated the aspect ratio of the graph and the y-axis in a couple different ways, and compared perceptions of these to the same data in nondistorted graphs. The results were staggering: " . . . the distorted charts lead to responses between 58.5% and 129.5% bigger than the control condition" (p. 9). The effects were especially pronounced for line graphs. That said, there are justifiable reasons for truncating the y-axis on a line graph and we will dig into this topic in Chapter 9. In such cases, the truncation is intentional, to better support honest decision making. It's a fine line to walk, because we must keep in mind that any alteration to the graph to change its shape can also alter the conclusions that can be drawn. Alteration to support decision making can be warranted. But, distortion is real, common, and harmful.

Data visualization is a powerful tool for communicating information. Thus, it is in everyone's best interest to learn how to display data in the best, most accurate way possible.

WHICH CHART TYPE IS BEST?

The surest way to defend against distortions and misrepresentations is to turn to the research about which type of graphs people interpret with accuracy. The foundational research in this area comes from Cleveland and McGill (1984). Parts of this research have been replicated or clarified in later research, which I mention in other chapters where it is relevant.

Cleveland is one of the grandfathers of data visualization, publishing pretty prolifically. Leading up to the 1984 publication, he ran many small studies testing how study subjects interpreted different graph types, essentially trying to figure out which graphs were the easiest and most accurate for people to understand. Easy and accurate. That's a nice goal, eh? Together with McGill, he published a hierarchy of graph types, placing the easiest and most accurate type of graphs at the top to the most confusing and error producing at the bottom (see Figure 1.5).

At the top of Figure 1.5, Cleveland and McGill showed that position on a common scale was the easiest visualization for people to interpret with accuracy. Position on a common scale? What does that look like? At the core, we are talking about dots on a line. You might be scratching your head on this one, or wondering if they meant a scatterplot. Excel's default chart options don't really include a graph type that reflects position on a common scale, but I introduce you to some in Chapter 3.

Next best, they said, is position on nonaligned scales. This means that if we have two graphs of dots, side by side, we can compare and interpret them pretty well, as long as the scales are the same. The key here to me is that the scales have to be the same, otherwise that is part of what can be manipulated to misrepresent data. Still, I realize this isn't totally helpful information yet. Hang in there.

FIGURE 1.5   Cleveland and McGill offer a hierarchy of graph types, from the most to the least accurate.

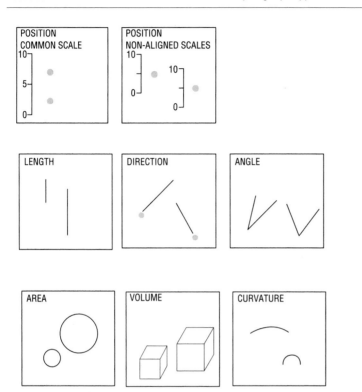

SOURCE: Adapted from Cleveland, W. S., & McGill, R. (1984). Graphical perception: Theory, experimentation, and application to the development of graphical methods. *Journal of the American Statistical Association, 79*(387), 531–554.

Below that level, we see length, direction, and angle. Length *is* how we encode column and bar charts. People are good at interpreting length accurately. Direction represents line charts, and newer visualizations like slopegraphs. Angle is how pie charts display data. The researchers ran several small studies just using these three types of graphs to see how this order was going to shake out. They found that, time and again, angle produced the most errors. Pie charts produced the most errors.

You'd think the pain would stop there, but it gets worse. Turns out humans are super bad at interpreting area, volume, and curvature—the graph types shown at the bottom of the figure. Area is found in visuals like bubble graphs. Volume is anything 3D. Curvature is how we would interpret a donut chart and other visualizations that can look more like art. The research does not support their functional use, but I will show the narrow acceptable uses of these graph types in other chapters.

Also listed at the bottom of this group is shading . . . but I've placed it off to the side of the hierarchy on purpose. Back in 1984, the only way researchers had to shade graphs was that terrible cross-hatching pattern fill. That sort of shading caused optical illusions in readers; Tufte (2001) called this a moiré effect. Yikes! Thankfully, technology continues to evolve and increase our capability to visualize with color. Research now shows that people can distinguish between four shades of one color before things start to get difficult (Ware, 2013).

The point is that we should be striving to graph as high up in this hierarchy as possible so that it is easy for our audience to interpret our visualizations accurately. That said, we can't and shouldn't make everything into bar graphs. In addition to this hierarchy, our decision on which graph type to choose is based on the story we need to tell about the data.

HOW TO USE THIS BOOK

I wrote this book to help your data stories shine. A huge part of telling the right story is knowing how to pick the right type of graph. If you Google "Chart Chooser," you will find a handful of other attempts to help you determine your graphing options. They all fall short for me mainly because they are created from the point of view of a data visualization-ist (visualizer? vizard?). By that I mean they group chart types into broad categories like "Distribution," which is not a user-friendly way to help you make your path down a decision tree. Few students, academics, researchers, office workers, or even data junkies think in terms of "oh I have a distribution here." Rather, my audiences think in terms of the stories they have to tell, and the things they need the audience to do when viewing the data.

It's those stories that make up this table of contents. Each chapter is a different story. Inside each chapter, you'll find the suite of graphing options that can best tell that story. They don't all have position on a common scale! That's because some graph types are more appropriate for certain situations than others, and I've spelled out those considerations for you. Scan the chapter titles for the story you need to tell, and then skip straight to that chapter to hone in on your data visualization possibilities. Flip to the inside front cover for a Chart Chooser Cheat Sheet that spells out the right chart for the right data.

Some of these are probably new graph types that you haven't seen before. They are also the graph types that often fit your data story the best. Sure, they aren't a default option in Excel, but in each chapter I'll show you the step-by-step instructions on how to make them there. Excel (maybe surprisingly) is one of the most flexible data visualization tools at our disposal. For most of us, it requires no new expense and (also maybe surprisingly) not all that much new skill. We will chop up the defaults of Excel with some ninja skills to use what Excel does have and create powerhouse visualizations. If you are storing your data in another program, or even if you are analyzing your data in something like SPSS, you need to covert the data table to Excel to work with it. Don't worry—I'll show you how the data tables need to be set up, too. I'll hold your hand while you transform your work into something magical.

You'll find the icons from the Chart Chooser Cheat Sheet throughout the book, next to the instructions on how to craft the data visualization in Excel. I'm running back and forth between Excel 2010 and Excel 2013. And I'm using a PC. The menus will look a little different if you are working in Excel on a Mac. That was a lie . . . they will look a lot different. But, all of these same features are available in the later versions of Excel, regardless of the hardware you are using.

Starting off each set of instructions, you will also see a ninja score rating. This is my fairly arbitrary attempt to help you know how much work you are in for when you choose a graph type. The scale runs from 0, which means it's the easiest possible visualization to make or isn't made in Excel, to 10, which means that we are going to engage in some hefty hacking of Excel's innards to pull out an amazing visual. You don't have to have tons of experience to start working on Ninja Level 10 visualizations—just some patience.

When you finish a new graph type, you're going to feel like a ninja rock star (you might think such a character doesn't exist, but just try it and you'll see). When your new graph types get accolades from your readers, you're going to feel like a superhero. Who knew being a data nerd could lead to such happiness? Well, it does. And more importantly, it leads to clear, effective communication.

EXERCISES

This 3D thing is no joke. Let's say we were at your favorite conference and we watched everyone eat breakfast from behind a fern. We tally up their choices into everyone's best friend, the 3D exploding pie chart (see Figure 1.6).

While eggs was most popular, which was second? Just a pile of bacon or cereal? Please base your decision off of the data in the chart, not your own personal preferences (I know how you feel about bacon). Hard to tell, isn't it? That's how much angle and area together can distort the data. For the answer in an improved visualization, check out **http://study.sagepub.com/evergreenedv**.

FIGURE 1.6   3D pie charts combine two things—area and angle—that people are bad at interpreting.

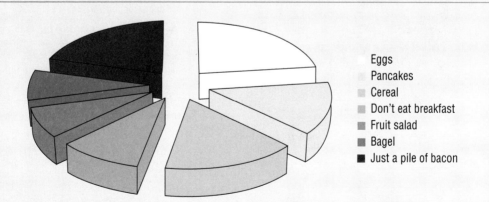

Eggs
Pancakes
Cereal
Don't eat breakfast
Fruit salad
Bagel
Just a pile of bacon

Download practice file at **http://study.sagepub.com/evergreenedv**. The first time you make a new graph type, it may be easiest to work with the same data I'm using in my examples. Once you get the hang of it, you can apply the same steps to your own data. In the practice file, you'll see a tab for each chart type shown in this book with the data table already inserted.

RESOURCES

Deception in data visualization is often unintentional. Check out the SlideShare compilation of graph violations that can lead to misinterpretation at http://www.slideshare.net/powerful point/presenting-data-webinar-presentation.

As much as I'm on the Excel bandwagon, *R* software is also becoming increasingly popular (I feel as if just typing that sentence sounds the death knell) because it is open source—free—and so flexible that it can do nearly anything you can imagine . . . or write code for. Yes, *R* requires coding, but, I put *R* tutorials for selected graphs from this book online at http://study.sagepub.com/evergreenedv

REFERENCES

de Graaf, A., & Hustinx, L. (2011). The effect of story structure on emotion, transportation, and persuasion. *Information Design Journal, 19*(2), 142–154.

Cleveland, W. S., & McGill, R. (1984). Graphical perception: Theory, experimentation, and application to the development of graphical methods. *Journal of the American Statistical Association, 79*(387), 531–554.

Evergreen, S. D. H. (2013). *Presenting data effectively: Communicating findings for maximum impact.* Thousand Oaks, CA: SAGE.

Kosara, R., & Mackinlay, J. (2013). Storytelling: The next step for visualization. *IEEE Computer (Special Issue on Cutting-Edge Research in Visualization), 46*(5), pp. 44–50.

Nyhan, B., & Reifler, J. (2013). *Blank slates or closed minds? The role of information deficits and identity threat in the prevalence of misperceptions* [Unpublished manuscript]. Hanover, NH: Dartmouth College.

Pandey, A., Manivannan, A., Nov, O., Satterthwaite, M., & Bertini, E. (2014). The persuasive power of data visualization. *New York University Public Law and Legal Theory Working Papers,* Paper 474.

Pandey, A. V., Rall, K., Satterthwaite, M., Nov, O., & Bertini, E. (2015). *How deceptive are deceptive visualizations?: An empirical analysis of common distortion techniques.* Proceedings of the ACM Conference on Human Factors in Computing Systems. Seoul, Republic of Korea.

Tal, A., & Wansink, B. (2014). Blinded with science: Trivial graphs and formulas increase ad persuasiveness and belief in product efficacy. *Public Understanding of Science,* 1–9. doi: 10.1177/0963662514549688

Tufte, E. R. (2001). *The visual display of quantitative information* (2nd ed.). Cheshire, CN: Graphics Press.

Ware, C. (2013). *Information visualization: Perception for design* (3rd ed.). Waltham, MA: Morgan Kaufmann.

WHEN A SINGLE NUMBER
IS IMPORTANT

SHOWING MEAN, FREQUENCY, AND
MEASURES OF VARIABILITY

LEARNING OBJECTIVES

After reading this chapter you will be able to

List several options for displaying a single number

Describe when each option is most suitable

Articulate the conditions under which a pie or donut chart is acceptable

Consider whether and how to show measures of variability

Translate statistical jargon into lay language

Sometimes, all we really need is for people to remember this one important number we calculated because the number itself is impactful. This chapter provides several options for displaying a single number, including some traditional and some newer or less familiar visuals that research corroborates as powerful choices.

Pie charts and donut charts get a bad rap—and for good reason. That's graphing by angle and curvature, respectively, and we humans don't interpret those properties all too well. But, if we just use one slice or one curved segment to highlight a single number, the results can be effective without becoming a burden on our cognitive abilities.

If the data don't comprise parts of a whole, we can use the same thinking by highlighting a single bar in a bar graph with an action color to call attention to one number while showing the rest of the bars for context.

Alternatively, simpler displays like an icon array can highlight one number while still being really accessible for audiences who are a bit data nervous.

Even simpler, why not just show a really big number? One huge number is an image more likely to burn into audience brains, so long as it is used sparingly.

Though I'm pushing for a pretty targeted message in this chapter, I know that many of us with academic statistical upbringings cringe when thinking about the information that can get lost, such as those measures of variability that describe a dataset. This chapter shows you several ways to add measures of variability to a graph under these conditions: your audience expects to see the variability reported, or you can translate your variability measure to the audience in lay language. As always, our goal is to help people interpret the story that our data disclose.

WHAT STORIES CAN BE TOLD WITH A SINGLE NUMBER?

Stories involving a single number tend to be fairly limited. However, a single number can represent a wide range of topics. And (super cool) single numbers can be either percentages or raw numbers (and some argue that raw numbers are BEST shown this way, especially if there are no other categories to compare or provide context). So the possible stories you can tell are numerous, including

- Our employees scored an 88 average on their ethics assessments
- On average, our mathematics student achievement is 64%
- We served 123,000 clients last year
- 9 out of 10 consumers prefer our pizza over our competitors
- Only 27% of children in this key neighborhood had a dental visit in the past year
- Chances of dying from a snake bite are just 1 in 50 million
- Median income in Kalamazoo, Michigan was $45,699 in 2013, the most recent year data are available

Essentially, the stories you can tell in this chapter stem from any time you are working with simple counts, frequencies, means, medians, modes, and natural ratios.

HOW CAN I VISUALIZE A SINGLE NUMBER?

Dear friends, you have 4 basic options.

23%   A SINGLE LARGE NUMBER

Seriously, if you want people to remember one important number, just show them the number, really big. Even though it's just text, by making it very large and perhaps putting it in an interesting font, it takes on a visual nature. This strategy is common in infographics. Flip through your closest magazine and you are likely to see a sidebar or callout box labeled "By the Numbers" with a series of data visualized as large numbers.

EXCEL NINJA LEVEL: ▮
(USE WORD OR
POWERPOINT)

I constructed this visual in PowerPoint, using separate textboxes for "1" "out" "of" "50" "million" and "will die of a snake bite" and reposted the source in the visual (Figure 2.1). The large numbers are in a font called ChunkFive Roman, size 199 points. The gray text is in Franklin Gothic Med Cond, size 72 point for "out of" and 56 point for "will die of a snake bite." It took me about 4 minutes to make this visual, but I didn't spend too much time on font choices (which can kill/enliven an afternoon, as we all know).

The concern, of course, is overload. Too many large numbers positioned on the same page may dilute the impact of this technique. If everything is large, size no longer matters. Use this strategy if you have a single large number or a single statistic you want to convey.

To be honest, I used to generally discount the single large number strategy altogether until I started talking to the people over at University of Michigan who run an amazing website called Visualizing Health (see www.vizhealth.org). They ran several studies with funding from the Robert Wood Johnson Foundation using online panels to research which types of data visualizations were most interpretable. One such study (Zikmund-Fisher, 2014) compared disease prevalence shown in an icon array, a pie chart, a bar chart, and a single large number. A large single number beat out the other visualizations when it came to accurate interpretation of the significance and scope of the disease.

FIGURE 2.1 This typical way of showing probability with natural ratios uses the large single number technique.

1 out of 50 million

million

will die of a snake bite.

SOURCE: Institute of Food and Agricultural Sciences

ICON ARRAY

Even though I pretty much just told you that a single large number rules over icon arrays, hang with me for a page or so.

Icon arrays are those visuals where one shape—sometimes a square, circle, or little dude—is repeated usually 10, 100, or 1,000 times and then some of the icons are color-coded to represent a percentage or proportion. Usually only one portion of the array is color-coded, but I have successfully snuck in up to 3 different percentages in one icon array. Be judicious in your colors. Also, careful on your icon choices. While Haroz, Kosara, and Franconeri (2015) found that graphs with representative icons (like a little dog icon to represent the proportion of dogs) increased engagement and memorability, icon styles that don't look alike or appear too much like clip art can misrepresent your professionalism.

I designed this icon array in PowerPoint (Figure 2.2). Follow *Insert>Shape*. Then I selected a three-quarters circle shape to represent pizza. I drew it out on the screen and then modified the shape so that it was .9" x .9." Then I copied and pasted it nine more times. I dragged my mouse over nine of the shapes so they were all selected and changed their fill color to a blue. I changed the last fill color to a light gray. Finally, I inserted a textbox and typed my headline in Gill Sans font, color-coding the text to the shape color and bolding the key text in front. Altogether it took me about 2 minutes.

EXCEL NINJA LEVEL: 1 (BUT STILL, MAKE IT IN POWERPOINT RATHER THAN EXCEL)

FIGURE 2.2   This very basic icon array is like those often seen in infographics.

Icon arrays have been shown to be especially effective for people with low numeracy skills (Galesic, Garcia-Retamero, & Gigerenzer, 2009). Low numeracy here means those who have trouble answering questions like "If the chance of getting a disease is 10%, how many people would be expected to get the disease out of 1,000?" Do you need to communicate with people like that? Many of us do. By the way, in the 2014 Zikmund-Fisher study that I referenced about single large numbers, the study participants had numeracy rates hovering around 4 on a scale of 1 to 5, where 5 is high—so not exactly a low numeracy crowd. It could be that your choices in this chapter depend on the number literacy of your primary audience.

In the icon array study (Galesic, Garcia-Retamero, & Gigerenzer, 2009), the researchers gave college students and older adults information about health risks both in simple narrative plain text terms, and those same terms paired with icon arrays. In both groups, young and old, those who had lower numeracy skills more accurately interpreted health risk when they saw icon arrays. Icon arrays also increased accuracy in high numeracy people, just not by as much. Of course, more research is needed, but the results sound promising enough that you should consider giving this type of graph a try.

I combined these first two visualization methods when I redesigned the keynote slides for Dr. Jody Fitzpatrick's presidential address to the American Evaluation Association in 2013 (Figure 2.3).

FIGURE 2.3   The revised slide combines a single large number with an icon array to be the visual support for Dr. Fitzpatrick's talk.

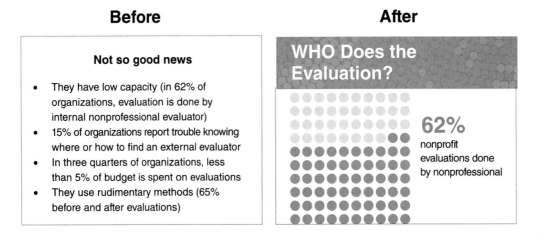

Same instructions apply here—insert a circle, copy/paste it 99 times, color-code 62 of them and insert a textbox with your single large number. Also notice how I'm really only visualizing the first bullet point in her "before" slide. That's the rule: One point per slide. The rest of those points deserve their own moment in the sun, too.

DONUT OR PIE GRAPH

The typical (typically bad) donut chart looks like a cousin of the traditional pie chart, with one major difference.

The middle of the pie is gone. The middle of the pie . . . where the angle is established, which is what humans would look at to try to determine wedge size, proportion, and data. Even though we aren't accurate at interpreting angles, the situation is made worse when we remove the middle of the pie. Now we are left to judge curvature, and as in Figure 2.4, compare wedges by both curvature and angle. It's making me ill.

Don't kick me out of the data visualization club for this one, but I think it is OK to use a donut graph on occasion. The only time they are OK to use is when you are showing just one chunk, to wrap a visual around a single number and give it a bit of eye-candy emphasis.

To make this chart (Figure 2.5) in Excel, highlight all of the data with your mouse, and click on the *Insert* tab. In the *Charts* family, click the drop-down arrow next to the tiny pie chart icon and select the last option there, the donut (Figure 2.6).

Now, right click on one of the pieces of the donut and in that menu, select *Format Data Series*. This opens a dialogue box where you can adjust the size of the donut hole. I reduced mine to about 32%. Now there's room for me to type a label. I really wanted to highlight those people who did not have a dental visit and I also wanted the largest wedge to start at noon, so I adjusted the angle of the first slice in that same dialogue box to 251° degrees (Figure 2.7).

EXCEL NINJA LEVEL: 3

FIGURE 2.4 The way donut charts are normally used does not support interpretation of the data.

FIGURE 2.5 The best way to use a donut chart is to highlight just one chunk to support a single number.

Smartphone market share continues to be dominated by Apple, followed closely by Samsung.
Source: comScore, Inc.

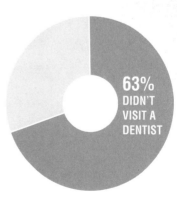

FIGURE 2.6   The donut chart type is hidden in the drop-down menu options for a pie chart.

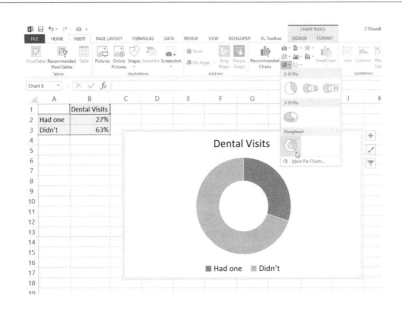

FIGURE 2.7   Decreasing the size of the donut hole creates a stronger visual impact.

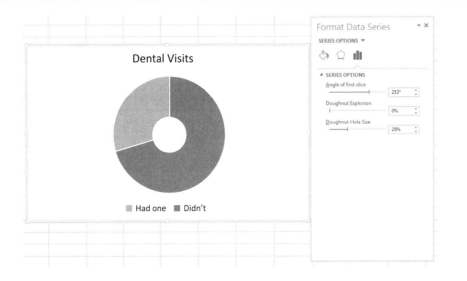

Next, I changed the color of the unimportant donut piece to gray, so it holds very little visual emphasis. To do this, click on the piece twice and then open the drop-down arrow by your paint bucket (located in the *Home* tab) and select a light gray from that palette. I also changed the fill color of my important piece of data representing those people who did not have a dental visit, to blue (Figure 2.8).

FIGURE 2.8   Use an action color to highlight a key piece of the data visualization.

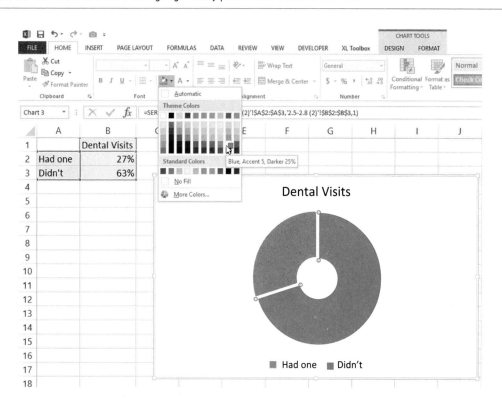

WHY CIRCLES CAN BE CHALLENGING

You wouldn't necessarily think it, because circles are so tidy and pleasing to the eye, but, they pose several problems when used as the main method of rendering data. I'm not talking about dot plots or markers on line graphs here, both of which are circles. I'm talking about when the size of the circle is what encodes the data.

Back in Chapter 1 we learned that angle is hard to interpret. That eliminates donut charts and pie charts. Area is even harder to interpret, thus calling into question the super popular bubble charts. The gurus/nerds who make data visualizations all day (me included) get into arguments on social media about whether bubble charts should be sized according to their diameter, radius, or circumference. And if the makers argue about how they are made, it doesn't leave much hope for the audience's ability to interpret them well.

But, aside from the mental calculations that are challenged by area and angle, readers also have somewhat visceral reactions to data graphed in circles. In a study run by Ziemkiewicz and Kosara (2010) respondents reported that bubble charts

(Continued)

(Continued)

seemed "unstable" and "uncontrolled." They said that the donut chart looked like it might "roll away." The study authors suggest respondents found the chart type "disconcerting."

Bubble charts were also seen as fun and easy-going, although the flip side of that is that they weren't taken very seriously. Whether we like it or not, chart type can influence much more than the simple encoding of our data. It affects interpretation and credibility.

FIGURE 2.9 Highlight just one wedge of the pie to support your point.

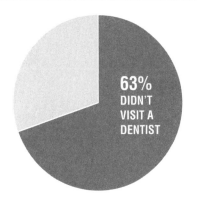

63%
DIDN'T
VISIT A
DENTIST

Finally, I deleted the legend (just click on it and hit your delete key) and added a text box to the graph with my main message.

The same process works for a pie chart (see Figure 2.9 and I'll tell you about how and when to use a pie with more slices in Chapter 6).

The big idea here is that people are bad at interpreting angles and curvatures so generally pies and donuts aren't ideal graph choices. However, in these examples, we aren't asking our audiences to do much mental work because we have muted all but one piece of the graph.

BAR GRAPH

As with donuts and pies, bar graphs can be effective at communicating a single data point, but with less social antagonism. By their very nature, bar graphs carry more pieces of data than the single slice we would highlight in a pie chart. But, we can still rework them to support a single number. The same ideas previously discussed can apply, where we turn down the color on all bars except one, which gets dressed in our action color.

In this example, I work with a graph of survey data. The survey sample was local Latino/Hispanic youth.

Humans are pretty decent at judging length, so I made this graph easier for my audience by ordering the bars from greatest to least. I can't make this happen within the graph itself, I actually have to sort my data table. Excel likes to do the opposite of what I want, so I have to sort the table from least to greatest.

FIGURE 2.10 A simple bar graph can be focused to help the audience remember a single number.

Nonparental adult relatives are important to Hispanic/Latino students. 57% reported talking with them about college aspirations.

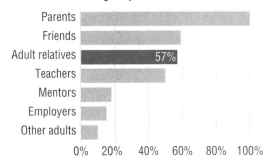

To replicate Figure 2.10, look all the way to the right in the *Home* tab and you'll see a button called *Sort & Filter.* Click the drop-down arrow next to it and select *Custom Sort.* This opens a dialogue box, where you can adjust each option to select the column you want sorted (the one with your percentages!) and the order of the sort—smallest to largest. (Figure 2.11)

FIGURE 2.11 Sorting the data table makes the graph more organized and easier to interpret.

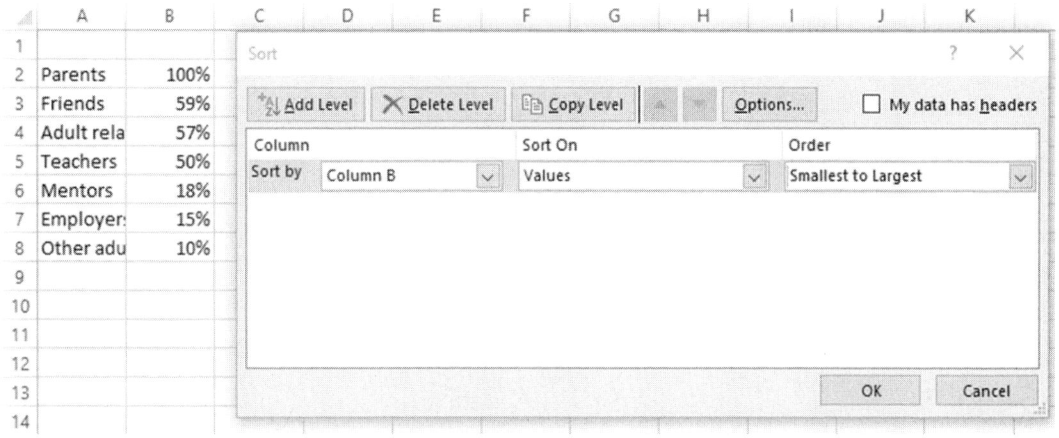

	A	B	C	D	E	F	G	H	I	J	K
1											
2	Parents	100%									
3	Friends	59%									
4	Adult rela	57%									
5	Teachers	50%									
6	Mentors	18%									
7	Employer:	15%									
8	Other adu	10%									
9											
10											
11											
12											
13											
14											

Sort dialogue box:

Add Level   Delete Level   Copy Level   Options...   ☐ My data has headers

Column	Sort On	Order
Sort by Column B	Values	Smallest to Largest

OK   Cancel

Now you highlight your sorted data along with its corresponding labels and insert a basic bar chart. (Figure 2.12)

Just as we adjusted the width of the donut slice, we can bulk up the bars by right-clicking on them and selecting *Format Data Series.* In the box that opens, decrease the gap width to around 60%, or something around that size that you like.

I changed the fill color for all the bars to a light gray and then clicked twice on the bar for *Adult relatives* so that it was the only one highlighted. Then I selected my blue action color as my fill.

Now, I want people to remember a single number here. And I don't want their visual field to be overloaded with numbers at the end of every bar. Therefore, I chose to keep the x-axis and the gridlines so the value of the other bars in the graph can be estimated, but I added a data label to the end of the *Adult relatives* bar. This way my single number is precise and isolated (Figure 2.13).

FIGURE 2.12 Choose the first option in the bar chart drop-down menu.

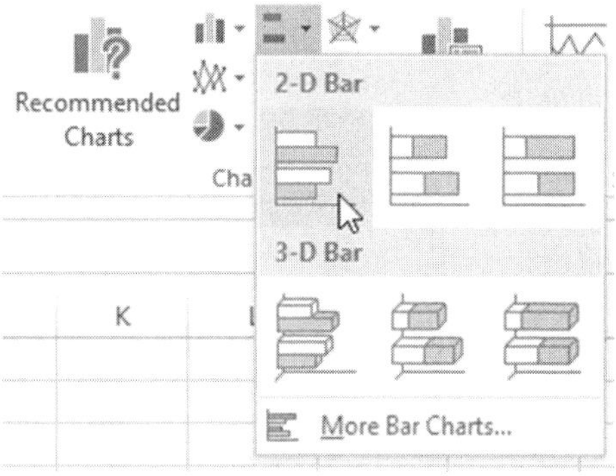

Recommended Charts

2-D Bar

3-D Bar

More Bar Charts...

FIGURE 2.13   Move the label to the end of the bar on the inside when there's room, which serves to reinforce focus on the visual display of the data.

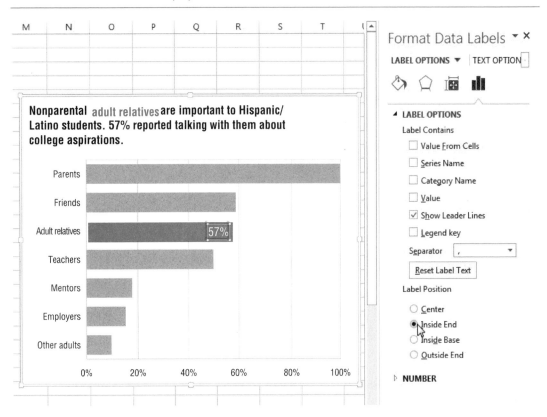

Here's how to make it happen: Click twice on the *Adult relatives* bar so it is highlighted all by itself. Then right-click on the bar and select *Add Data Labels* from that menu. You'll see Excel add your percentage outside the end of the bar. I prefer my percentages on the inside of the bar whenever there is room because it keeps the visual focus squarely on the data. So click on the label twice and then right-click on it (lots of clicking) and select *Format Data Label.* In the dialogue box that opens, look for *Label Position* and change the radio button from *Outside End* to *Inside End.* As a last step, you'll want to change the text color for that label to white, so it is visible against the action color of the bar.

We generally do not need both data labels and an x-axis. That's just repetitive information. But, in this case we are intentionally repeating with a data label on a single bar to give it more of the limelight and help our audience focus on remembering that number.

These strategies give laser focus to a single number that you want to boost. However, I have that academically trained voice in the back of my head that whispers "single number is fine, but standard deviations can tell a bigger story." I argue with that little voice frequently, and sometimes I let it win.

HOW CAN I SHOW MEASURES OF VARIABILITY?

I answer that question with another question: Do you **really** need to show measures of variability? Think hard about that question because chances are your mainstream audiences don't know what measures like confidence intervals or standard deviation actually mean (Muscatello, Searles, Macdonald, & Jorm, 2006). Presenting measures of variability can have the unintended effect of confusing your readers. They want to know you calculated your standard deviations. They want to know you were meticulous in your number crunching. But, most likely they do not want you to actually tell them the standard deviation. Tuck those details in an appendix or something. If you feel confidence intervals are key because the data are really uncertain, it should be a signal that the data shouldn't be graphed in the first place. If you truly feel you should show measures of variability, here are some smart options.

Correll and Gleicher (2014) tested three alternatives to the typical column plus error bar graph to visualize means and margins of error using a crowd-sourced sample—that is, members of the general public (see Figure 2.14). They immediately rejected the column plus error bar graphic, citing other research revealing that viewers misinterpret the half of the error bar that extends down into the column. They believe that the means should be represented by a point or a line rather than a bar, with the error distributed around the mean symmetrically. But exactly how?

Among the four visualizations they tested, gradient plots and violin plots solved some of the bias in the column plus error bar style, and respondents produced more statistically accurate interpretations of the data. These have in common a central line to indicate mean and then a band of color distributed around it, which visually encodes the variability.

Even though the respondents represented average North Americans, I doubt most audiences are able to interpret such diagrams, mainly because we don't demand that they do on a regular basis. The study's respondents were asked to use similar graphics to determine factors like the likelihood that a candidate will get 55% of the vote, which puts the reader in a specific position of really needing those error bars to make sense out of the

FIGURE 2.14   The two visual graphs on the left tend to produce bias. The two on the right produce more accurate interpretations.

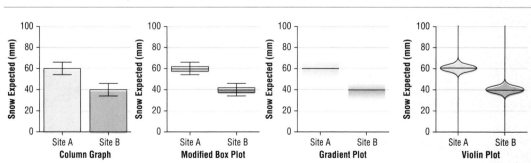

question. Most of the time, we don't require such tasks of our audiences, nor do they want to take the 8 minutes it took the study's respondents to muddle through the answer.

More sophisticated, numerically literate, hard-core data nerd groups like scientific peers likely need and want to see you report your measures of variability. Even in that group, Correll and Gleicher (2014) noted serious difficulty with interpretation of these graphs visually, so I recommend reserving these only for those occasions when dealing with that particular audience.

If you are really committed to showing a more traditional dot and whisker plot, we can at least lighten the mood. This revision was sent to me and published on my blog by a researcher with a dedication to presenting data effectively. At her organization, they felt it was important to add confidence intervals in their reporting. They had been presenting them in the pretty standard heavy way (see Figure 2.15).

FIGURE 2.15   Heavy gridlines and dark labels make the data hard to see.

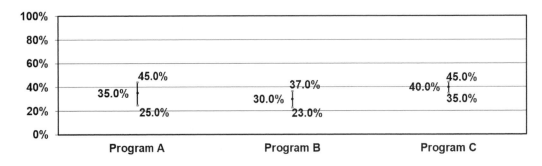

SOURCE:Angie Ficek (2014). "CI Before." PDA Stats. Used with permission.

In her original graph, the confidence ranges were hogging way too much attention. The confidence interval labels are the same color and size as those representing the means. The dots along each line are also the same size, and get this, you can't see it in this black and white reproduction, but the dots at either end showing confidence intervals are a bright, Rudolph-nose red. It's the only thing that really catches your eye in the whole graph; and it's probably the least important part.

The reworked graph does a much better job of emphasizing the means, the real reason for this graph's existence. Angie, the researcher, changed the confidence bands and the gridlines to gray, decreased the size of the confidence interval labels and grayed them out as well. In Figure 2.16 you can also see that she added a line to represent their goal—a smart idea that we explore in more depth in Chapter 4.

FIGURE 2.16   Muting some background information lets the data stand out.

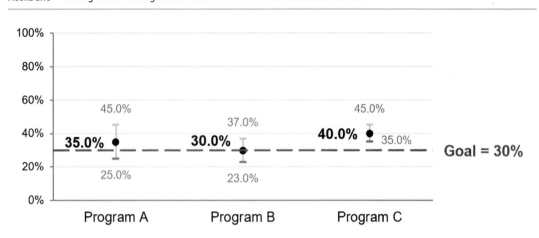

SOURCE: Angie Ficek (2014). "CE After." PDA Stats. Used with permission.

In the References section at the end of this chapter, you can find a link to the guest blog post where Angie describes her redesign thinking and points out even more changes she would make, some of which I'm sure you have considered, too.

EXCEL NINJA LEVEL: 2

To make a simple, but muted box and whisker plot like Figure 2.16, type in your means and your confidence interval ranges. Highlight the labels and the means and insert a line graph with markers. Then right-click on the line and select *Format Data Series.* In the box that pops up, click the radio button by *No Line* so you are left with only markers.

Now we add the whiskers!

In Excel 2013, follow *Chart Tools>Design>Add Chart Element.* Follow the drop-down menu for *Error Bars* and pick *More Error Bars Options.* In that menu, adjust the error amount by picking the radio button by *Custom,* clicking on *Specify Value,* and then selecting your CI range data for both upper and lower confidence intervals. While in there, click on the paint can and change the line color to a light gray (see Figure 2.17).

From there on out, it's all formatting, baby. Add some data labels, enhance with a powerful title, and add a subtitle that explains what those bars indicate, for example which measure of variability (if that part is too much of a struggle, it may be a clue that your audience wouldn't appreciate knowing the confidence intervals; also see the box on page 26).

Figure 2.18 on page 25 is another option that eliminates the whiskers all together. It shows frequencies for different sites, with the focus on the performance for Site E. Upper confidence level is included via a gray bar on top of the actual impact data bar.

EXCEL NINJA LEVEL: 2

The set up for this visualization really happens in your data table (Figure 2.19). You have one column with your actual performance data. You have another column with your actual upper confidence interval, and then you create a third column that is the sum of the two. The second column is the chunk that appears gray in the graph.

FIGURE 2.17   Use the Error Bars options to add confidence intervals.

To make this graph, select your actual performance data, its associated labels, and your second column of confidence intervals. Insert a regular stacked bar (not the 100% stacked bar). Turn the confidence interval chunks into a gray color.

Add data labels to those gray chunks by inserting textboxes and typing in your third column of summed data.

Textboxes are also how we can position "base" and "upper confidence interval" on the side of the graph.

FIGURE 2.18   Half of your measure of variability could be shown by graphing a stacked bar.

Our analysis estimates show that Site E is furthest behind, with only 74% impact.
Gray segments indicate that base scores could be higher, suggesting we also keep an eye on Site F.

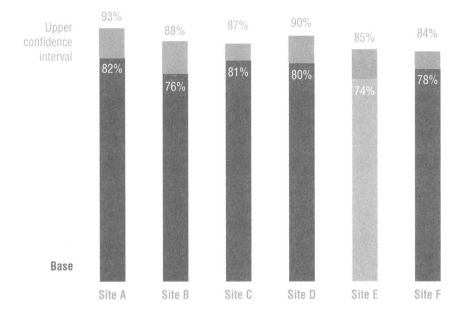

We can add data labels to the inside end of the base bars by right-clicking on the bars and selecting Add *Data Labels*. If that puts your labels in the middle of your bars, right-click on them and select *Format Data Labels*. From there you can choose the radio button for *Inside End*.

As with the other graphs, you can change the color of a single bar by clicking it twice so that it is the only thing highlighted and then choosing a different fill color.

Finally, here's a pretty easy way to visualize measures of variability in your graph inside Excel that uses bands of color distributed around a point,

FIGURE 2.19   You add Base to your gray confidence intervals to create a third column that is your upper confidence limit.

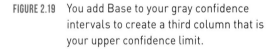

	A	B	C	D	E
1		Base	Gray	Upper confidence interval	
2	Site A	82%	11%	93%	
3	Site B	76%	12%	88%	
4	Site C	81%	6%	87%	
5	Site D	80%	10%	90%	
6	Site E	74%	11%	85%	
7	Site F	78%	6%	84%	

similar to what Correll & Gliecher (2014) suggested. It can be way more readable than the clutter-y dot and whisker plot, and can be more easily interpreted than the bars

TRANSLATING SCIENTIFIC JARGON FOR A LAY AUDIENCE

My main rule of thumb is that you can show measures of variability in your graph so long as you can explain what they mean in an extremely concise subtitle. Translating scientific jargon for a lay audience may be the most challenging aspect of communicating data. Work from some of these suggestions to capture the translation in your own words, in a way that makes sense for both you and your audience. Try your best not to get too tangled up in academic technical precision, which usually requires an entire chapter of explanation. The idea is to be brief and effortless.

Standard deviation:	"Where the core middle of our respondents fell;" "Most answers fell in this range;" "How spread out (how much above and below) something is from the average."
Confidence interval:	"Statistically, there's a chance the actual score falls in this range;" "This represents where the actual answer plausibly could be;" "We are statistically as close as possible to certain that the answer is within this span."
Statistical significance:	"Statistically speaking, this difference is significant;" "Our calculations show that this growth did not just happen by chance;" "What we are measuring (values) between Group A and Group B are different because of real differences between the groups, not something that happened by chance."
Margin of error:	"Our answers could be off by a few percentage points in either direction."

Put it in your own words, but always explain the measure of variability in the graph via a subtitle or annotation when presenting to an audience that is not composed of your scientific peers.

(Newman & Scholl, 2012). This visualization (Figure 2.27) represents the standard deviation via a gray band behind the mean scores, using a stacked area chart. Sounds complicated, I know, but it's actually pretty simple and these are the step-by-step instructions (Figures 2.20–2.26). In this example, we are visualizing mean reading scores for schools across the state.

Step 1, we calculate means and standard deviations for each of the 5 years we are reporting on.

Step 2, add the standard deviation to the mean to calculate the upper end of the standard deviation range. And subtract the standard deviation from each mean to get the lower end of the standard deviation range.

Step 3, the difference between the upper range and the lower range is the full standard deviation range, so calculate that by subtracting the lower range from the upper range.

Step 4, graph. Highlight the values in the lower range and the full range, and insert a stacked area chart, using this guy in Figure 2.23.

EXCEL NINJA LEVEL: 5

You'll get something pretty unappealing, but as my notes in Figure 2.22 suggest, you'll change the bottom segment of the area chart to no fill or white. Change the part that represents your measure of variability to gray. We choose gray here because the measure of variability needs to be in the background, deemphasized, since it is likely not the most important thing about the data visualization.

Step 5, add the mean values. First, right-click on the graph, click on *Select Data,* and add your mean values as a new series. It'll look like Figure 2.24.

You don't want it to look like that, but don't freak out. Just keep going.

Step 6, click on that new area representing your means so that it is highlighted. Then look in your *Chart Tools>Design>Type* family for the button that says *Change Chart Type.* You want to select a line with markers (see Figure 2.25).

Great, now your means are showing as a line on top of your gray measure of variability, right? So far so good, but Excel will probably make your line

FIGURE 2.20   Type your means and measures of variability into Excel.

	Y1	Y2	Y3	Y4	Y5
means	52%	57%	60%	63%	63%
stddev	0.1328	0.1321	0.1303	0.1266	0.1225

FIGURE 2.21   Calculate your upper and lower range.

	Y1	Y2	Y3	Y4	Y5
means	52%	57%	60%	63%	63%
stddev	0.1328	0.1321	0.1303	0.1266	0.1225
upper range	66%	70%	73%	75%	75%
lower range	39%	44%	47%	50%	51%

FIGURE 2.22   Subtract to get the full range represented by your measure of variability.

	Y1	Y2	Y3	Y4	Y5		
means	52%	57%	60%	63%	63%		
stddev	0.1328	0.1321	0.1303	0.1266	0.1225		
upper range	66%	70%	73%	75%	75%		
lower range	39%	44%	47%	50%	51%	<--- turn white	
full range	27%	26%	26%	25%	24%	<--- turn gray	

FIGURE 2.23   Pick the top middle graph in the area graph drop-down menu.

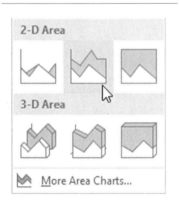

FIGURE 2.24   Excel added your mean values as another segment of the area chart, but we will change that.

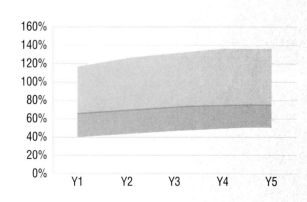

FIGURE 2.25   You will represent your mean values with markers on a line.

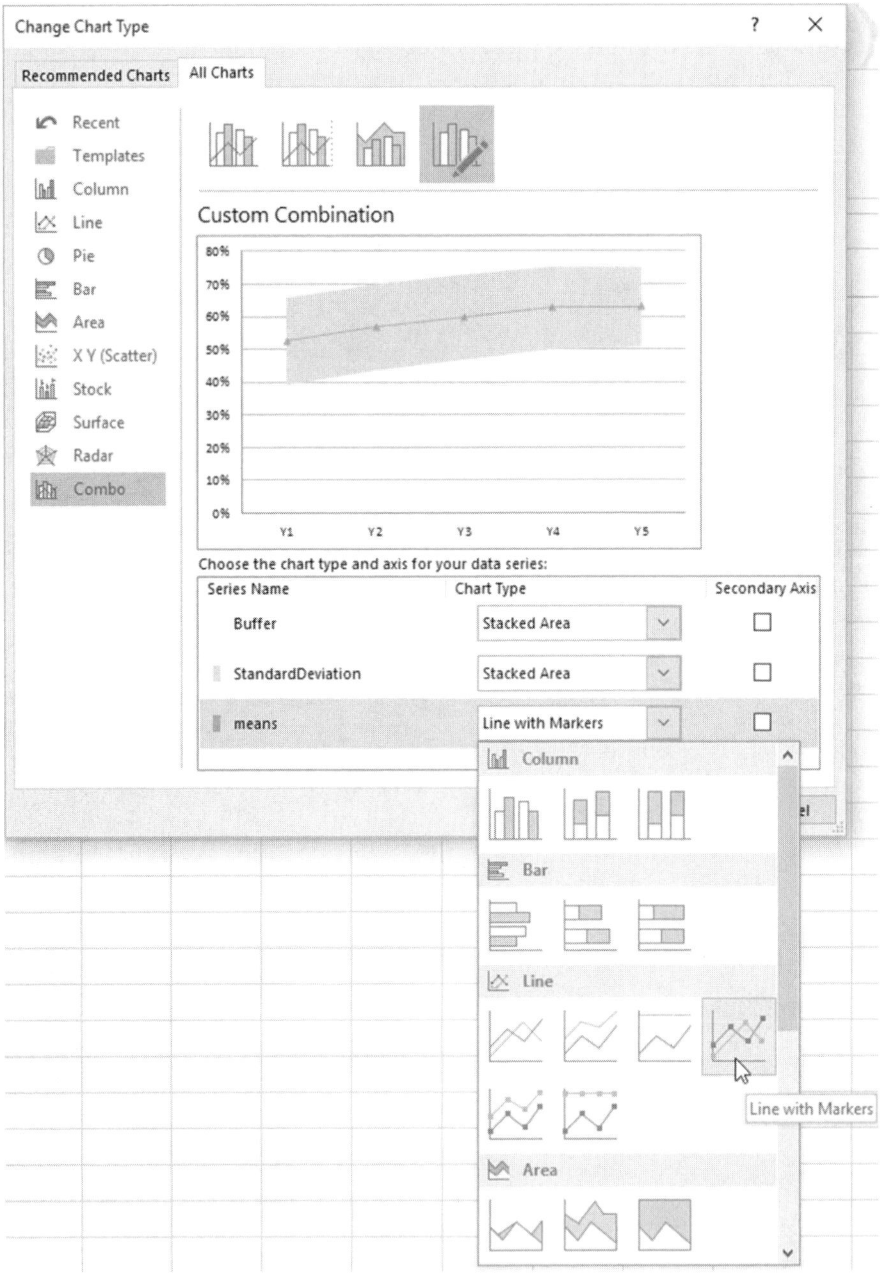

green. In my case, my markers were triangles, too (see Figure 2.26). Just as we have done with other graphs in this chapter, right-click on the line, select *Format Data Series* and change the line color to black.

While in that dialogue box, look for *Marker Options*. Let's switch from clunky rect-angles to simple circles. Select the radio button by *Built-in* and then click the drop-down arrow next to *Type* to see the menu of marker options. At first glance, it doesn't look like Excel even has a circle option. To me, it has always appeared to have a jagged edge, like it was a sunflower or a starburst. But actually, that's Excel's circle. Click it. And then change the fill and border color there to black to match your line.

Step 8, format! Add an explanatory title and a legend-like subtitle to convey what standard deviation actually means.

I'm kind of cheating here because this specific dataset is showing change over time, which we discuss in another chapter, but this is still a good strategy to keep in mind for showing measures of variability that might be easier to interpret.

And there you have it. Remember, wield these strategies with care, okay? Measures of variability, while important to us data nerds, can elicit deer-in-the-headlight stares from many audiences.

FIGURE 2.26 Change your marker type to a circle.

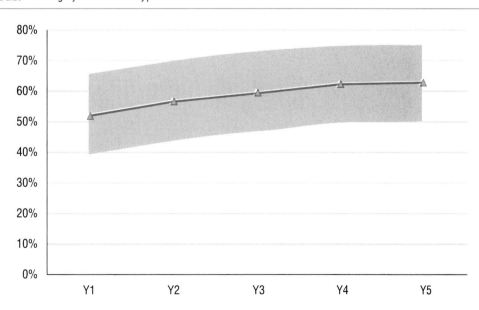

FIGURE 2.27   Finish off the graph with a strong title and an explanation for standard deviation, in public-friendly terms.

**Reading scores increased steadily each year,
with the majority of the students scoring above 40%.**
Black indicates average score.
Gray indicates spread, where most of the student scores fell.

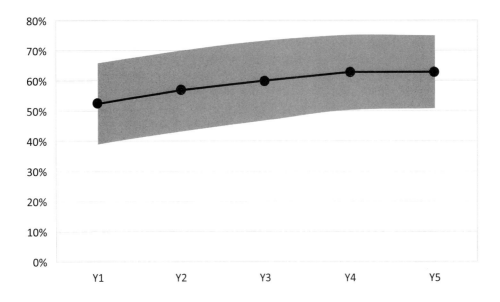

EXERCISES

Look for a large number visualization in a few magazines. Note their colors, fonts, and sizes. Note how many large numbers are communicated together. How many do you think is too many?

Identify a place in your most recent work that could be conveyed through an icon array. Quickly sketch what that array might look like. Decide if your icons can be as simple as a circle or whether more distinction is needed. If so, then head over to one of my favorite icon sites listed in the Resources and find the right icon for you.

Choose a visual from your nearest statistical book's chapter on measures of variability (if there is no image, search for one online). Revise the display of the variability following one of the options in this chapter. Include a subtitle for the revision that explains the measure of variability in a single easy-to-understand sentence.

RESOURCES

Check out the gallery of data visualizations at the website Visualizing Health at **http://www.vizhealth.org/** and even walk through a wizard that helps people in healthcare choose the right chart type.

Some of my favorite places for icons are Flat Icon at **http://www.flaticon.com/**, where they are free and vector (so if you make them large, they don't become fuzzy), and the Noun Project **http://thenounproject.com/**, which costs very little per icon and boasts the largest collection anywhere (for example, they have an icon for Lady Gaga).

Read Angie Ficek's explanation of her redesigned confidence interval chart on my blog at **http://stephanieevergreen.com/charting-confidence-intervals/**

Haroz and his team developed a fun (or maybe frustrating) site that showcases their work on memory and icons. Read through a high-level review of their research and then test your own memory skills with their interactive experiments. **http://steveharoz.com/research/isotype/**

REFERENCES

Correll, M., & Gleicher, M. (2014). Error bars considered harmful: Exploring alternate encodings for mean and error. *IEEE Transactions on Visualization and Computer Graphics, 20*(12), 2142–2151.

Galesic, M., Garcia-Retamero, R., & Gigerenzer, G. (2009). Using icon arrays to communicate medical risks: Overcoming low numeracy. *Health Psychology, 28*(2), 210–216.

Haroz, S., Kosara, R., & Franconeri, S. L. (2015, April). ISOTYPE Visualization–Working Memory, Performance, and Engagement with Pictographs. In *Proceedings of the 33rd Annual ACM Conference on Human Factors in Computing Systems* (pp. 1191–1200). New York, NY: Association for Computing Machinery (ACM).

Muscatello, D. J., Searles, A., Macdonald, R., & Jorm, L. (2006). Communicating population health statistics through graphs: A randomized controlled trial of graph design interventions. *BMC medicine, 4*(1), 33.

Newman, G. E., & Scholl, B. J. (2012). Bar graphs depicting averages are perceptually misinterpreted: The within-the-bar bias. *Psychonomic bulletin & review, 19*(4), 601–607.

Ziemkiewicz, C., & Kosara, R. (2010). *Implied dynamics in information visualization.* Paper presented at AVI (Advanced Visual Interfaces) in 2010 in Rome, Italy. Downloaded from **http://kosara.net/publications/Ziemkiewicz_AVI_2010.html**

Zikmund-Fisher, B. J. (2014, June 27). *Image request IR5: Risks in a population: Emergent disease case counts.* Retrieved from **https://vizhealth-assets.s3.amazonaws.com/media/use-cases/IR5_GCSSSI_findings_2014-01-22.pdf?Signature=464CQ5v3GpRd1q3z%2FAnSUAdoCtA%3D&Expires=1417807888&AWSAccessKeyId=AKIAINE2JWH6QJMAQ5KQ**

3

HOW TWO OR MORE NUMBERS ARE ALIKE OR DIFFERENT

VISUALIZING COMPARISONS

LEARNING OBJECTIVES

After reading this chapter you will be able to

Construct multiple new graph types

Understand how different graph types will highlight different angles of your story

Choose the graph that best shows the story of your data

Save new chart types as a template

Export your graph out of Excel for placement in other software programs

Execute a trick that will save any graph that looks complicated

This chapter shows several ways to visualize comparisons between two numbers—whether dealing with means, frequencies, medians, or any other data. Visualization options include comparing means, such as pretest and posttest, and *groups* of means, such as a set of survey responses from teachers and principals. This chapter is chock full of newer, research-backed visualizations that are easy to produce in many software programs.

Side by side, or clustered, column and bar charts are probably the most popular options here, but their interpretive ability is limited to just comparing two things. Any more than that and it becomes a challenge to compare the lengths of the columns that are nonadjacent, even though we can interpret length well.

Slopegraphs are an excellent alternative to the clustered bar chart, even though they also only compare two numbers. Their strength is in showing when one category has decreased while others increased, or when one category increased at a rate faster than the others.

Another new graph type—dot plots—plunks dots on a line, the easiest visualization for humans to interpret with accuracy. Depending on the dataset, you can fit multiple comparisons on each line.

The dumbbell dot plot, cousin to the dot plot, draws a line between two dots, emphasizing the story of the growth or gap between the two comparison points.

Back-to-back graphs, also known as population pyramids, are best at showing and comparing the overall shape of two datasets rather than comparing individual points within the datasets.

And the secret trick to uncomplicating any graph: break it down into small multiples.

All of these graph types foster comparisons, but choose the one that best showcases the most important angle of your story.

WHAT STORIES CAN BE TOLD ABOUT HOW TWO OR MORE NUMBERS ARE ALIKE OR DIFFERENT?

What stories *can't* be told? Most of the essential questions we ask in research are based around the comparison of two or more numbers. Comparisons are how we determine if a treatment was effective; if results are equal among subgroups; or if one candidate is favored over another. Stories run along these lines, to name just a few:

- Option A is better than Option B
- Posttest scores are higher than pretest scores in almost all subject areas
- Group F and Group G disagreed on five of the eight measures
- There were no differences between the treatment and control groups
- Youth rates are significantly lower than adult rates
- We have equal participation from boys and girls with the exception of girls aged 10 to 13
- All sites increased performance, but Site L did so at a faster rate than other sites
- The performance of Class L is in contrast to Class K

How two or more numbers compare is essentially the story we are trying to tell whenever we are discussing implementation of pre and post designs, experiment/control designs, or the results of t-tests. In this chapter rather than strictly showing the comparison of two numbers, we do hedge into showing change over time, and we show some graphs that could fit into our chapter on visualizing qualitative data, Chapter 8. A couple of the visualizations represented here are adaptable enough to show comparisons at a single point or over time.

HOW CAN I VISUALIZE HOW TWO OR MORE NUMBERS ARE ALIKE OR DIFFERENT?

Perhaps more so than in any other chapter, the choices in this chapter come down to the particulars of your dataset and which graph type is going to best highlight your key point.

Read through each one of these options to learn how to make your data the most charming. If you still aren't sure, you probably want to test drive your data in a few different graphs to see which one does the best job of speaking for you. Most of these visualizations are best for comparing two numbers, but dumbbell dot plots and small multiples, at the end, are capable of handling more.

SIDE BY SIDE COLUMN

EXCEL NINJA LEVEL: 2

Side by side column or bar charts—maybe also referred to as clustered columns or bars—are possibly the most ubiquitous way of showing how two or more numbers compare, but the cold hard truth is that they have significant limits on their effectiveness. It's difficult for people to compare between nonadjacent bars (Talbot, Setlur, & Anand, 2014). At most, side by side column graphs should only compare two categories.

Humans are pretty good at judging length and comparing two different lengths, but effectiveness really stops with two comparisons: Youth and adult, male and female, treatment and control, my beer and your beer. In this case, it also helps that we have some extra white space between each set of clustered columns. This creates three groups and two columns to compare within each group. Our brains can process groups of three to five things and compare two more numbers within each group (Cowan, 2000). Once we start slicing in a third, fourth, or fifth column within each group, we are asking brains to do too much.

FIGURE 3.1   The effectiveness of side by side column graphs is limited to comparing just two things.

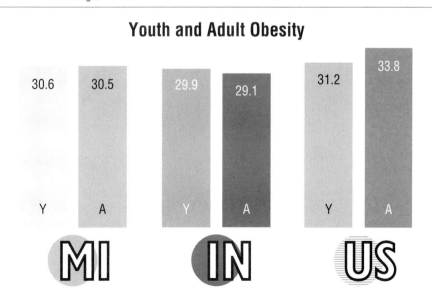

Figure 3.2 is the sort of overloaded side by side column graph that I see all the time.

I see graphs like this wherever I travel, everywhere in the world, inside organizations of all sizes, and in every industry. It's so common because it's so easy to make. It's just that it's very hard for an audience to make any kind of sense out of graphs like that. The graph itself can overwhelm a viewer because there is too much happening, so even if a viewer tries to look at the graph, she or he will find that it is difficult to make comparisons across multiple columns. A side by side column graph best fits just two categories. (Scratch your head about how to fix this one and then keep reading—I'll show a solution by the end of the chapter.)

Now, let's break out of the default options usually presented in Excel and explore more compelling ways to show how two or more things are alike or different.

FIGURE 3.2   This side by side column has too many columns.

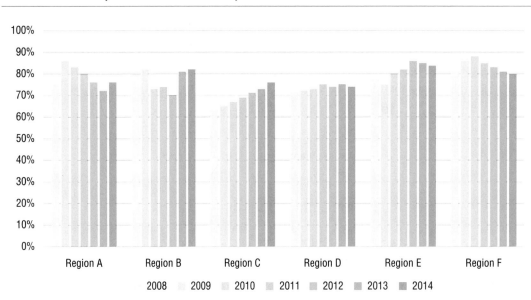

SLOPEGRAPH

Slopegraphs are a newer graph type. They rely on Excel's line graphing feature, but they don't necessarily have to show change over time. Slopegraphs play into our ability to judge slope fairly well. For this reason, they are perfect for highlighting the story of how just one category decreased when other categories increased, or to show that one changed at a rate much faster than the others.

Let's say that we are comparing sales in each department of a grocery store, before and after they moved locations. As a side by side bar graph, it would look like Figure 3.3.

Even though humans are good at detecting length, the story of what's happening in this grocery store is difficult to detect in this graph. It's a bit hard to see that sales of cheese are actually down at the new site, for example. It's easy to miss that there is only one New Site bar that is shorter than its corresponding Old Site bar. A slopegraph will make the story clearer.

The table for a slopegraph is probably quite familiar—just two columns of numbers (see Figure 3.4).

EXCEL NINJA LEVEL: 5

FIGURE 3.3   This side by side bar graph clouds the story.

Sales by Department (in thousands)

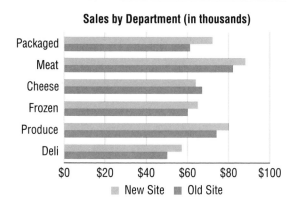

FIGURE 3.4   Sites are in columns and departments are in rows.

	A	B	C
1	Sales by Department (in thousands)		
2		Old Site	New Site
3	Deli	$50	$57
4	Produce	$74	$80
5	Frozen	$60	$65
6	Cheese	$67	$64
7	Meat	$82	$88
8	Packaged	$61	$72

In order to produce a slopegraph using this data, you need to follow a few steps. First, highlight the rows and columns and insert a line graph. I prefer a line graph with markers, but maybe I'm just obsessed with dots (see Figure 3.5).

It doesn't quite look right—the departments are on the x-axis and they shouldn't be. Click the *Switch Row/Column* button, located in the green *Chart Tools>Design* tab (or in Excel 2010, look in *Chart Tools>Layout*).

You can see the beginnings of the slopegraph in this modified line graph already (Figure 3.6). The differences between this line graph and a true slopegraph are minor, but interpretively important. Slopegraphs usually have no space between the end of the line and the end of the plot area. The lines are pushed to either side of the graph. To delete that gap, we are going to click a single magic button inside Excel. Really, this is pretty much where it all happens.

Right-click on the x-axis and select *Format Axis* from that menu. In the *Format Axis* box that opens, look for the area with the heading *Axis Position* (in Excel 2010, it's called *Position Axis,* not *Axis Position,* because Excel likes to mess with us). Under that, pick the radio button next to *On tick marks* (Figure 3.7).

By default, the *Between tick marks* button is selected, but if you select the *On tick marks* button, it will push the lines to the edges of the graph (Figure 3.8).

FIGURE 3.5 Insert a line graph.

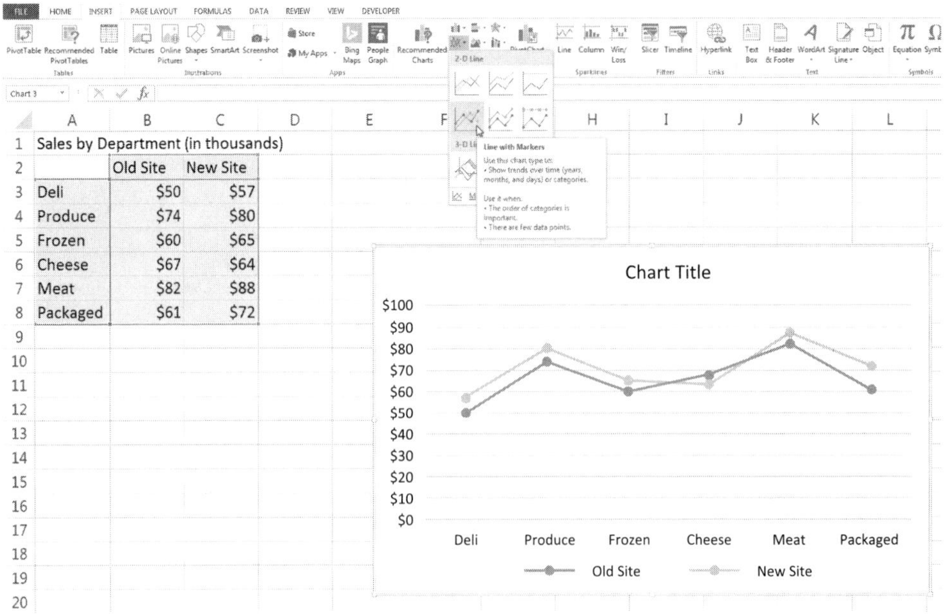

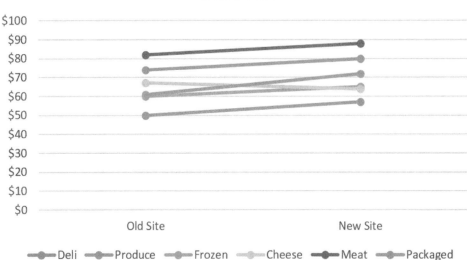

Sales by Department (in thousands)
Old Site
New Site
Deli $50 $57
Produce $74 $80
Frozen $60 $65
Cheese $67 $64
Meat $82 $88
Packaged $61 $72
Chart Title
$100
$90
$80
$70
$60
$50
$40
$30
$20
$10
$0
Deli
Produce
Frozen
Cheese
Meat
Packaged
Old Site
New Site

FIGURE 3.6 Now the sites are on the x-axis—and it's almost a slopegraph already!

Chart Title
$100
$90
$80
$70
$60
$50
$40
$30
$20
$10
$0
Old Site
New Site
Deli
Produce
Frozen
Cheese
Meat
Packaged

From here on out, it's all formatting baby!

Slopegraphs tend to be long and narrow, unlike line graphs, which are usually wide and short. So resize the whole graph by stretching the corners. This also puts some distance between points that are nearly on top of one another.

We also need some space on either side of the line to add labels. Currently, there's a y-axis there. Delete the y-axis (just click on the numbers and hit the Delete key). Do the same for the y-axis gridlines. That buys a little bit of room on the left, but not enough. So click inside the plot area—the white space in the middle of the graph—and drag it's side handles in on both sides. The graph space will narrow, but the overall chart area will stay the same (Figure 3.9).

At this point, it should already be really obvious that one line is going down. We can also see that another line is increasing more so than the others. Slopegraphs highlight this story better than any other chart type. Ultimately, we will use action colors on those two lines to call attention to them and make the other lines gray to reduce emphasis.

Let's start formatting the graph to bring out the story. The primary formatting will take place in the labels and the colors. I'm not gonna lie, formatting a slopegraph is a tedious process because you have to click on every single part of the graph multiple times. Here's the most streamlined way to do it:

FIGURE 3.7   Select *On tick marks* to make the slopegraph.

FIGURE 3.8   Now the lines of data extend to the edges of the plot area.

FIGURE 3.9   Shrink the plot area to make room for labels on their side of the line.

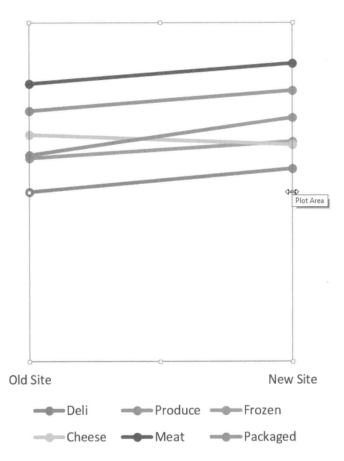

Right click on the top line and select *Format Data Series*. In the box that opens up, change the line color, marker fill color, and marker border color all to a medium-light shade of gray. Look at Figure 3.10.

The line should still be highlighted inside your graph. Right-click on it and select *Add Data Labels*. This will add the dollar values to both markers. Click on the labels and change their color to match the lines. With those labels highlighted, carefully click again on just the left label so that it is the only one highlighted. Then right-click on that label

FIGURE 3.10   There are three places to change colors for a single line: line color, marker fill color, and marker border color.

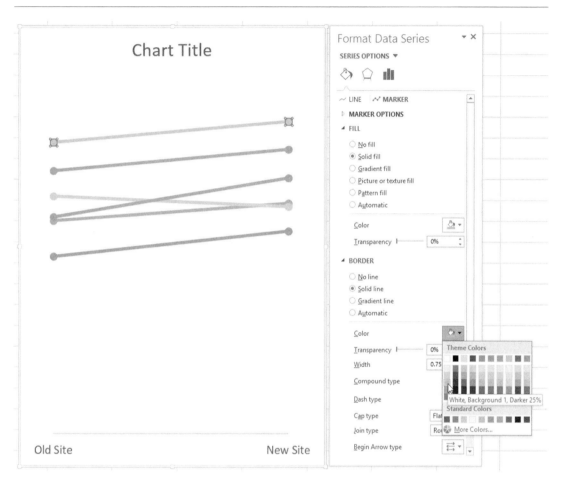

and select *Format Data Label* (it should be singular). New box opens! Check *Series Name* so that the corresponding grocery department label will be added, but only on the left. Uncheck *Show Leader Lines* (this will matter more later). Personally, the comma that separates the label from the value offends me. In the Separator drop-down menu, pick the option that says *space*. Then look for the *Label Position* choices and pick *Left*. All of this is pictured in Figure 3.11.

FIGURE 3.11   Move the left label to the left of the graph and add the Series name to indicate the department.

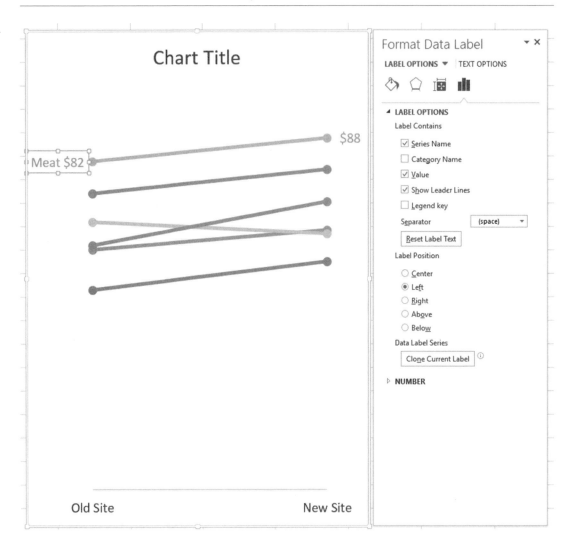

Yes, lots of steps there, but the payoff is clear labeling, and smart color coding that supports the story inside this data. Repeat this process for the rest of the lines, choosing a medium dark color for the rapidly increasing line and a dark color for the decreasing line (Figure 3.12). Dasgupta, Chen, and Kosara (2012) made the good point that we should be careful that the colors chosen on the slopegraph are distinguishable from one another, especially since the lines cross. Try looking at the graph in black and white to see if the color choices will be distinct.

FIGURE 3.12   The slopegraph now shows that the Cheese department is the only one that isn't performing as well and that the Packaged department is making impressive gains.

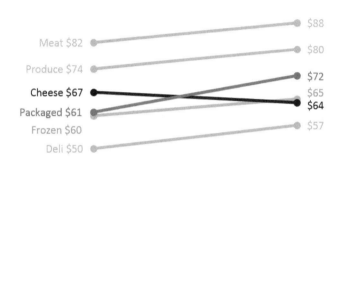

As you labeled these lines you probably noticed that the labels for Packaged and Frozen were overlapping each other. To fix that, just click on each label and drag it up or down a little to space them apart. This is why we unchecked *Show Leader Lines* earlier. With that box checked, each label would have an ugly, cluttering little line tying it to its part of the slopegraph.

It's OK to add a great title and stop here. I like to add a final touch by inserting vertical lines that shoot up from Old Site and New Site. Right-click on the x-axis and in that menu, select *Add Major Gridlines*. BOOM! I also delete the x-axis line. To do so, right click on the x-axis again and select *Format Axis*. In the new box, look for the line color area and select *No line*.

The slope of the slopegraph markedly accentuates increases and decreases when comparing two sets of numbers.

FIGURE 3.13   The final slopegraph helps readers make clearer interpretations about growth at the two sites.

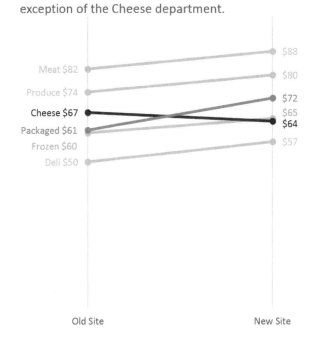

BACK-TO-BACK BARS

Now serving back-to-back bars, two ways. Both solutions depict two sets of bar graphs that share a spine. Our brains seek symmetry, so we can detect where the bars on one side do not mirror the bars on the other. The object here is not to ask people to compare specific values from each bar graph. Such comparisons are difficult to make when the bars are back-to-back. These visualizations are best for showing the shape of the overall data-set. When you are trying to show natural distributions or bell curves in the two datasets, this is the graph type for you (in this case, this type of graph is sometimes referred to as a "population pyramid"). Back-to-back bars are useful for getting at-a-glance assessments of whether two groups are similar.

Solution 1—Two Separate Bar Graphs

Let's say we're interested in comparing how two groups—oh, teachers and principals—responded to a survey. One way to visually display that comparison would be a side-by-side bar graph, where each question had two bars, one for teachers and one for principals. That choice is helpful in some ways, but such a display can make it difficult to also see how

EXCEL NINJA LEVEL: 4

JUST teachers or JUST principals responded. You would need to be able to mentally unsee one set of bars in order to see the shape of the other clearly—and that's hard to do! Thus was born the need for a back-to-back graph.

Figure 3.14 contains the data used to begin to graph.

Highlight just the column of Teacher data and insert a regular plain bar graph. Highlight the Principal column and do the same. Two regular plain bar graphs.

FIGURE 3.14   Survey questions are in rows while the two respondent groups are in columns.

	A	B	C
1		Principals	Teachers
2	Teachers hold principals accountable.	44%	40%
3	Principals support teacher decisions.	73%	75%
4	School climate is positive.	76%	65%
5	Teachers give individualized care to students.	77%	85%
6	Principals hold teachers accountable.	82%	78%
7	Staff have camradarie.	86%	80%
8	Support staff are treated well.	95%	96%
9	Principals listen to teacher concerns.	96%	75%

The Principal data is ordered so that in the graph it displays greatest to least (Figure 3.15). That is easy for the eye to detect when those bars are facing the other direction, so let's switch the direction of the Principal graph. Again, the magic trick here is just

FIGURE 3.15   Look for Values in reverse order to send the bars right to left.

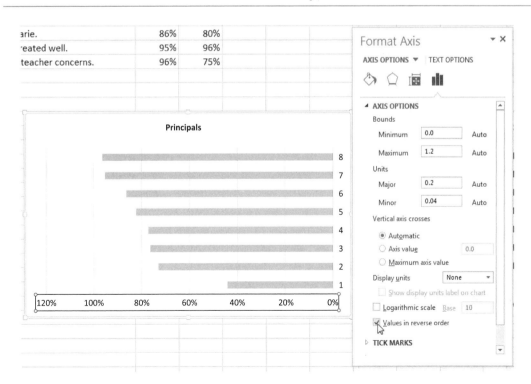

FIGURE 3.16   When working with multiple graphs and textboxes, the Align functions are essential friends.

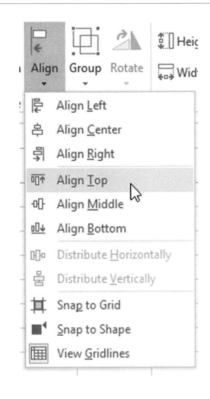

one single checkbox inside Excel. Find it by right-clicking on the x-axis for the Principal graph and selecting *Format Axis*.

In that new dialogue box, look for the checkbox next to *Values in reverse order*—and check it! So simple, isn't it??

While in that dialogue box, change the maximum for the x-axis to 100% or 1.0. Excel likes to give us more than we need, but this survey data can only go to 100%. And remember, whatever you do to one graph here, you'll need to do to the other. Change the x-axis maximum for the Teacher's graph, too. Delete both y-axes, since one to eight isn't helpful.

We need to insert the questions as the labels, but we don't want the questions to be associated with either Principals or Teachers. They need to sit in the middle, impartial and neutral. Make room for them by moving the Teacher graph over to the right. Just drag it over. I can't drag in a perfect line, so when I do this, my two bar graphs are no longer aligned. To fix this, hold down the Control key on your keyboard and click inside both graphs so they are both highlighted. Then look in the orange *Drawing Tools* tab and find the *Align* button. Click the arrow under it and choose *Align Top* (Figure 3.16).

Now we are good to add the survey question labels. We do this by inserting textboxes (see Figure 3.17). It may seem tedious, but the way to make it perfect is to insert one textbox per question. Just draw the textbox in the empty space between the two graphs. Link it back to your survey question by clicking on the textbox border and then typing an equal sign in the formula bar and then clicking into the cell with your survey question. Hit Enter to insert that question into your textbox.

In Figure 3.17 notice how the formula bar shows =$A$9—this is the link back to the cell with the survey question so I don't have to retype every question over again.

Also notice that the text is aligned to the center of the textbox and aligned to the middle—so centered both horizontally and vertically. I stretch the textbox so it touches each bar in the separate graphs, making it easier to visually judge that everything is aligned. I'll eventually delete the textbox border, but I find the border guides me in making sure the textbox is equidistant. Repeat this process for all of the survey responses. When you are finished, make sure the top textbox and the bottom textbox both look like they are centered with their corresponding bars. Then hold down the Control key and click on all the textboxes. Align them Center and then, in that same Align menu, Distribute vertically. This will make sure that each of the textboxes match up with the bars in the bar graphs. Add a helpful title with a new textbox.

FIGURE 3.17   Connect the textbox to the cell that holds the survey question.

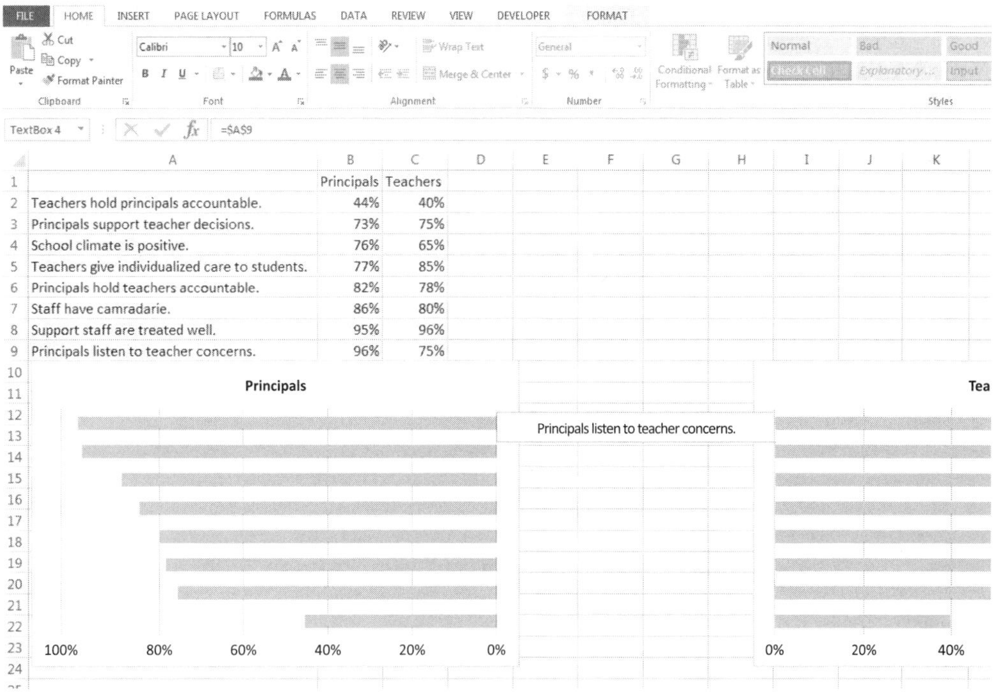

While this may look like a lot to handle, we are going to finish the visualization quickly. Start by removing borders from all textboxes and both graphs. Just right-click on them, select *Format,* and then select *No Line.*

I also shrunk each graph a little bit so that the entire visualization was narrower. Changing size is OK, just take care to change the size of both graphs. With one graph selected, look in the green *Chart Tools* area, within the *Format* tab. All the way to the right is information that tells you the height and width of the graph. Shrink one graph down and note the new dimensions. Then click on the other graph and type those same dimensions into the height and width area to match sizes. You may want to recheck alignment, too.

Finally, I used a darker color on the bars I referenced in the title of the graph.

I'm telepathically picking up your question about how to get all of these pieces out of Excel. Check out the sidebar for a few options. This method of making a back-to-back graph is appropriate for potentially political situations where you don't want to have the questions more associated with one group or the other. If that's not so important for you, the next section has another method that creates the entire visualization within one single graph.

FIGURE 3.18   This back-to-back bar graph is composed of 11 different elements.

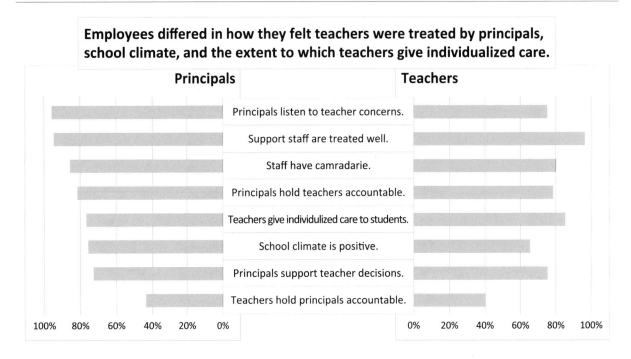

Employees differed in how they felt teachers were treated by principals, school climate, and the extent to which teachers give individualized care.

FIGURE 3.19   The finished back-to-back graph shows overall shape of each dataset and highlights areas of major difference.

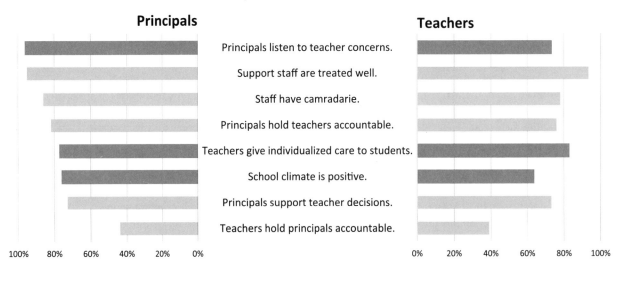

Employees differed in how they felt teachers were treated by principals, school climate, and the extent to which teachers give individualized care.

HOW DO I GET MY GRAPH OUT OF EXCEL?

Exporting a graph from Excel can be a little challenging when you have multiple graphs and textboxes. Here are four potential solutions.

1. If your ultimate destination is PowerPoint, construct your entire visualization there. PowerPoint has the same graphing functionality as Excel. You can make your initial graphs in Excel and then copy and paste each one into PowerPoint (Ninja trick: Look under the *Paste* button for *Paste Special* and then select Microsoft Excel Chart Object). Insert the textboxes and continue the rest of your formatting right from PowerPoint.

2. If your graph is going into a report, you probably want to insert a picture rather than get frustrated over messing with textboxes inside Word. To make a picture, hold down the Control key while you select all the textboxes and graphs in Excel. Then click the *Copy* button. Navigate over to Word and right-click to see the *Paste* options. You want the third icon, *Paste as Picture*.

FIGURE 3.20   PasteOptions

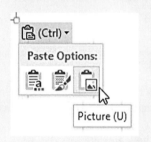

Paste as Picture is the little icon of a clipboard with a photograph on it.

3. One more way to export the bundle is to take a screenshot. Screenshots are notoriously low resolution, but the real issue is the quality of the actual screen you are using. New hi-def computer monitors allow for higher-resolution screenshots.

4. Does your department allow you to install plug-ins? If yes, start your fist-pumping. The XL Toolbox is a tiny plug-in for Excel that allows you to export including vectors. It makes my heart really happy graphics in many formats, including because vector images can be resized without losing their clarity. Refer to http://xltoolbox.sourceforge.net/

Solution 2—Secret Buffer Data

EXCEL NINJA LEVEL: 7

Friends, Solution 2 is where you earn your ninja ranking. To construct a back-to-back graph inside a single visualization, we are going to use secret buffer data. As a groomed academic you might bristle at the thought of putting anything secret inside your datasets, but no one will know. Remember, this method is suitable for graphing situations where the labels do not need to appear neutral.

The data here show the top 10 leading causes of death for males and females in the United States (suicide is not in the top ten for women and septicemia is not in the top

FIGURE 3.21   Actual data are in the middle with buffer columns to either side that when paired with their actual data, add up to 100%.

	A	B	C	D	E
1		Male Buffer	Male	Female	Female Buffer
2	Heart disease	75.4%	24.6%	22.9%	77.1%
3	Cancer	75.9%	24.1%	21.8%	78.2%
4	Unintentional Injuries	93.7%	6.3%	3.7%	96.3%
5	Respiratory	94.6%	5.4%	6.0%	94.0%
6	Stroke	95.8%	4.2%	6.1%	93.9%
7	Diabetes	96.9%	3.1%	2.8%	97.2%
8	Suicide	97.5%	2.5%		100.0%
9	Alzheimer's	98.0%	2.0%	4.7%	95.3%
10	Flu & Pneumonia	98.0%	2.0%	2.3%	97.7%
11	Kidney Disease	98.2%	1.8%	1.8%	98.2%
12	Septicemia	100.0%		1.5%	98.5%
13		^turn white			^turn white

FIGURE 3.22   Select the third option under the bar graph icon.

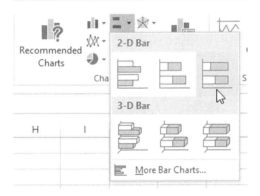

ten for men). Actual death rates are listed in the middle, in Columns C and D, in black text. On either side I've inserted a buffer column of secret data.

The Male Buffer and the Male data together need to add to 100%. So I subtracted the Male data from 100% and put the remainder in the Male Buffer column. Then, I did the same for the Female data. Across each row, the data should add to 200%.

Now, highlight all the data from A1 to E12 and insert a 100% Stacked Bar.

Initially, the resulting chart will look confusing, but if you use your imagination you can probably already see the back-to-back graph buried in the middle (Figure 3.23).

To bring the actual data to the forefront, change both buffer segments of the stacked bar graph from a color to white. Right-click on one segment and select *Format Data Series*. In the pop-up box, navigate to the *Fill* area (mine has a paint bucket icon) and select *White* from the *Solid Fill* color options (Figure 3.24).

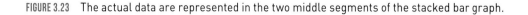

FIGURE 3.23   The actual data are represented in the two middle segments of the stacked bar graph.

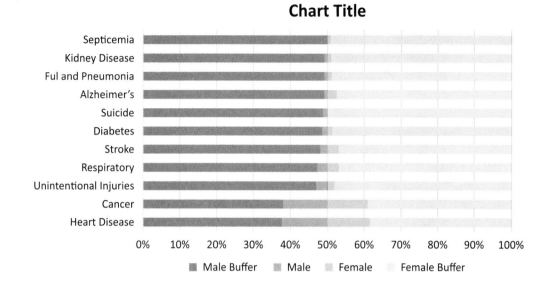

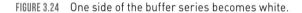

FIGURE 3.24   One side of the buffer series becomes white.

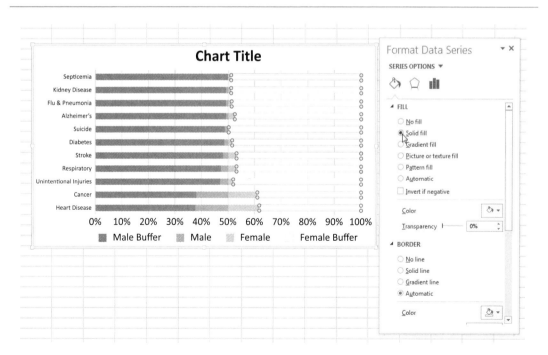

Continue the same process to change the other side of the buffer series to white.

With the buffer segments white, the actual data are all that's left to see. However, it's pretty scrunched in the middle of the graph (see Figure 3.25). So, let's adjust the scale of the x-axis. Again, don't let this offend your data loyalty and sensibilities—we will ulti-mately delete that scale anyway; it's just here as a ninja tool for now. But, before we do, we need to make sure the data can be adequately viewed and interpreted. Right-click on the x-axis and select *Format Axis.* Set the minimum (in this case) to 35%, which looks to be lower than the leftmost Male bars. Set the maximum to 65%, which is to the right of the rightmost Female bars.

Now that the scale is better suiting the data, delete the x-axis and the gridlines. The visualization is nearly complete.

Since we are talking about leading causes of death, it makes sense to start with the most prevalent at the top. Right-click on the y-axis, select *Format Axis* and then check the box next to *Categories in reverse order.* While you have the same formatting box open, look for the line settings and select *No Line.* This eliminates the y-axis line, which remained even after deleting the graph's gridlines.

We no longer have an x-axis to help us interpret the values of the bars, so I'm going to add in data labels. Right-click on one set of bars and select *Add Data Labels.* Excel popped my labels into the center of the bars so I right-clicked again, selected *Format Data Labels,* and chose the option *Inside Base.* Repeat these steps for the other side.

FIGURE 3.25   Adjust the axis so it begins and ends closer to your actual values.

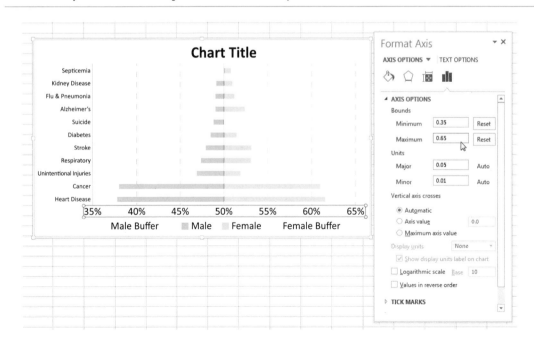

FIGURE 3.26   Make the bars more visible by decreasing the width of the gaps between the bars.

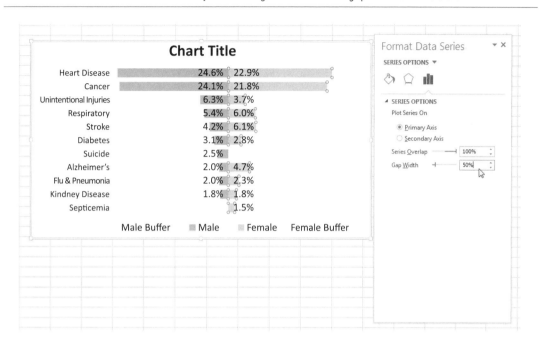

Now that the labels are in the bars, it seems to me that the bars are too thin. Thicken them up by right-clicking on any set, selecting *Format Data Series,* and then cranking the *Gap Width* way down to something like 50% (see Figure 3.26).

The final touches are simple—adjust colors (please not pink and blue), add a title, and create a new legend at the top of each set of bars.

For the final graph, Figure 3.27, I prefer the reader be able to see the bars themselves, especially since we are asking them to compare the shape of each dataset. So, I carefully clicked on individual data labels that were overlapping the end of the short bar and dragged them to the outside of the bar. I also added textboxes to explain why bars were absent for both groups. This back-to-back graph makes it clear that there are key disparities between genders regarding unintentional injuries, stroke, suicide, Alzheimer's, and septicemia.

Buffer columns are a secret ninja move that you can use to force Excel to make visualizations that aren't a part of the default options, but can sometimes tell your story in the most compelling way. Keep these buffers in your back pocket—we will use them in other chapters and they might help you invent new graph types, too!

Now you have two ways to create back-to-back graphs that support the comparison of the overall shape of two datasets.

FIGURE 3.27   The shape of each dataset makes key differences in leading causes of death obvious.

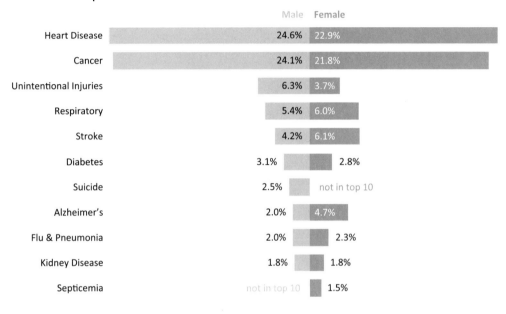

Leading causes of death for males and females are similar, with a few notable exceptions.

	Male	Female
Heart Disease	24.6%	22.9%
Cancer	24.1%	21.8%
Unintentional Injuries	6.3%	3.7%
Respiratory	5.4%	6.0%
Stroke	4.2%	6.1%
Diabetes	3.1%	2.8%
Suicide	2.5%	not in top 10
Alzheimer's	2.0%	4.7%
Flu & Pneumonia	2.0%	2.3%
Kidney Disease	1.8%	1.8%
Septicemia	not in top 10	1.5%

DOT PLOT

This is my all-time favorite graph. Dot plots are flexible and easy to read. Back in Chapter 1 we learned about Cleveland's early experiments on visual perception, which found that humans most accurately interpret locations on line, when those lines share a common axis. We are more accurate at interpreting dots on a line than we are at judging length for example in a bar chart (Jacoby, 2006).

However, the problem is that most of us use Excel, and dot plots are not a default chart option in Excel. But, we will use ninja skills to make it work. And I think you'll agree that the dot plot really does allow for a better comparison between two points as opposed to a side by side bar.

My data table is shown in Figure 3.28. Fall and Spring columns hold my actual values (kindergarten readiness scores). The DOT SPACING values are just my secret ninja place-holders that turn this into a dot plot. They'll put the Fall and Spring values on equally spaced lines.

To make the graph in Excel, first I select "Fall" and it's values and—holding down the Control key—"DOT SPACING" and it's values, and insert a scatterplot. Doing that produces Figure 3.29.

EXCEL NINJA LEVEL: 8

FIGURE 3.28   Insert an extra column called Dot Spacing and type in values that are equally spaced apart.

	A	B	C	D
1		Fall	Spring	DOT SPACING
2	Literacy	34	69	5
3	Language	63	77	4
4	Mathematics	67	75	3
5	Science	92	98	2
6	Creative Arts	96	100	1

FIGURE 3.29   The Dot Spacing values pushed the Fall values onto separate equally disbursed lines.

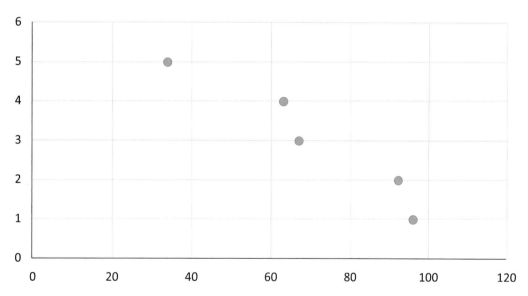

DOT SPACING

This is usually the time when people write me emails, freaking out. Because the graph is titled "Dot Spacing" and that is supposed to be our secret. Don't panic—that title will disappear. Also, don't panic if your points are not circles. We will change those.

FIGURE 3.30   Click the tiny arrow icon to activate your mouse and then highlight the cells you want to enter into each section of this dialogue box.

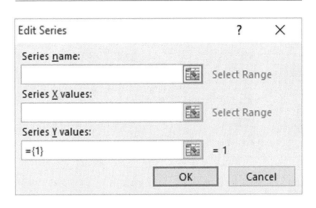

Right-click on the graph, choose *Select Data.* In that dialogue box, edit the name of this series so that it points to the cell that contains the word Fall. Then click *Add* to make a new series for Spring.

Use the little orange cell picker icon next to each blank box to select the right cells (Figure 3.30). Series name is Spring, so click inside the cell that says Spring. You will select the Spring data for the x-axis values and again select Dot Spacing data for the y-axis values. Those actions produce Figure 3.31. Take it slow here if you need to. This is the step that can trip people up.

If you have a legend, delete it.

Next, format each set of scores so they look like big dots. Right-click on one set and select *Format Data Series.* In that box, look for *Marker Options.* You will want to check the radio button next to *Built In.* Then, choose the circle shape from the drop-down menu. You don't see a circle shape? I know! Excel makes it appear like a sunburst, with jagged edges, but it is really a smooth circle (Figure 3.32).

FIGURE 3.31   Fall and Spring scores now appear on the graph.

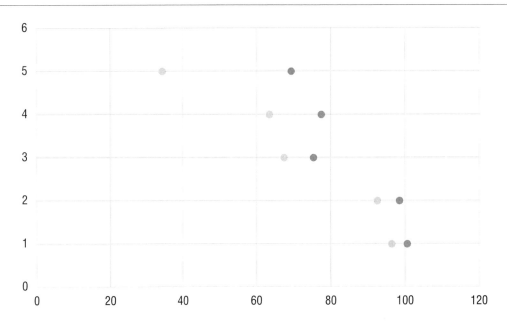

FIGURE 3.32   Choose the built-in marker icon and make it large.

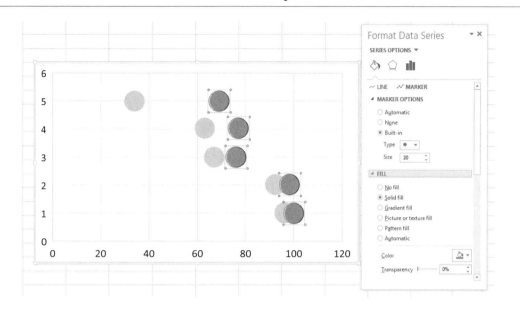

Then increase the marker size to something around 20. At this point, I change the fill and border colors of the markers so that the reference point (Fall) is a gray and the most recent point is an action color (blue).

While the markers are highlighted, add data labels (right-click on the markers and select *Add Data Labels*). This is the second time when people write me panicky emails because Excel labels the dots with the secret y-axis values. No problem! Right-click again and select *Format Data Labels*.

Change the settings there so that the labels display the x-values (uncheck *Y-Value*), are centered over the dot, are white, bold, and approximately size 14.

Next, adjust the y-axis so the top line is gone. To do this, right-click on the y-axis numbers and select *Format Axis*. Just change the maximum number on the axis to the highest number you have listed in the dot spacing values (in this example, 5). Then click on the y-axis again and delete it.

Also adjust the x-axis. This dataset naturally caps at 100. Changing the maximum value there will also help spread apart some of the dots that are tightly clustered. (If that still doesn't do the trick for your clustered dots, try using a condensed font. And if that doesn't work, it could be that the dot plot isn't the right graph type for displaying your data.)

Truth be told, since the dots are all labeled with their values, we really don't need the x-axis at all. But, in this case, I think it can be valuable. Dot plots are a new kind of visual for most people. And while they are easy to digest, it may help credibility to have the x-axis in there as an anchor. However, we don't need to have all of the intervals along the x-axis. So in the same *Format Axis* box, change the major units from 20 to 100 (Figure 3.34).

FIGURE 3.33   Add the x-axis values to the labels and change the position to Center.

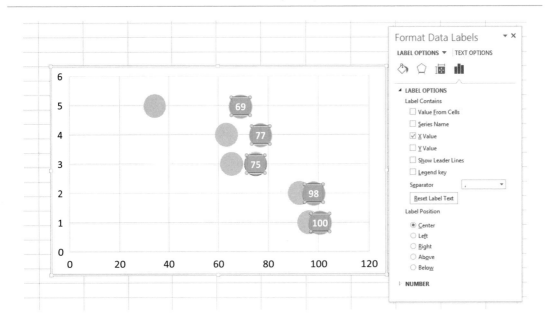

FIGURE 3.34   Anchor the graph with an x-axis that just runs from 0 to 100.

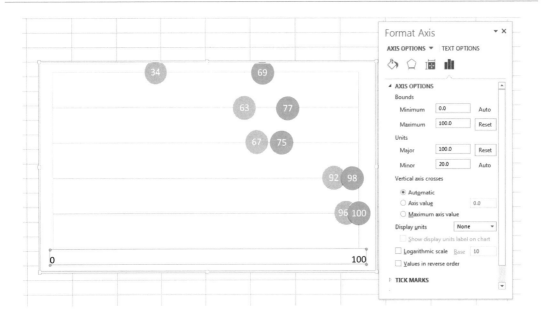

Right-click on the x-axis again and select *Format Major Gridlines*—then select *No Line.*

Add a title and subtitle. There are a few ways to get the subject area labels in the graph, but in this case I went the simplest route and just inserted linked textboxes right inside the chart. Some people prefer to have all the labels aligned on the left of the chart—do whatever works best for you. My final product is shown in Figure 3.35.

So, the key is to set up a hidden y-axis of spacing values that serve only to put your data points on lines that are evenly spaced apart from one another.

I'm sure you noticed that this example actually reflects change over time. This is the nice thing about dot plots—they are flexible. I've even successfully gotten away with adding a third dot to each line—comparing 3 things. But, it really depends on the extent to which your data points overlap one another.

FIGURE 3.35   Dot plots can be easier to interpret than side by side bar charts.

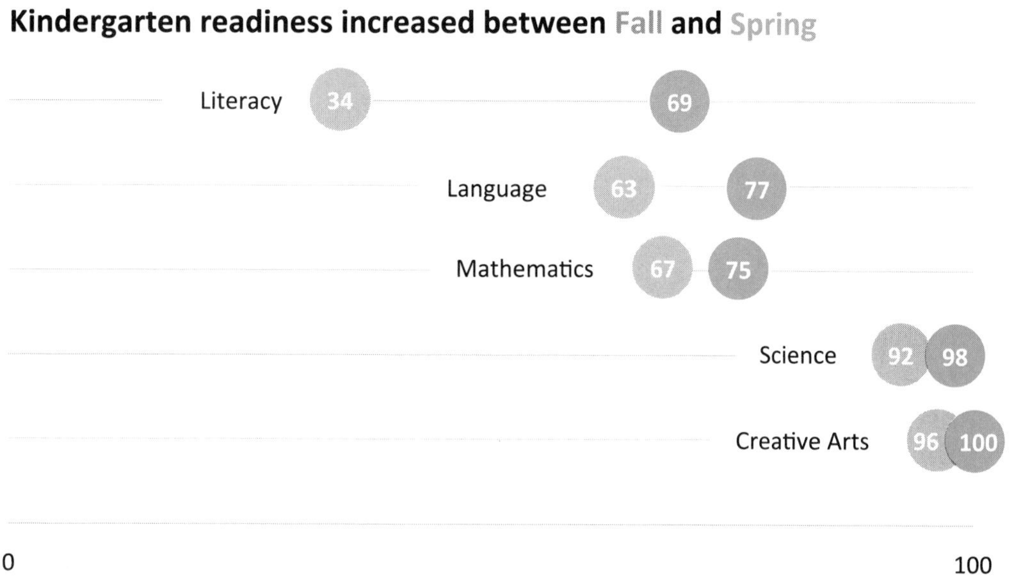

Kindergarten readiness increased between Fall **and** Spring

0   100

DUMBBELL DOT PLOT

In case it wasn't clear, I love dot plots. They are amazingly easy to read, beautifully simple in their display. I was making these babies for some clients a little while ago, before and after dots for about 25 variables in one graph. And they said "Uh, hey Stephanie? Could you, like, draw a tiny line between the pair of dots on each line?" >.< That was my face when I imagined painfully inserting 25 lines, perfectly aligned between the dot pairs. But, I love challenges like this. Could I find a way to make Excel do this for me? Yes I could! I'm an Excel ninja!

Dumbbell dot plots (also known as connected dot plots) have an advantage over the regular dot plot: the line that connects each pair of dots emphasizes their distance. If you are trying to tell a story about the gap or growth between two things, try a dumbbell dot plot.

A regular dot plot is made with a basic scatterplot as its backbone. But, we will use a connected scatterplot to make a dumbbell dot plot. The construction of the data table is a little bit different (see Figure 3.36).

I need a set of y-values to accompany each of my x-values (the stuff I really care about displaying). The y-values are just placeholder values that allow my actual data to appear on equally spaced lines. Note that I ordered the scores from least to greatest in terms of the growth that occurred between 2013 and 2015. I won't plot the Growth data, but I did use it to sort the table. Dumbbell dot plots emphasize the gap or growth, so ordering them in this way makes the story even easier to read.

First, I insert a connected scatterplot without selecting any data and then right-click in the empty space inside the graph and click *Select Data*. Each pair of dots will need to become its own series. So, you'll click on *Add* to make a new series in that *Select Data Source* window.

A new little window will open up (Figure 3.37).

EXCEL NINJA LEVEL: 10

FIGURE 3.36   You will need a secret y-values column for each set of x-values.

	2013	2015	2013 Dot Spacing	2015 Dot Spacing	Growth
Agency 11	25%	9%	1	1	-16%
Agency 2	58%	46%	2	2	-12%
Agency 8	66%	60%	3	3	-6%
Agency 5	20%	22%	4	4	2%
Agency 13	9%	15%	5	5	6%
Agency 7	21%	29%	6	6	8%
Agency 15	41%	50%	7	7	9%
Agency 1	22%	32%	8	8	10%
Agency 14	17%	28%	9	9	11%
Agency 4	12%	26%	10	10	14%
Agency 9	19%	34%	11	11	15%
Agency 12	4%	23%	12	12	19%
Agency 3	9%	31%	13	13	22%
Agency 16	1%	24%	14	14	23%
Agency 6	0%	31%	15	15	31%
Agency 10	20%	52%	16	16	32%

For Series name, click on the name of the Agency (let's start with Agency 11). For Series X-values, select Agency 11's 2013 and 2015 scores. For Series Y-values, select Agency 11's 2013 Dot Spacing values and 2015 Dot Spacing values. Note how this added the first set of connected dots to the graph (see Figure 3.37).

FIGURE 3.37   Add each Agency's data as its own series.

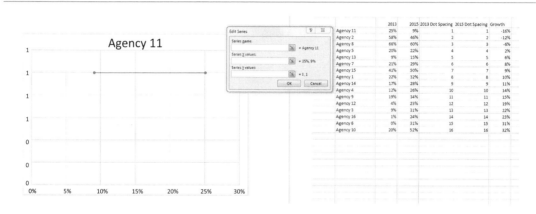

Click OK and then repeat this for each Agency until they are all displayed on your graph. This looks like a lot of work, but it took me about 2 minutes of clicking to add them all.

Delete any gridlines so you can see the dumbbells clearly.

For some agencies, the dot on the left is 2013 and for others, it is the dot on the right. Color coding the dots by year will help audiences keep track of whether agency performance increased or decreased. We also want larger dots so we can label the percentage inside the dot. Unlike regular dot plots, where we could click on the Spring dots and change all the markers at once, with a dumbbell dot plot, you have to change each dumbbell one at a time.

To make the changes, right-click on the markers and click *Format Data Series*. Change the marker size and add the labels, using the same methods outlined for the regular dot plot.

Change the color of each marker to correspond to the year, following the same steps as changing marker colors in the regular dot plot. In this case, 2013 is a light blue and 2015 is a dark blue. Also, since the connecting line doesn't get associated with either year, change it to a shade of gray. Changing every single color and adding the data labels took me 10 minutes. It's not the most exciting part of visualizing data.

Time to label! Do you really want to insert, nudge, and align 16 textboxes for all agencies? Me neither. Let's leverage Excel to help us. Delete both axes to make room for labels. Then go back to the table and add another column called *Labels* and fill the column with zeros (see Figure 3.39).

Right-click back on the graph and click *Select Data*. Add a new series, which you can call *Labels*. This time, the x-values will be the whole column of zeroes you just typed.

FIGURE 3.38   The dumbbells show the growth between two points.

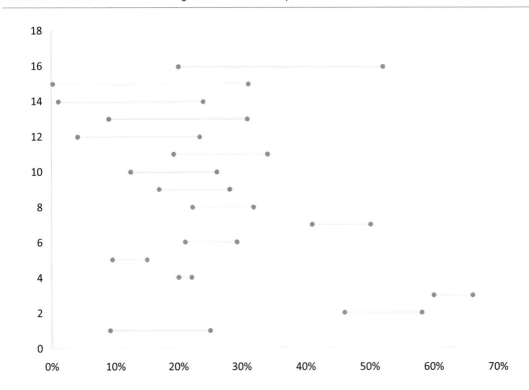

FIGURE 3.39   Make a placeholder column for the labels.

	2013	2015	2013 Dot Spacing	2015 Dot Spacing	Growth	Labels
Agency 11	25%	9%	1	1	-16%	0%
Agency 2	58%	46%	2	2	-12%	0%
Agency 8	66%	60%	3	3	-6%	0%
Agency 5	20%	22%	4	4	2%	0%
Agency 13	9%	15%	5	5	6%	0%
Agency 7	21%	29%	6	6	8%	0%
Agency 15	41%	50%	7	7	9%	0%
Agency 1	22%	32%	8	8	10%	0%
Agency 14	17%	28%	9	9	11%	0%
Agency 4	12%	26%	10	10	14%	0%
Agency 9	19%	34%	11	11	15%	0%
Agency 12	4%	23%	12	12	19%	0%
Agency 3	9%	31%	13	13	22%	0%
Agency 16	1%	24%	14	14	23%	0%
Agency 6	0%	31%	15	15	31%	0%
Agency 10	20%	52%	16	16	32%	0%

The y-values will be either of the dot spacing columns, doesn't matter which one. Click OK and you should see a line with markers running vertically down the left of the graph (see Figure 3.40).

FIGURE 3.40   Add a new series to make a vertical line with markers.

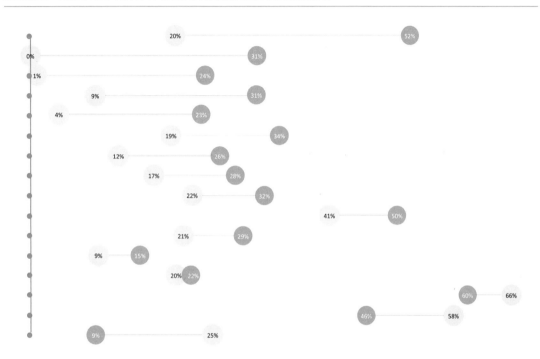

The labels for the markers on this new line will be the Agency names. Make room for the labels by dragging the left side of the plot area over to the right. Then right-click on the labels line and select *Add Data Labels*. Excel will label with the y-values. So right-click again and select *Format Data Labels*. In Excel 2013, I have the option to relabel by selecting the values from other cells. Check *Value From Cells* and pick the agency names. Uncheck *Y-Value*. Then select the radio button under *Label Position* that says *Left* (see Figure 3.41). So sweet and easy.

If you are working in an earlier version of Excel or plan to send your Excel file to someone who is working in an earlier version of Excel, pick *Left* for your label position and then use the linked textbox trick to change the contents of each label to its proper agency name.

Then format the labels line so that it is *No Line* and *No Markers*.

If that isn't enough ninja skill for you, let's add in another point of comparison. Let's say these agencies have a benchmark of 50% for 2015. Use the same technique we just used with the labels line to insert a vertical benchmark line. Add a column to the table named Benchmark and fill it with 50% for each agency listed (see Figure 3.42).

FIGURE 3.41   Check Value From Cells and highlight the cells with the agency names.

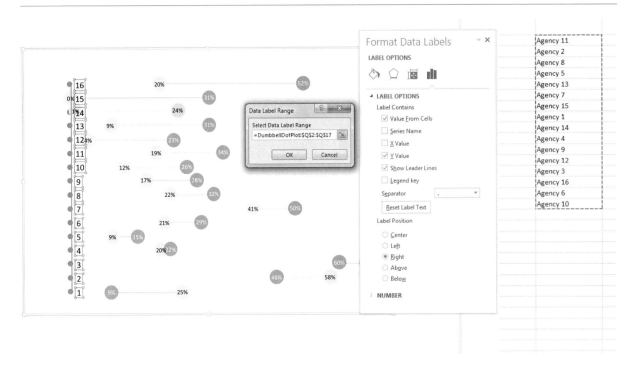

FIGURE 3.42   Drop in a new column for the Benchmark line.

	2013	2015	2013 Dot Spacing	2015 Dot Spacing	Growth	Labels	Benchmark
Agency 11	25%	9%	1	1	-16%	0%	50%
Agency 2	58%	46%	2	2	-12%	0%	50%
Agency 8	66%	60%	3	3	-6%	0%	50%
Agency 5	20%	22%	4	4	2%	0%	50%
Agency 13	9%	15%	5	5	6%	0%	50%
Agency 7	21%	29%	6	6	8%	0%	50%
Agency 15	41%	50%	7	7	9%	0%	50%
Agency 1	22%	32%	8	8	10%	0%	50%
Agency 14	17%	28%	9	9	11%	0%	50%
Agency 4	12%	26%	10	10	14%	0%	50%
Agency 9	19%	34%	11	11	15%	0%	50%
Agency 12	4%	23%	12	12	19%	0%	50%
Agency 3	9%	31%	13	13	22%	0%	50%
Agency 16	1%	24%	14	14	23%	0%	50%
Agency 6	0%	31%	15	15	31%	0%	50%
Agency 10	20%	52%	16	16	32%	0%	50%

FIGURE 3.43   Add a title with color-coded words to identify the years associated with each dot.

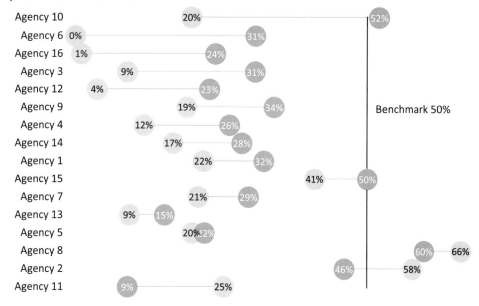

Many agencies made significant progress from 2013 to 2015, but few surpassed the benchmark.

Right-click on the graph, click *Select Data,* and add a new series where the x-values are the Benchmark data and the y-values are either of the dot spacing columns. Then format the line so that there are no markers and the line is your favorite benchmark color. I also typically add a data label to just one point on the benchmark line. Finish it off with a title.

I thought we were good to go, but my clients said they'd prefer if the graph make it even more obvious where the scores actually decreased. It would seem as if we could simply change the line style so that it began or ended with an arrowhead, but in actuality the arrowhead is obscured by this awesome size 20 dot. So, I manually inserted a tiny triangle shape, which wasn't too painful, especially since we only applied it to a small portion of the dumbbell dot plot pairs.

Whew! That may be the most complicated maneuvering of Excel ninja skills possible. The whole thing, start to finish, takes approximately 20 minutes. Dumbbell dot plots are worth the time investment because nothing else shows the gap or growth in the dataset quite as well. If you have pages of these to make, check out the exercises on code at the end of the chapter and read about macros in Chapter 9.

FIGURE 3.44   Tiny arrows can further emphasize places where performance decreased.

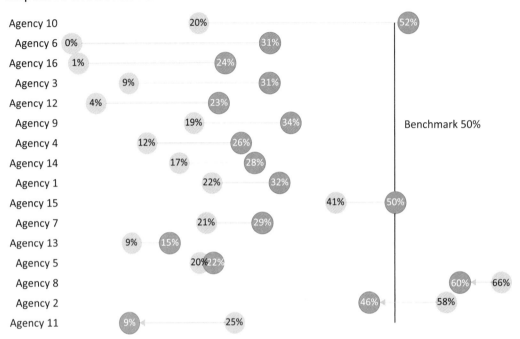

FIGURE 3.44   Tiny arrows can further emphasize places where performance decreased.

Many agencies made significant progress from 2013 to 2015, but few surpassed the benchmark.

SMALL MULTIPLES

In the last section, we started comparing more than two numbers in the same graph. However, trying to compare too many numbers at once can quickly become overwhelming and meaningless.

Remember the bar graph with way too many columns that we saw earlier in this chapter (Figure 3.2)? It was too much information to comprehend easily. But, I bet you noticed that the columns in that graph actually represented years. I know we haven't hit the chapter where we review this yet, but the most common way people show change over time is through a line graph.

How's Figure 3.45 working for you? Personally, I can barely see anything. The values in that dataset are all so close together that this graph has basically become a bowl of spaghetti. Well now what?

FIGURE 3.45   The line graph may be the most traditional way to compare trends over time, but this example isn't easy to read.

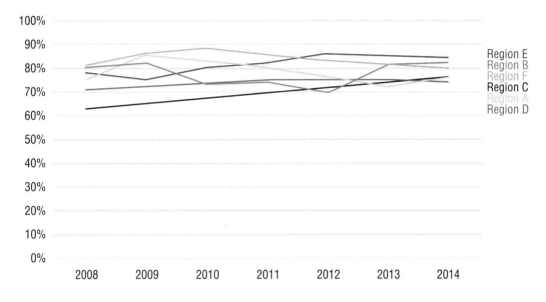

Region progress since 2008

When we are trying to compare multiple categories, but the graph gets complicated, one good solution is to break it apart into small multiples. Small multiples are several graphs, all on the same scale, arranged together. Figure 3.46 is what the same dataset looks like using small multiples.

Now I can see stuff, like how Region C is looking good!

FIGURE 3.46   Plotting each trend on its own graph makes them easier to compare—as long as the graphs are on the same scale.

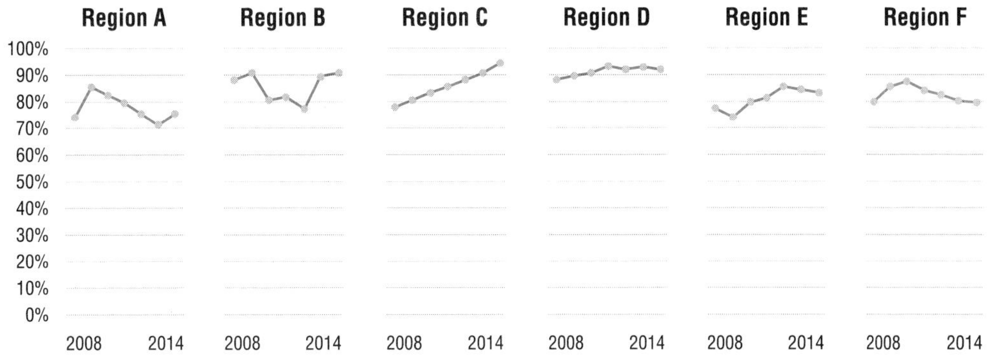

The thing is, in the first two graphs (Figure 3.2 and Figure 3.45), I couldn't see the data well enough to pull anything meaningful out of it. I couldn't even come up with a good title because I couldn't locate something important to highlight. The small multiples version makes things about a billion times easier.

In another chapter, I'll show you how to make small multiples that fit inside one big graph, but that doesn't work as well with line graphs. To construct the small multiples here, I created six separate line graphs, one for each region.

The first line graph, for Region A, is tall and skinny, with an axis. I format it just the way I want it—with markers on the lines, a y-axis labeled at 10% increments, and so on. Then I copy and paste the graph, and point the new graph to new data.

EXCEL NINJA LEVEL: 4

I right-click on the second graph and click *Select Data.* The box will open and Region A will appear as my data series. Click the *Edit* button and then use the cell picker icons to point the graph onto the next set of data, for Region B (see Figure 3.47).

The graph's formatting essentially stays the same, but importantly Excel revised the scale of the y-axis so that it maxes out at 90% in the new graph. In a small multiples series, the axes need to be the same. Format the y-axis so the maximum is 100% or 1.0. Then go ahead and delete that axis. We really only need the axis labeled on the far left of this visualization. Repeat these steps for each of the regions.

FIGURE 3.47   Edit the data series and highlight the next set of data.

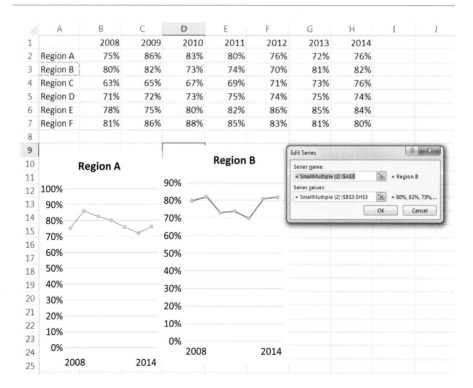

The tricky part is making sure all of the graphs have the same sized plot area, including the first one on the left, which houses the axis (refer to Figure 3.46). Chances are, when you deleted the axis from the second through sixth graphs, the plot area resized and now they are wider than the first graph. How in the world do we make the plot areas the same size? Not even kidding, I literally got my kid's ruler and measured the length of the gridlines behind the graph for Region B and then resized the graph for Region A until the gridlines were the same length. It sounds more complicated than it is. Plus, how often do you get to break out the ruler?

Select all graphs by holding down the Shift key and clicking on them all. Then look in the *Drawing Tools* tab and under the *Align* button and select *Align Top*. They end up all perfect and tidy and you end up looking like a data visualization rock star.

We talk more about graphing change over time later, but the big idea here is that you should keep small multiples in your back pocket. They are nearly always the right answer when the data display, while technically correct, is still overcomplicated.

Each of the chart choices in this chapter offer strong storytelling support, each one bolstering a different story. Think about your dataset carefully and decide which graph type will display it clearly.

EXERCISES

Small multiples are such an elegant solution to so many graphing problems. Chapter 9 shows an area graph, which is a default graph type, but one that can be a bit complicated to read. Use the data table from that chapter and break out the data into a small multiples array of area charts. Compare the stacked area chart with the small multiples array of area charts that you constructed and articulate the strengths and weaknesses of both visuals.

These Excel ninja graphs make you feel good, but they can also leave you feeling a bit daunted by the idea of churning them out at scale. Three possible solutions that I want you to try:

1. Save the finished graph as a new chart type. Just right-click on the graph and you should see a menu option called *Save as Template*. It opens some magical place on your computer—don't move from that spot. Just name your new chart type and save. Then you'll see a new area in your regular menu of chart choices called Templates. This process will get you 60% to 85% of the way there, depending on the graph type. You'll still have to do some adjusting, but it gives you a head start in your graph development. Try making a template for a slopegraph.

2. More advanced users should try recording a macro. Sounds intimidating, but it isn't that scary once you get started. Macros are accessible through a new tab you have to tell Excel to add to your toolbar. Follow *File* to *Options* and then look in the *Customize Ribbon* menu. From there you can add the *Developer* tab to your ribbon. In it, you'll see a button called *Record Macro*. Essentially, this records your movements around the spreadsheet and writes code based on those movements. So, you begin recording the macro (name it after your graph type), then you make

(Continued)

(Contined)

your ninja graph, and then press *Stop Recording.* In the future, you'll simply go to the *Macros* menu and play your recorded steps. Try recording a macro for one of the graphs in this chapter. Be patient. It takes some trial and error. Skip ahead to Chapter 9 for more details on macros for slopegraphs and dot plots.

3. When you recorded your macro, the code Excel wrote in the background is a powerful, if intimidating, way to generate copies of graphs with speed. In Excel-speak, this is called Visual Basic for Applications or VBA code and people have written dozens of coding instructions to make Excel do all sorts of cartwheels and tricks. Conduct a quick Internet search on VBA code to copy graphs with new data. You'll see several options that you can dump into a new *Visual Basic* window (right next to the *Macros* button). Again, code can be complex to work with so allow yourself a lot of time . . . and coffee.

RESOURCES

Two smart colleagues each wrote a blog post suggesting alternatives to the side by side bar chart within a week of each other. Jon Schwabish's post walks through a redesign into a modified dumbbell dot plot at http://policyviz.com/killing-the-paired-bar-chart/. Ann Emery offers six possible redesigns, including a slopegraph and a dot plot at http://annkemery.com/clustered-bar-chart/.

Snag action colors for your graph from your own organizational branding (search "branding guidelines" on your website) or identify them through a lightweight application called *Colorblind Assistant,* which generates color codes to replicate the color of whatever you hover over. Check under the *Apps* tab at http://www.littlesky.org/

REFERENCES

Cowan, N. (2000). The magical number 4 in short-term memory: A reconsideration of mental storage capacity. *Behavioral and Brain Sciences, 24,* 87–185.

Dasgupta, A., Chen, M., & Kosara, R. (2012). Conceptualizing visual uncertainty in parallel coordinates. *Computer Graphics Forum, 31*(3), 1015–1024.

Jacoby, W. G. (2006). The dot plot: A graphical display for labeled quantitative values. *The Political Methodologist, 14*(1), 6–14.

Talbot, J., Setlur, V., & Anand, A. (2014). Four experiments on the perception of bar charts. *IEEE Transactions on Visualization and Computer Graphics, 20*(12), 2152–2160.

4

HOW WE ARE BETTER OR WORSE THAN A BENCHMARK

DISPLAYING RELATIVE PERFORMANCE

LEARNING OBJECTIVES

After reading this chapter you will be able to

List multiple methods for showing progress against a benchmark

Choose a method for displaying a benchmark that fits your need for precision and context

Understand how adding a benchmark increases interpretability of the data

Add performance data and visuals to your existing graphs

Regardless of the type, whether a standard, target, benchmark, average, national norm, or long-term goal, it is too often missing from our data displays. I find that the people I work with tend to know their department goal—sure, it's written down in a memo somewhere—but it is rarely included in the data visualization. Without that context, we limit the amount of information a reader can pull from our graphs.

The easiest, most direct method for adding in a comparison point on your graph is to insert a line. This works especially well when all of the data share the same comparison point or goal.

When there are different goals or benchmarks for each category, you can use a combo chart or some variation of a bullet chart. Bullet charts have gray shaded areas of comparison behind a bar or column, or a target line for each bar or column (and sometimes both gray shaded areas and target lines).

If your visualization needs are pretty basic, you can get away with using Data Bars as a modified bullet graph. These are programmed using Excel's conditional formatting function, where the gray background area represents the target and the Data Bar would meet the end of the cell when the target is met. It's a bit crude, but can suffice for many circumstances, particularly for internal purposes.

Use a true bullet chart for more precise and context heavy visualizations, where the use of both shaded background areas and a target line pack in the interpretive power. These charts can be vertical or horizontal, the latter of which are most useful in dashboards.

Finally, indicator dots are another way to maximize the readability of a dashboard. These dots indicate when there's a problem that needs attention by staff, popping right out of the screen and sounding the alarm bells.

No matter which method you choose to show your relationship to a benchmark, these visuals play an important role in painting the whole picture about what's happening with your data.

WHAT STORIES CAN BE TOLD ABOUT HOW WE ARE BETTER OR WORSE THAN A BENCHMARK?

Adding benchmark information increases and deepens nearly any story told in this book. This tiny bit of extra detail in a graph answers the first set of questions readers are likely to ask about the data: "Compared to what?" The stories that can be told include

- Our key indicators met the preestablished targets in three out of seven areas
- Regions A and B did not meet quarterly benchmarks
- Here is how our groups compared to the national norm
- Students in the Chemistry Department are above average on final exams this year
- The salmon hatchery initiative is halfway to completion
- We did not meet our fundraising goal, but we got very close
- Our click rate was 25.6% while the industry standard is 4.3%

The stories that can be told with benchmark data help a reader determine whether performance was good, bad, or close to the mark.

HOW CAN I VISUALIZE HOW WE ARE BETTER OR WORSE THAN A BENCHMARK?

Your decision among these options will depend on whether your benchmark changes (year to year, across different variables, etc.); how precise of a visual you need; and your Excel ninja level (some of these require backflips). Don't worry—I'll show you how to take every step.

BENCHMARK LINE

Adding a benchmark line to a graph gives loads of context for the viewer; this simple line packs so much power. Here's how to make one right inside Excel, using a combination of two different graph types. It's so easy you might pass out.

EXCEL NINJA LEVEL: 2

My data table is shown in Figure 4.1.

Highlight the group names and their data and insert a simple column graph.

Then right-click on the graph (Figure 4.2) and click *Select Data*. In the box that pops up (see Figure 4.3), click the *Add* button to add a new series. In *that* new dialogue box, select your Benchmark data. You'll see a second set of columns added to the graph in the background.

Now it's time to change that benchmark data from columns to a line. This is where the Excel magic happens.

In Excel 2013, I right-click on the benchmark columns and click *Change Chart Type* and then choose *Line* (Figure 4.4). You can do this in 2010, too, just click on the benchmark columns and then click the *Change Chart Type* button in your Layout tab and select a line graph.

FIGURE 4.1   I have my data and I have the benchmark value listed next to each.

⊿	A	B	C
1			Benchmark
2	Group A	55%	65%
3	Group B	58%	65%
4	Group C	67%	65%
5			

FIGURE 4.2   Forget the benchmark data for a second and just insert a basic column graph of your data.

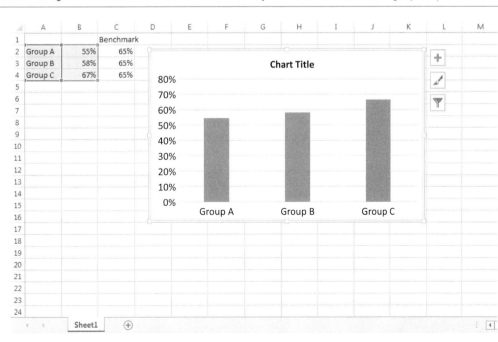

FIGURE 4.3   Add in a new series—your benchmark data!

FIGURE 4.4   When you change chart type in Excel 2013, you'll get a drop-down menu of chart options for each series of data. Choose *Line* for your benchmark data.

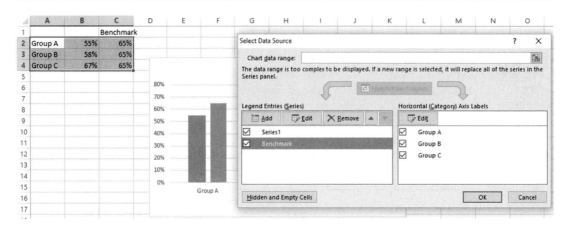

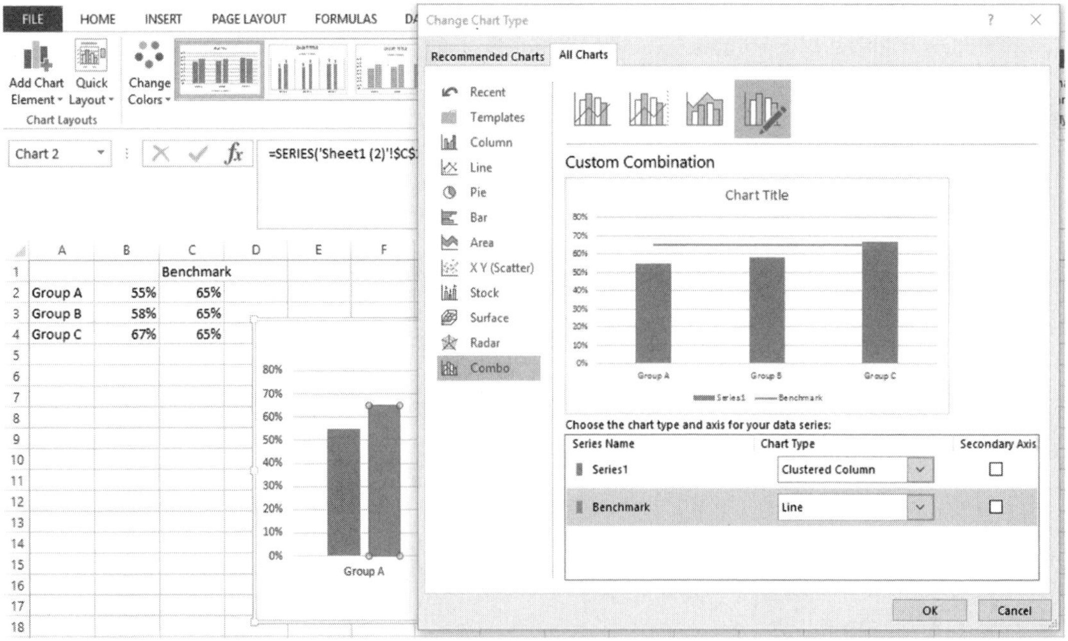

At this point, it is all about formatting. Change the colors to something meaningful for you and your organization. Add a data label to one point of the line so it says "Benchmark." Of course, Excel tried to give me the value of the point, but just right-click on the point again and click *Format Data Label* and then select *Series name* and unselect *Value*. Then drop in a crystal clear title.

So this is cool, but if you'd like your benchmark line to be a bit longer, like I have it in Figure 4.5, you can just fiddle with the data table a little and select blank cells to add some space to the set of columns and then associate the benchmark 65% with each blank spot.

FIGURE 4.5   In the full color version of this graph, the benchmark line is orange. Orange, red, and black are common benchmark colors.

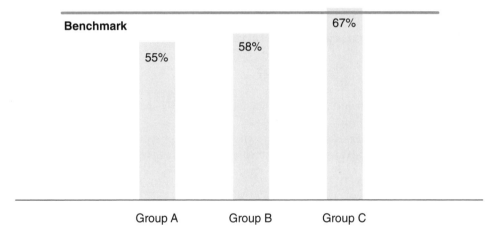

Two of the three grantee groups did not meet performance benchmarks this year.

Did that sentence make any sense? It was heavy on the nerd-speak. Just make your data table look like Figure 4.6. Then go back in to *Select Data* and edit each series to include rows 2 through 6.

And now the graph is WAY more powerful! We've added so much interpretation to the data visualization, helping the viewer understand how far the first two groups are from the target and by how much Group C exceeded it. Your viewers want to be able to interpret the data . . . is it good? . . . bad? . . . the worst in history? . . . best in the nation?

This option is fine when the benchmark is the same for everything you need to graph, but what about when relative performance is different for each group?

FIGURE 4.6   Bulk up the benchmark numbers in your data table to make a longer line.

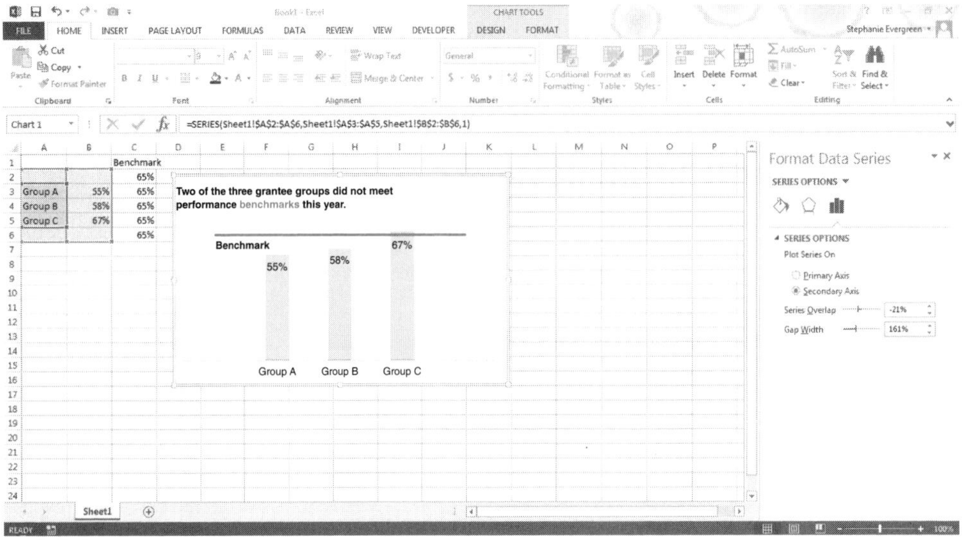

COMBO CHART

It's no big deal at all, just adjust your data table accordingly and your line will move, so it looks like this Figure 4.7

In this particular example, the presence of the comparison group (State average) actually *makes* the story that these researchers need to tell with their data.

EXCEL NINJA LEVEL: 2

CAN I ADD A SECOND LINE?

Hello, do you know how I can include two goal/benchmark lines in a bar graph? For example I want to track the Donations progress . . . I want to show a first goal at $85, then a second goal at $100. I would like to be able to see the current donations progress measured against those two goals. Thank You!!!

Justin P

Yes, Justin, you can add two benchmark lines. Just follow these same steps and add another column of data to your table for your second benchmark line. You'll want to take care to distinguish the lines from one another. Perhaps make one gray and the other black. Possibly one could be dashed and the other solid. Too many lines could get confusing, of course, so you definitely wouldn't want gridlines on the graph. Another way you could go about this could be to make it more like a bullet graph, where your goals are gray bands in the background. Instructions are on page 79. Good luck with your fundraising!

FIGURE 4.7   The norm group in this case also changes over time, so the benchmark line looks like it would in a more traditional line graph.

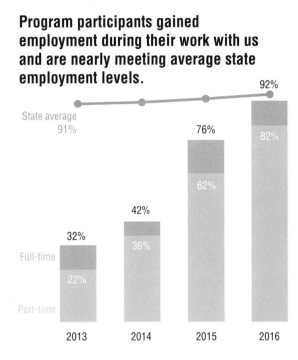

Program participants gained employment during their work with us and are nearly meeting average state employment levels.

State average 91%

92%

76%

82%

62%

42%

36%

32%

Full-time

22%

Part-time

2013   2014   2015   2016

BULLET GRAPH

Have you seen a bullet graph before? They are a relatively new chart type, birthed into being by data viz legend, Stephen Few. Figure 4.8 is the anatomy diagram.

Few (2013) says that a bullet chart encodes your actual data as a bar (usually black), plotted with a target line (usually red), and against gray ranges of performance, like unacceptable/acceptable or poor/satisfactory/good. You don't normally see a single bullet graph isolated like this. More commonly, they are packed into data dashboards, where each variable has its own bullet graph, all arranged on one sheet of paper.

If those ranges of performance made you scratch your head, you aren't alone. I've introduced bullet charts to many clients over the years and almost none of them had ranges of performance they needed to measure against, just a single target. So let's start with the simplest type of bullet graph with no ranges of performance in the background and work our way up to the most complex type.

FIGURE 4.8   As defined by Stephen Few, a bullet chart has several key design elements.

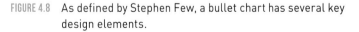
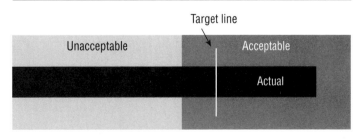

Target line

Unacceptable

Acceptable

Actual

The Easiest—Data Bars

My client said, "Dearest Stephanie, we don't need those gray shades in the background. Our metrics don't have performance levels. You either meet the target or you don't. And furthermore, we don't need a target line. The target should be the end of the graph so that when the actual bar hits the end of the graph, we know we have met our target."

And you know what? That way of visualizing the bullet chart made . . . so . . . much . . . sense, at least for me when dealing with this particular case and several others I've worked with since then. Technically, without those background areas, this doesn't qualify as a bullet chart. Excel calls these Data Bars, but why quibble about the name? This is a good time for me to mention that if I ever open a pub for data nerds, I'm going to call it the Data Bar. Let's get graphing.

And BONUS: this method uses in-line graphing with Excel, so the graphs don't move out of alignment or require extensive size and positioning, compared to the others I mention in this chapter. We're using conditional formatting to make these (and it works in Excel 2010, too!). Here's how:

FIGURE 4.9   Duplicate your actual data into a third column, which will become your data bars.

	A	B	C	D
1	Census QuickFacts Kalamazoo			
2		Kalamazoo	Target (MI Average)	
3	Living in same house 1 year & over, percent, 2008-2012	78.5%	85.4%	78.5%
4	Foreign born persons, percent, 2008-2012	4.7%	6.0%	4.7%
5	Language other than English spoken at home, pct age 5+, 2008-2012	6.6%	9.0%	6.6%
6	High school graduate or higher, percent of persons age 25+, 2008-2012	92.4%	88.7%	92.4%
7	Bachelor's degree or higher, percent of persons age 25+, 2008-2012	33.7%	25.5%	33.7%
8	Mean travel time to work (minutes), workers age 16+, 2008-2012	20	24	20
9	Homeownership rate, 2008-2012	65.2%	72.8%	65.2%
10	Housing units in multi-unit structures, percent, 2008-2012	27.9%	18.0%	27.9%
11	Median value of owner-occupied housing units, 2008-2012	$141,200	$128,600	$141,200
12	Persons per household, 2008-2012	2	3	2
13	Per capita money income in past 12 months (2012 dollars), 2008-2012	$25,860	$25,547	$25,860
14	Median household income, 2008-2012	$46,011	$48,471	$46,011
15	Persons below poverty level, percent, 2008-2012	18.9%	16.3%	18.9%
16	Crime rate, percent, 2008-2012	-8%	4%	-8.0%

EXCEL NINJA LEVEL: 4

1. We are graphing Census data (listed in Figure 4.9) from Kalamazoo, Michigan (where I currently live) against our target, Michigan's average. First, create another column to the right of Michigan's average, where you duplicate the Kalamazoo data. But, don't just copy and paste. We want these linked, so type an equals sign in the first cell of your new column and then click on the first cell of the Kalamazoo data and hit Enter. Excel copied in your data and now they are linked such that if you change the values in that Kalamazoo cell, it will change in your new column too. Yeah? Got it? Good! Now copy your new cell all the way down that whole column. This third column of duplicated data is where the bullet charts will eventually go. Your table should look like Figure 4.9.

Go ahead and change the fill color of the cells in that third column to a shade of gray. Just one shade. It will represent your target by the time we are finished.

2. Put your cursor in the first cell where you want the bullet chart. So in this example, that'll be D3. Then click on the *Conditional Formatting* button in the Home tab and pick *New Rule*. It'll open up the dialogue box shown in Figure 4.10.

By default, the highlighted drop-down menu in the middle will say 2-color scale, so click the arrow and select *Data Bar*.

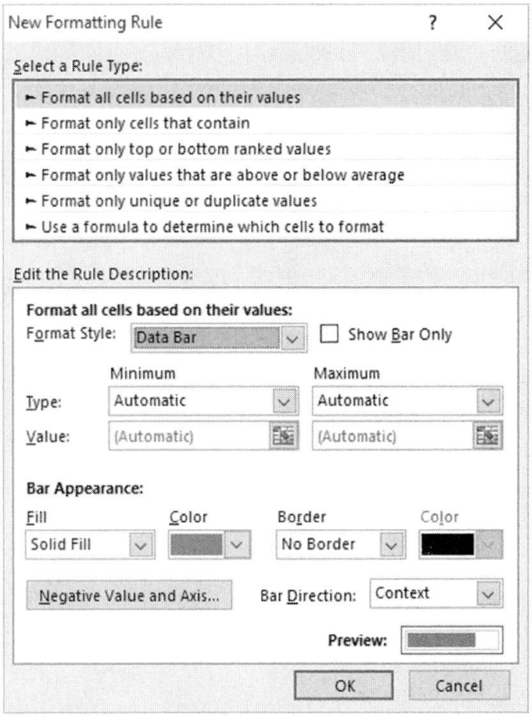

3. Adjust the settings in the dialogue box, like I have done in Figure 4.11.

Take a deep breath and let's walk through this bit-by-bit.

Check the box that says *Show Bar Only,* which will replace your copied data with just the bullet graph.

Where it says *Minimum,* you'll want to change the type from *Automatic* to *Number.* The *Value* box will populate with a 0. Generally, don't alter that box.

Where it says *Maximum,* you'll want to point Excel to your target value, since that's the way we are conceptualizing the bullet graph here, where the end of the cell/gray space *is* when the target is reached. To do so, change the type from *Automatic* to *Formula.* In the *Value* box, type in the cell that contains your target value. Note that you need to have an equals sign (=) at the front and dollar signs before the letter and number ($).

FIGURE 4.10   Make a new rule using conditional formatting.

Where it says *Bar Appearance,* you can change the fill color to match your brand.

Finally, under *Bar Direction,* select *Left-to-Right.* And click OK.

BOOM! Bullet graph! (See Figure 4.11.)

It's embedded in the cell, so it won't jump around on the screen like regular graphs can. It'll copy into new spreadsheets with ease. And it's pretty easy to set up, compared to some of the other methods I've seen. Not to totally deflate that BOOM!, but you still have to go through this process for each variable. You can't simply copy and paste the bullet you just made all the way down the column. This is because Excel's conditional formatting is stubborn in that it can only refer to one cell, just that cell, nothing but that cell. That's what the dollar signs were all about in that formula. They bind the data bar to that particular target cell. So, you'll have to

FIGURE 4.11 This is where we set up the structure of the data bar for each variable.

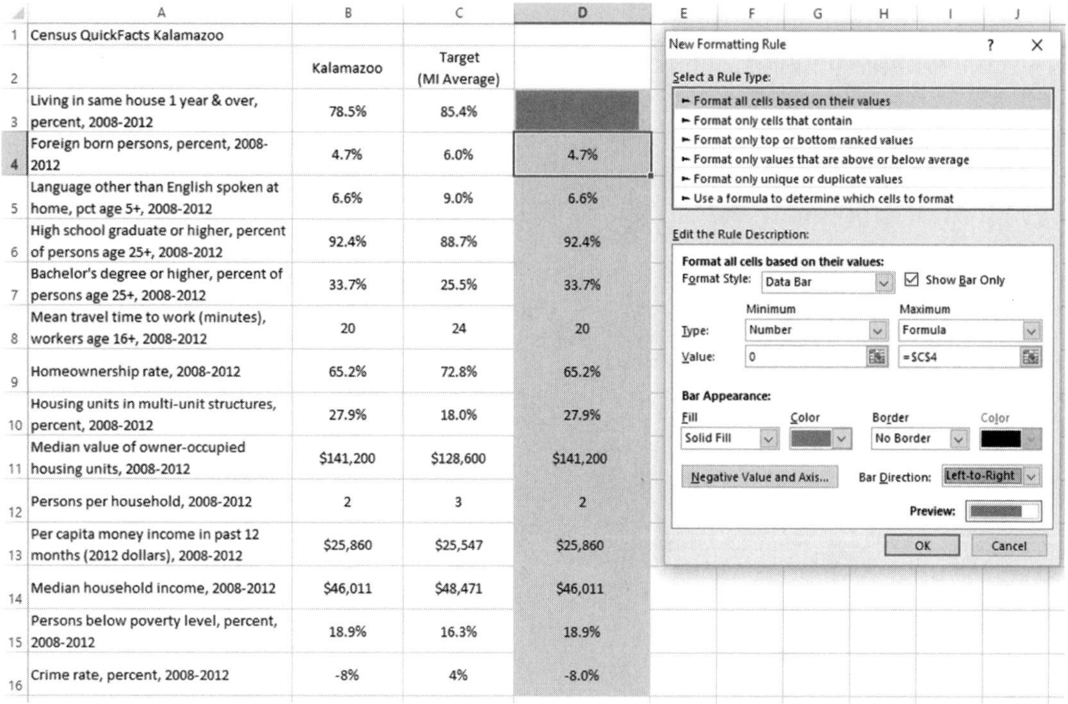
A
B
C
D
E
F
G
H
I
J
1 Census QuickFacts Kalamazoo
2 Kalamazoo Target (MI Average)
3 Living in same house 1 year & over, percent, 2008-2012 78.5% 85.4%
4 Foreign born persons, percent, 2008-2012 4.7% 6.0% 4.7%
5 Language other than English spoken at home, pct age 5+, 2008-2012 6.6% 9.0% 6.6%
6 High school graduate or higher, percent of persons age 25+, 2008-2012 92.4% 88.7% 92.4%
7 Bachelor's degree or higher, percent of persons age 25+, 2008-2012 33.7% 25.5% 33.7%
8 Mean travel time to work (minutes), workers age 16+, 2008-2012 20 24 20
9 Homeownership rate, 2008-2012 65.2% 72.8% 65.2%
10 Housing units in multi-unit structures, percent, 2008-2012 27.9% 18.0% 27.9%
11 Median value of owner-occupied housing units, 2008-2012 $141,200 $128,600 $141,200
12 Persons per household, 2008-2012 2 3 2
13 Per capita money income in past 12 months (2012 dollars), 2008-2012 $25,860 $25,547 $25,860
14 Median household income, 2008-2012 $46,011 $48,471 $46,011
15 Persons below poverty level, percent, 2008-2012 18.9% 16.3% 18.9%
16 Crime rate, percent, 2008-2012 -8% 4% -8.0%
New Formatting Rule
Select a Rule Type:
Format all cells based on their values
Format only cells that contain
Format only top or bottom ranked values
Format only values that are above or below average
Format only unique or duplicate values
Use a formula to determine which cells to format
Edit the Rule Description:
Format all cells based on their values:
Format Style: Data Bar
Show Bar Only
Minimum
Maximum
Type: Number
Formula
Value: 0
=$C$4
Bar Appearance:
Fill
Color
Border
Color
Solid Fill
No Border
Negative Value and Axis...
Bar Direction: Left-to-Right
Preview:
OK
Cancel

change the target cell for each data bar. Sounds tedious, but not as bad as making your readers wonder about the significance of what you are showing.

4. (Optional) Handle negative values. I made up this data about Crime Rate at the bottom, but let's pretend the rate since 2008 has decreased in Kalamazoo. In this situation, adjust the *Minimum* for the bullet graph by selecting *Lowest Value.*

Then click on this gray button at the bottom of the dialogue box that says *Negative Value and Axis.* It'll bring up a new dialogue box as shown in Figure 4.13.

Here is where you can change the color of the bars when they are negative (red is default, but it was too bright for my branded color scheme so I chose a dark gray). Note it also makes an axis line appear, which better visualizes that the value is negative.

FIGURE 4.12   Usually we don't need to mess with the settings for Minimum—only if trying to graph negative values.

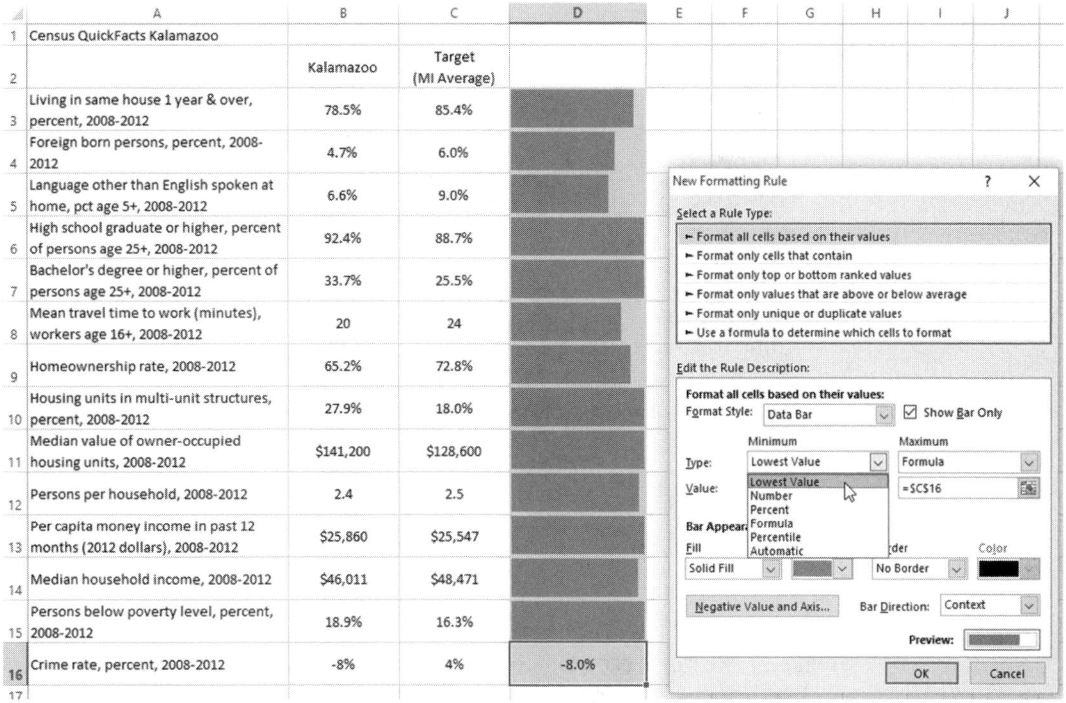

	A	B	C	D	E	F	G	H	I	J
1	Census QuickFacts Kalamazoo									
2		Kalamazoo	Target (MI Average)							
3	Living in same house 1 year & over, percent, 2008-2012	78.5%	85.4%							
4	Foreign born persons, percent, 2008-2012	4.7%	6.0%							
5	Language other than English spoken at home, pct age 5+, 2008-2012	6.6%	9.0%							
6	High school graduate or higher, percent of persons age 25+, 2008-2012	92.4%	88.7%							
7	Bachelor's degree or higher, percent of persons age 25+, 2008-2012	33.7%	25.5%							
8	Mean travel time to work (minutes), workers age 16+, 2008-2012	20	24							
9	Homeownership rate, 2008-2012	65.2%	72.8%							
10	Housing units in multi-unit structures, percent, 2008-2012	27.9%	18.0%							
11	Median value of owner-occupied housing units, 2008-2012	$141,200	$128,600							
12	Persons per household, 2008-2012	2.4	2.5							
13	Per capita money income in past 12 months (2012 dollars), 2008-2012	$25,860	$25,547							
14	Median household income, 2008-2012	$46,011	$48,471							
15	Persons below poverty level, percent, 2008-2012	18.9%	16.3%							
16	Crime rate, percent, 2008-2012	-8%	4%	-8.0%						
17										

5. When the actual value exceeds the target, we'd expect to see a blue bar that goes past the gray background, but Excel has these in-cell margins, so there's always a tiny sliver of gray that shows up so that it can look like the actual values haven't met the target yet even when they have. You'll see this in rows 6 and 10 of Figure 4.12, as examples. To fix that, highlight all of the data bars and right-click. In that menu, select *Format Cells*. In the box that opens, change the border on the left and right to white. This should make things line up as they should. Still, you'll notice that if your actual value exceeds your target, the data bar doesn't keep growing into the next cell, which makes this method slightly more rudimentary, but still sufficient in many circumstances.

FIGURE 4.13   Adjust the fill color and axis settings for negative values.

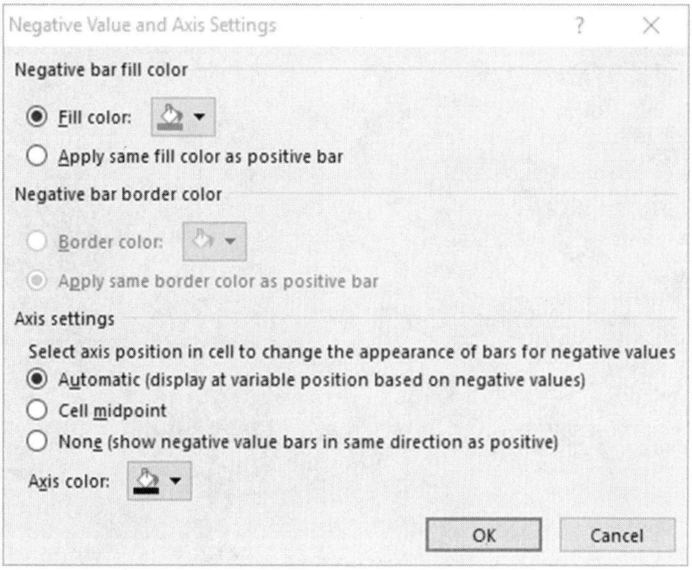

Negative Value and Axis Settings   ?   ✕

Negative bar fill color

○ <u>F</u>ill color: 🪣 ▼

○ Apply same fill color as positive bar

Negative bar border color

○ <u>B</u>order color: 🪣 ▼

◉ Apply same border color as positive bar

Axis settings

Select axis position in cell to change the appearance of bars for negative values

◉ A<u>u</u>tomatic (display at variable position based on negative values)

○ Cell <u>m</u>idpoint

○ No<u>n</u>e (show negative value bars in same direction as positive)

A<u>x</u>is color: 🪣 ▼

[OK   ]   [Cancel]

From here, we can order from greatest to least (without having to reshuffle lots of graphs!), add more data, and maybe other in-cell indicators like those we discuss later in this chapter, and make it ten thousand times easier for our viewers to get a sense of performance at a glance.

FIGURE 4.14   Every piece of the final visual has a value associated with it in the table.

◢	A	B
1		Region A
2	Poor	33.3%
3	Good	33.3%
4	Excellent	33.3%
5	Value	70%
6	Target	75%

Somewhat Harder—Vertical Bullets

This time, let's be proper and include the ranges of performance in the background of the bullet graph. The backbone behind this version is two sets of overlapping data. Except we are going to leverage a totally amazing and misunderstood feature of Excel.

Here is how I set up my table (Figure 4.14). The first three rows are the performance areas that will become the background of the bullet. The value row is my actual value and will ultimately show up as a black column in my bullet chart. The target value will become a red line.

To make the visual, highlight everything and insert a stacked column chart. Careful, now—not the 100% stacked column, just the regular stacked column. It'll come out looking like Figure 4.15.

EXCEL NINJA LEVEL: 7

FIGURE 4.15   This doesn't look like a stacked column, but hang in there!

FIGURE 4.16   After switching the row and column, the data are now in one stacked bar.

Not cool, Excel. This isn't what I want. Look up in the green *Chart Tools>Design* tab and click *Switch Row/Column* and now your chart should look like Figure 4.16.

Well OK, so that's not really doing it for you, either, is it? Let's start by making the target into a line instead of a bar. Right-click on the target slice of this stacked bar and select *Change Chart Type.* (In Excel 2010, this is a button in your banner, not part of your right-click menu.) In the box that pops up, select *Stacked Line with Markers.*

HOLD UP! Don't close the box. While here, we are going to execute some Excel ninja skills. Right now everything is stacked as one bar (and a line), but we really want the performance areas as one stacked column in the background and our value and target line in the foreground. Do you know how we shift them to the foreground? It's by moving them to the secondary axis. Yeah! That crazy thing we always see in Excel! It actually has a purpose! So, in that dialogue box you should also see a checkbox that says *Secondary Axis.* Do it! Click now! (In Excel 2010, right-click again on the target part of the graph and select *Format Data Series.* You should see a radio button there for *Secondary Axis.*)

Then right-click on the target line and select *Format Data Series.* Adjust the marker option so that it is a *Built-in* marker type and select the dash marker from the drop-down menu of marker choices. Make it big, for example a size 15. Change the fill color to red and in the Border area, select *No Border.* Your chart should end up looking like Figure 4.17.

That was the hardest part. Almost there.

Now, let's move Value so it's also on the secondary axis. Right-click on the Value slice of the stacked bar and select *Format Data Series.* In the window that pops up, you'll see an option to move it to the secondary axis. CLICK! It'll look super weird so before you close that window move the slider bar on the Gap Width up to like 250% so the Value bar gets skinny. Then you'll be able to see the others behind it. While in the formatting dialogue box, change the fill color of Value to black. Hopefully, your graph now looks a lot like Figure 4.18.

It's all formatting from here on out, baby. You'll want to change the maximum for both axis so they stop at 100%. Right-click on each axis, select *Format Axis,* and then in that

FIGURE 4.17   The graph is starting to take the correct shape—the target is now a red line.

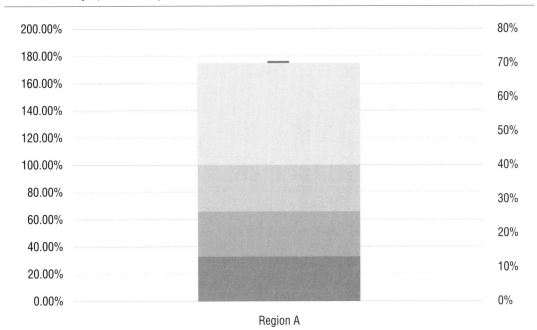

FIGURE 4.18   Value and Target should now be in front of the performance ranges.

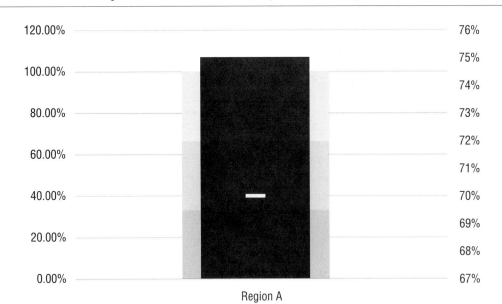

new dialogue box, locate the *Maximum* information, click on the radio button by *Fixed* and change it to 1.0 or 100% (see Figure 4.19).

After you have fixed both axes, go ahead and delete one of them. We don't need to display both. Then adjust the colors of the performance areas so that they are shades of gray.

Then, suppose your boss says you also need to report on Regions B through D. Go through that whole process again? Thankfully, no. Just click on the graph such that the original data table is highlighted in blue. Drag the bottom corner handle of the new column so it covers all of your data as in Figure 4.20.

FIGURE 4.19   Both axis should stop at 100%.

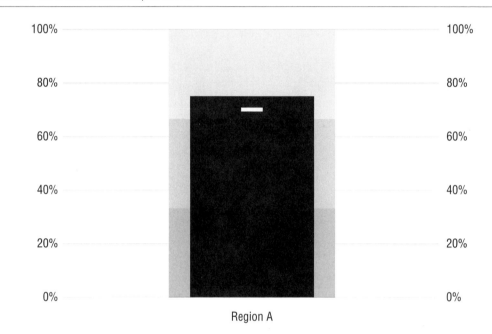

FIGURE 4.20   Use the corner handle to include the new data in your table.

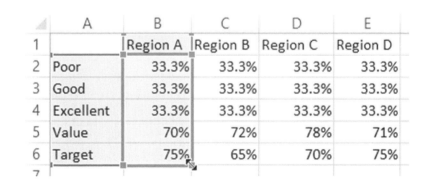

	A	B	C	D	E
1		Region A	Region B	Region C	Region D
2	Poor	33.3%	33.3%	33.3%	33.3%
3	Good	33.3%	33.3%	33.3%	33.3%
4	Excellent	33.3%	33.3%	33.3%	33.3%
5	Value	70%	72%	78%	71%
6	Target	75%	65%	70%	75%
7					

Add an informative title. Add data labels to show the value on your black columns. You're looking at the finished product in Figure 4.21.

FIGURE 4.21   Finish formatting the chart with a helpful title. You could also add labels for your performance areas, if your main audience won't know how to interpret those.

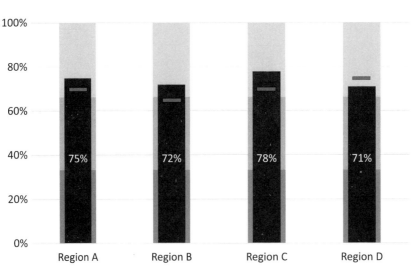

All regions except D met revised performance targets this quarter.
What's up, Region D?

Coming up with solutions like this just takes thinking through the backbone of the graph and what Excel default graphs are available to make your vision happen. This method of bullet chart construction takes no extra plug-ins, no crazy math, just a teeny bit of ninja skill to lean on the secondary axis. So super simple.

The Hardest—Horizontal Bullets

EXCEL NINJA LEVEL: 10

You can do this!

Don't ask me why (ask the people at Excel), but you can't use our last method to make bullets that are horizontal bars. We need a new hack. This will require working our magic on Excel's connected scatterplot, a technique I adapted from Jorge Cameos (more about him in the Resources section). You are going to feel like such a rock star when we are done.

Check out how we set up this table. It's pretty extensive, so let's walk through each piece.

The first column is the name of each region. Next to that, I have each region's target. Next to that, I have two columns under the heading "value." We will connect these two points in the connected scatterplot with a really thick line in between, to essentially

FIGURE 4.22   The dataset comes in three parts—Data, Performance Areas, and Spacing.

	A	B	C	D	E	F	G	H	I	J	K	L
1			Data				Performance Areas				Spacing	
2		target	value		low		med		high			
3	Region A	80	0	35	0	33.33	33.33	66.66	66.66	99.96	4	4
4	Region B	80	0	54	0	33.33	33.33	66.66	66.66	99.96	3	3
5	Region C	75	0	50	0	33.33	33.33	66.66	66.66	99.96	2	2
6	Region D	70	0	65	0	33.33	33.33	66.66	66.66	99.96	1	1

create a bar, like in a bar chart. Excel needs to know where the bar starts and ends. All the value bars will always start at 0, but where they end is where I type the actual performance data for each region.

In the Performance Areas section, I have two columns each for low, medium, and high performance zones. These will become the gray background segments. The same logic applies here, where Excel needs to know where to start and end each segment. Low starts at 0 and runs for 1/3 of the length. Medium picks up where Low left off and runs for another 1/3. High follows suit. Everything we have in here so far is going to be the x-values we need to plot in the connected scatterplot.

What about the y-values that the scatterplot will need? That's the purpose of those extra Spacing columns. We need a y-value for each of the x-values we plot. Don't worry if this doesn't totally make sense yet. Follow the steps and you'll see how this will all come together, ninja-style.

Ready? Without highlighting any data, insert a blank connected scatterplot (Figure 4.23).

Now right-click in the empty graph and click on *Select Data*. We are going to add each piece here, one at a time. In the *Select Data* box, click *Add* to add a new series. Let's add Region A's values, saving target for later.

We get a new box and in here we click in the name for Region A (this is helpful to keep things straight later), select the two cells that make up the value (cells C3 and D3 in this example) for the series x-values, and the two corresponding spacing cells for the series y-values. Click OK and you'll see the connected set of dots in the background (see Figure 4.24). Yay!

Let's go ahead and format the value into a bar instead of a connected dot. Right-click on the connected dot and select *Format Data Series*.

In the *Line* menu, change the color to black—in bullet charts the values are usually black. Then make it really thick, like width size 10. Under *Cap* type, change the default to flat so that it isn't rounded in appearance. To get rid of the markers on either end, look under *Marker,* then *Marker Options,* then change the marker to *None.*

That's hacking a connected scatterplot to make it into a bar chart.

Repeat this process for the low, medium, and high values for Region A, assigning them shades of gray. The big difference here is that the performance zones should be wider than the actual bar, so instead of a width of 10, choose something more like 20. You'll keep

FIGURE 4.23   The connected scatterplot option is the 2nd one shown.

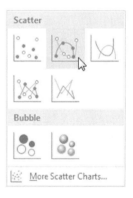

FIGURE 4.24   Add a new series and select the values and spacing for Region A.

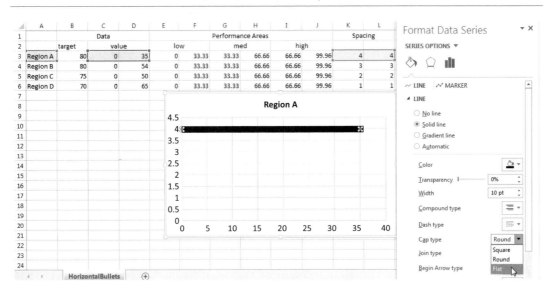

FIGURE 4.25   Format the line so it is thick, black, and with flat caps.

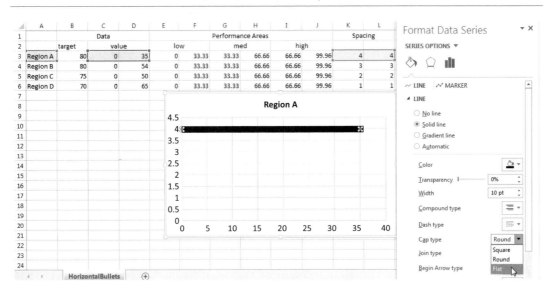

using the same spacing values (those 4s) as the y-values. Doing so keeps the connected dot series all on the same line. After repeating all those steps, you should get here to Figure 4.26.

FIGURE 4.26   Adding the three performance zones creates a stacked bar.

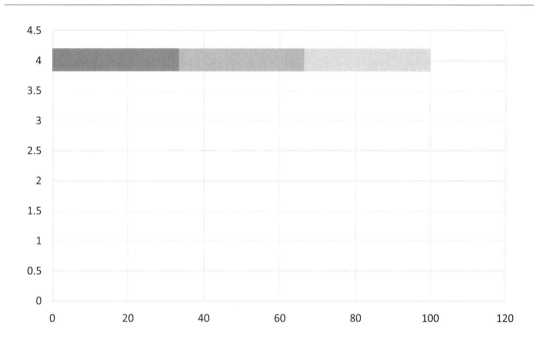

We ninja'ed the connected scatterplots into a stacked bar by staggering their start and end points, you see? But, what happened to the black bar we created? Well, it's hiding in back of these thicker bars. To bring it to the front, right-click on the graph and pick *Select Data*. All you'll need to do is reorder the list of data series. Click on the one called Region A and then hit the down arrow button to move the Region A series to the bottom of the list.

Time to add the target. While in this *Select Data Source* menu, click *Add* to add a new legend entries series and this time, choose the target for the x-value and only select one of the y-value cells. The target won't be a bar, it just needs to be a point, so only one y is necessary. You can format that single marker that shows up as anything you'd like. From the marker options drop-down list, I'll often use an x (see Figure 4.28).

If you really want to use a vertical line, you won't see one in Excel's list of marker options, but fret not. You can hack one. In the drop-down menu, you'll see the option to use a picture as the marker type. Usually this would be a pretty dangerous affair. But, you can draw a vertical line in another program (like PowerPoint) by inserting a shape and then you can save that shape as a picture and import it here as your marker style.

FIGURE 4.27   By reordering the legend entries, you can push the stacked bars to the background.

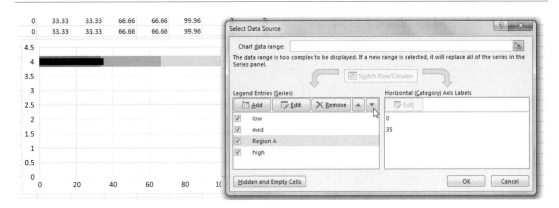

FIGURE 4.28   Choose a marker style from the drop-down list.

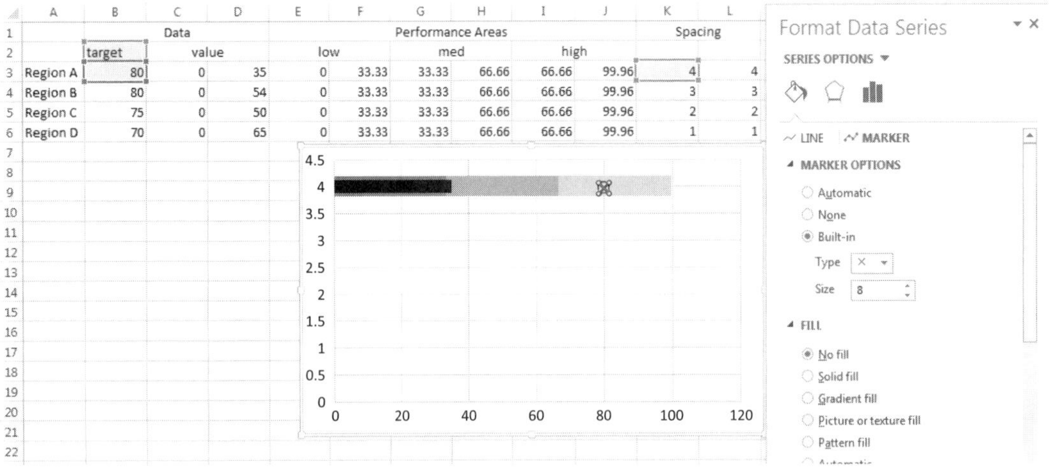

To polish off Region A, I'm going to add a data label to the left side of the black bar and change the label position so that the label is out to the left. Then I repeat this process for the other regions. If you find you have trouble clicking any particular series, click on another and then use the arrow keys on your keyboard to toggle between series.

My final steps are to delete the y-axis and gridlines and adjust the maximum of the x-axis so that it stops at 100. Then I add a title that tells my story.

And now you know why this chart is an Excel ninja level 10. We really had to break out a lot of elbow grease to turn a connected scatterplot into a horizontal bullet graph. You kind of feel like a rock star now, don't you?

The lovely part about these bullet graphs is that you can handle different performance ranges for each region, if that's your reality. You can add many more regions and have a very tall bullet graph. You can remove the title and the labels and pop this on the end of a table of numbers to give your spreadsheet more interpretive power.

FIGURE 4.29   The final horizontal bullet graph shows progress toward targets, against performance areas.

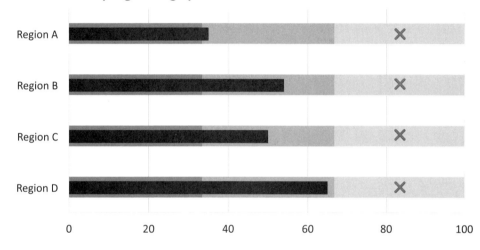

Region D nearly met its target but all regions entered the "progressing" performance zone.

Metric A ●
Metric B ○
Metric C ●

INDICATOR DOTS

EXCEL NINJA LEVEL: 7

Indicator dots are little colored markers that show up next to a target value listed in a table. They indicate whether or not the target has been met. They are so handy, giving instant assessment for a viewer and really boosting the power of a data dashboard. I'll show you two examples of their muscle.

Let's say I'm working with a high school Math teacher with way too many students. She keeps track of student scores on homework, exams, and so forth in a spreadsheet (see Figure 4.30), but she told me she needed something that would jump out at her if students were failing or on the edge of doing so.

I begin to help her by inserting an indicator dot next to each student's average score so she can see who needs attention.

Lucky for us, Excel 2010 has built in a set of icons that we can use for this purpose. These are a part of Excel's conditional formatting, a place I used to be too intimidated to use. Click into the first average value—that's cell I2 in this example—and then click the drop-down arrow by *Conditional Formatting*. At the bottom of that menu, you'll see an option that says *New Rule*. Click it. It will open up this dialogue box (Figure 4.31). In the menu in the center of the box, choose *Icon Sets*.

FIGURE 4.30   My data table holds the student ID number, the student scores, and an average of all scores.

	A	B	C	D	E	F	G	H	I	J
1	Student ID	Homework1	Homework2	First exam	Homework3	Group Project	Homework4		Average to date	
2	1	67	75	78	85	48	62		69.2	
3	2	86	75	57	63	48	87		69.3	
4	3	46	36	52	46	48	47		45.8	
5	4	53	62	35	47	48	75		53.3	
6	5	57	66	73	75	74	78		70.5	
7	6	88	87	86	80	74	85		83.3	
8	7	76	74	67	66	74	60		69.5	
9	8	97	96	99	96	74	94		92.7	
10	9	85	85	69	75	78	68		76.7	
11	10	32	37	33	36	78	44		43.3	
12	11	78	74	72	77	78	73		75.3	
13	12	45	47	64	66	78	75		62.5	
14	13	34	36	32	38	37	48		37.5	
15	14	64	62	74	61	37	59		59.5	
16	15	75	84	74	54	37	64		64.7	
17	16	63	57	60	44	37	45		51.0	
18	17	71	66	62	71	69	79		69.7	
19	18	78	85	60	94	69	91		79.5	
20	19	73	86	67	99	69	95		81.5	
21	20	26	35	40	52	69	65		47.8	
22	21	86	81	71	79	85	80		80.3	
23	22	75	82	90	98	85	93		87.2	
24	23	57	57	66	73	85	73		68.5	
25	24	42	68	55	47	85	58		59.2	
26	25	96	96	97	96	88	98		95.2	
27	26	54	47	52	44	88	40		54.2	
28	27	64	75	80	83	88	87		79.5	
29	28	32	37	39	41	88	48		47.5	

FIGURE 4.31   The Icon Sets option prepopulates with the stoplight color scheme—we'll modify those.

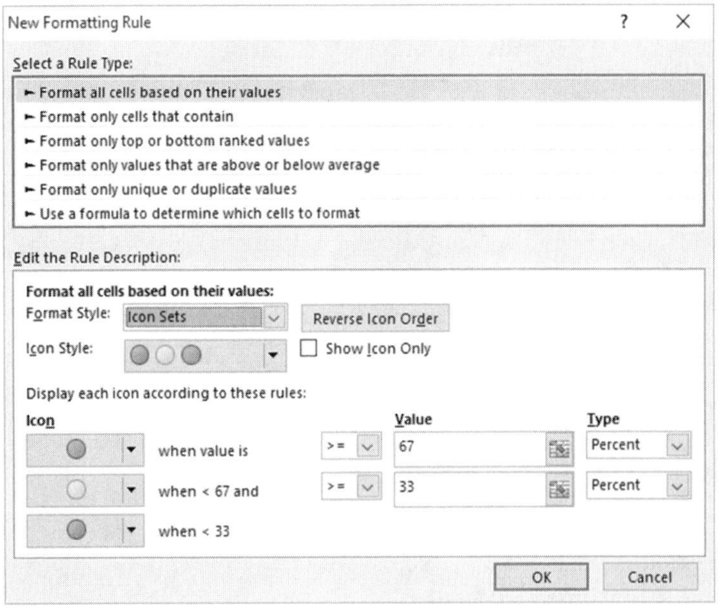

Two problems, though. First of all, the predesigned icon set in the red/yellow/green spectrum isn't helpful to the colorblind. And it's kinda ugly (qualifier: views expressed are my own!). The other problem is that this system will put an icon on everything in a spreadsheet or dashboard—every value will have a red or yellow or green dot. And that is a sure way to make things overwhelming, fast. Here's how to fix that issue.

We really only want a red dot to show students who are failing (scores under 50). And let's use a light red dot to show those on the borderline (scoring between 50 and 60). I want no cell icon for the students with passing grades. Use the arrows next to each pre-populated icon to select these better choices (Figure 4.32).

Next—and this is probably the most mentally taxing part—think through how the rule will logically apply for each of these indicator icons.

In order to work out the logic of your entries, try to read each row of this rule as a sentence. In the example (Figure 4.32), the first line reads: We will see No Cell Icon when the value in the table is greater than 60, which is a Number. Makes sense right? Second line: We will see a pink dot when the value in the table is less than or equal to 60 and greater than 50 (which is also a Number—be sure you are changing those types to Number). Last row: We will see a red dot when the value is 50 or lower.

FIGURE 4.32   Adjust the values and types in the New Formatting Rule box to set up the
logic for your indicator icons.

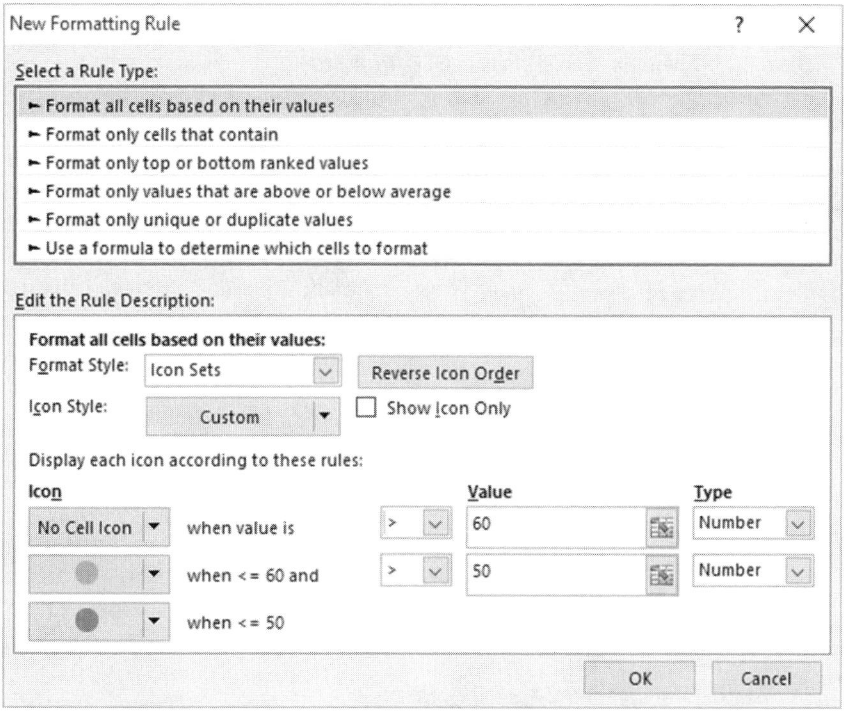

Click OK. If you did this right, you won't see anything but 69 in that first cell—and this is a good thing! A dot will only show up if that value is 60 or less. Copy that cell and paste it down your entire column of averages. Doesn't that make you so happy? Me too!

Now the icons highlight the average student scores that need attention. I also added in sparklines to show each student's progression of grades over time. Sparklines are tiny line graphs, visualized inside a cell.

Place your cursor in the empty column between the scores and the averages—so cell H2 in this example. In Excel's toolbar, click *Insert.* Look for the Sparkline family of options. Inside there, click *Line* (see Figure 4.33).

FIGURE 4.33   It isn't a regular line graph—see how it is in the Sparkline family?

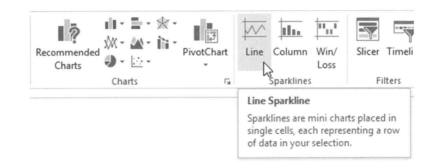

A dialogue box will open that looks like Figure 4.34.

Where it asks for your *Data Range,* highlight the first student's scores. *Location Range* is where the sparkline will be located and it is already populated with H2, where we clicked when we started. Hit OK and you'll see a sparkline in H2. You can format it if

FIGURE 4.34   Here is where we tell Excel which data to encode in the sparkline.

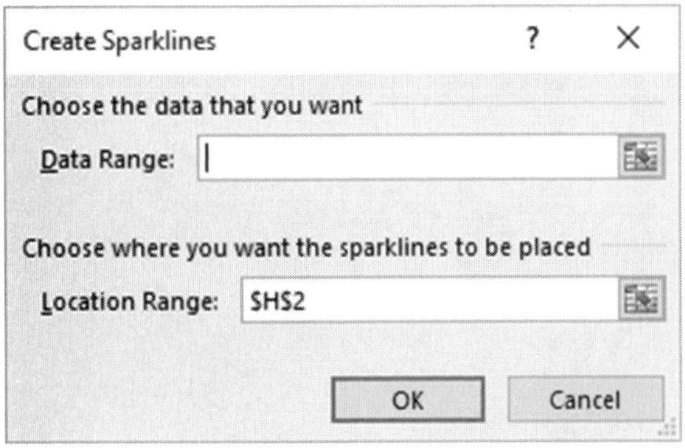

Create Sparklines   ?   ✕

Choose the data that you want

Data Range: |

Choose where you want the sparklines to be placed

Location Range: $H$2

OK   Cancel

you'd like, using the new yellow *Sparkline Tools* tab, changing the color or adding beginning and end markers. When you have it looking the way you want, copy it all the way down your spreadsheet so each student's scores are visualized as a sparkline.

The combination of the sparkline and the indicator dots gives us a lot of information at a glance. Student ID 20, for example, has a bright red mark, indicating failing. But, that student's sparkline shows a generally improving trend since the first assignment. A different remediation approach might be warranted for this student than for Student 10, whose sparkline has stayed flat for most of the semester.

FIGURE 4.35   The spreadsheet packs more interpretive punch with sparklines and indicator dots.

	A	B	C	D	E	F	G	H	I	J
1	Student ID	Homework1	Homework2	First exam	Homework3	Group Project	Homework4			Average to date
2	1	67	75	78	85	48	62			69.2
3	2	86	75	57	63	48	87			69.3
4	3	46	36	52	46	48	47		●	45.8
5	4	53	62	35	47	48	75		●	53.3
6	5	57	66	73	75	74	78			70.5
7	6	88	87	86	80	74	85			83.3
8	7	76	74	67	66	74	60			69.5
9	8	97	96	99	96	74	94			92.7
10	9	85	85	69	75	78	68			76.7
11	10	32	37	33	36	78	44		●	43.3
12	11	78	74	72	77	78	73			75.3
13	12	45	47	64	66	78	75			62.5
14	13	34	36	32	38	37	48		●	37.5
15	14	64	62	74	61	37	59		●	59.5
16	15	75	84	74	54	37	64			64.7
17	16	63	57	60	44	37	45		●	51.0
18	17	71	66	62	71	69	79			69.7
19	18	78	85	60	94	69	91			79.5
20	19	73	86	67	99	69	95			81.5
21	20	26	35	40	52	69	65		●	47.8
22	21	86	81	71	79	85	80			80.3
23	22	75	82	90	98	85	93			87.2
24	23	57	57	66	73	85	73			68.5
25	24	42	68	55	47	85	58		●	59.2
26	25	96	96	97	96	88	98			95.2
27	26	54	47	52	44	88	40			54.2
28	27	64	75	80	83	88	87			79.5
29	28	32	37	39	41	88	48		●	47.5

So, the strategy here was to add simple, limited indicators to show our cut points and spur action. As with most things in Excel, the defaults are nice, but insufficient and some tweaking will be needed to maximize their benefit.

Here's another example that combined everything discussed in this chapter so far. I love this example because it really shows how presenting data effectively changes the kinds of conversations that can happen inside organizations. Better presentations shape an improved culture of decision making.

In late 2012, I got a call from an evaluation officer who was working at the Walton Family Foundation (Yep—*those* Waltons. Whatever your opinion of Walmart, the foundation is doing some good work. While I can't tell you the details of their data, you'll just have to trust me that their investments in environmental initiatives are truly impressive.) She said her group was ready for change, ready to learn ways to present better.

We shared a thought provoking workshop together, and at the end they made the decision that they were ready to overhaul their reporting. You see, they had been submitting their data to their board of directors in this format (see Figure 4.36), with the expectation that the board would make actionable decisions based on it.

FIGURE 4.36   A board of directors does not want to try to make decisions off of a table of numbers that look like this.

Education Performance Dashboard

Outputs	2010	2011	2012	2013		5-year target (2014)
Metric 1	490	495	515	530		600
Metric 2	5%	6%	9%	11%		22%
Metric 3	4	16	20	21		120 cumulative
Short-term Outcomes	2010	2011	2012	2013		5-year target (2014)
ST Metric 1	600 (3)	630 (4)	755 (4)	810 (5)		1975 (10)
ST Metric 2	35%	41%	39%	45%		93%
ST Metric 3	18% (12/65)	16% (11/70)	25% (18/73)	27% (20/75)		35%
ST Metric 4	70%	76%	81%	83%		90%
Medium-term Outcomes	2010	2011	2012	2013		5-year target (2014)
MT Metric 1	22.9 (18.1%)	21.8 (19.2%)	22.9 (20.3%)	21.9 (22.5%)		23.2
MT Metric 2	95%	92%	93%	94%		97%
MT Metric 3	32%	46%	59%	48%		60%
MT Metric 4	2.0%	4.3%	6.8%	10.4%		40%
MT Metric 5	3.0%	5.2%	4.8%	7.6%		11%
MT Metric 6	19.8%	20.2%	25.1%	24.1%		35%
Long-term Outcomes	2010	2011	2012	2013		5-year target (2014)
LT Metric 1	16.2	17.0	17.1	17.7		18
LT Metric 2	15.8	15.7	16.6	16.2		18

*Some caveat goes here

SOURCE: Marc Holley (2013). "WFF Dashboard Before," Walton Family Foundation. Used with permission.

Yeah, that wasn't happening. Rows and rows of numbers are extremely hard to read, much less interpret. It's very difficult for our brains to make sense of that many digits and pull out any kind of pattern, let alone gain insight that can lead to strategy. I suggested we swap out all tables for graphs, but Karen at Walton said, "Uh, no the board really wants to see all the raw numbers." Inside my head I said "Suuuuuuure they do," and out of my mouth I said, "No problem, let's keep them all in there and dashboard this thing." Figure 4.37 shows my redesign.

We really only made 3 small changes.

1. I added a sparkline, to show the row of numbers preceding it so that the overall pattern is clear. That green dot at the end of the sparkline? That's the target they are aiming for in 2019. Sparklines can refer to hidden data—I really have several hidden blank columns in this spreadsheet, representing all the years in between now and the target year.

2. The target is listed numerically in the column next door. And in that target cell, you'll see that some have a red dot. I used our old friend conditional formatting to set up a formula which calculates their predicted value in 2019 based on their current data (again, in a hidden column) and the red dot shows up when they aren't

FIGURE 4.37   We added three simple visuals to show comparison to a target.

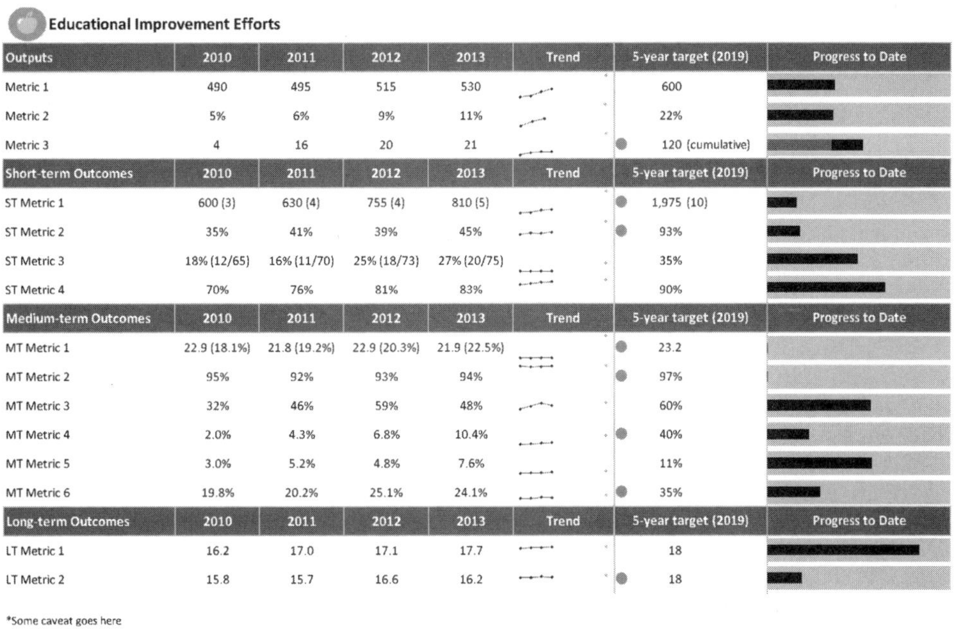

Educational Improvement Efforts

Outputs	2010	2011	2012	2013	Trend	5-year target (2019)	Progress to Date
Metric 1	490	495	515	530		600	
Metric 2	5%	6%	9%	11%		22%	
Metric 3	4	16	20	21		120 (cumulative)	
Short-term Outcomes	**2010**	**2011**	**2012**	**2013**	**Trend**	**5-year target (2019)**	**Progress to Date**
ST Metric 1	600 (3)	630 (4)	755 (4)	810 (5)		1,975 (10)	
ST Metric 2	35%	41%	39%	45%		93%	
ST Metric 3	18% (12/65)	16% (11/70)	25% (18/73)	27% (20/75)		35%	
ST Metric 4	70%	76%	81%	83%		90%	
Medium-term Outcomes	**2010**	**2011**	**2012**	**2013**	**Trend**	**5-year target (2019)**	**Progress to Date**
MT Metric 1	22.9 (18.1%)	21.8 (19.2%)	22.9 (20.3%)	21.9 (22.5%)		23.2	
MT Metric 2	95%	92%	93%	94%		97%	
MT Metric 3	32%	46%	59%	48%		60%	
MT Metric 4	2.0%	4.3%	6.8%	10.4%		40%	
MT Metric 5	3.0%	5.2%	4.8%	7.6%		11%	
MT Metric 6	19.8%	20.2%	25.1%	24.1%		35%	
Long-term Outcomes	**2010**	**2011**	**2012**	**2013**	**Trend**	**5-year target (2019)**	**Progress to Date**
LT Metric 1	16.2	17.0	17.1	17.7		18	
LT Metric 2	15.8	15.7	16.6	16.2		18	

*Some caveat goes here

SOURCE: Stephanie Evergreen (2013). "WFF Dashboard After." Walton Family Foundation. Used with permission.

going to meet their target as things stand without some serious intervention. Talk about being able to make actionable decisions!

3. And then the modified bullet graph shows progress to date. In this case, the target is the background of gray, such that when they meet their target, the black bar is at the right side of the gray rectangle.

So only 3 changes, really, plus some light graphic design in terms of colors and such.

Karen and her team showed this dashboard to their board, who saw it as a real improvement. We went on to build several other dashboards together. So, good for me and my business, but let's talk about what happened inside the Walton Family Foundation.

The culture changed. Karen recently told me that the drive toward better design "really impacted everyone at Walton Family Foundation." She went on to say, "Dipping our toe in the waters of better data visualization with the dashboards has set off a chain reaction. Our entire organization is really poised to improve how we present information to our Board and publicly. Data visualization helps us tell a story about the foundation's impact and leads to improved decision-making across the organization."

And *that's* the kind of difference that can be made with effective data visualization.

Benchmarks Inside Sparklines

Excel doesn't give us much to work with in terms of using ninja skills on sparklines, but we can use what little it does provide to slice in a benchmark line. Let's return to our math teacher spreadsheet (Figure 4.30) and let's say our math teacher friend says that the cut score for earning an A in the class is 85. We can't add a second sparkline in the same cell, but we can use ninja moves on the sparkline's axis to fake a second line.

The axis is by default set at zero. We can turn it into a benchmark line at 85. We have to do this by creating a second table, where we subtract 85 from each one of our original scores.

FIGURE 4.38   Make a secret table that recalculates your original scores as deviations from your benchmark value. Student 1's recalculated score for Homework 1 is shown.

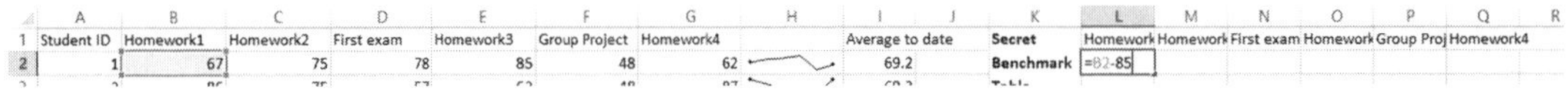

	A	B	C	D	E	F	G	H	I	J	K	L	M	N	O	P	Q	R
1	Student ID	Homework1	Homework2	First exam	Homework3	Group Project	Homework4			Average to date	Secret	Homework	Homework	First exam	Homework	Group Proj	Homework4	
2	1	67	75	78	85	48	62			69.2	Benchmark	=B2-85						
			85	75	57	62	48	87			69.2	Table						

We will essentially recast each score reflecting its distance from the benchmark. Complete the new scores for Student 1 and then click in your original sparkline for Student 1.

In the *Sparkline Tools* tab, look over on the left for the *Edit* button. In that drop-down menu, select *Edit Single Sparkline's Data*. In the dialogue box that pops up, you'll highlight your recalculated scores for Student 1.

FIGURE 4.39   Edit the sparkline's data so they refer to your recalculated secret table.

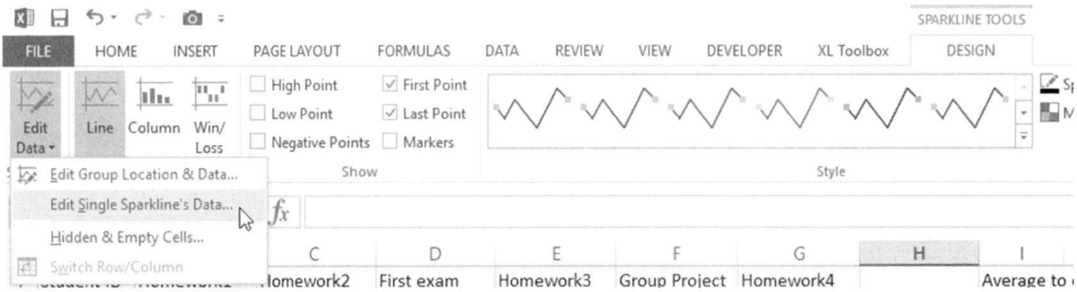

Then, in the same *Sparkline Tools* tab, look over on the right for the button that says *Axis*. In the drop-down menu there, click a checkmark next to *Show Axis*.

FIGURE 4.40   The sparkline looks the same as before, but now there's a benchmark line as well.

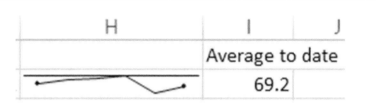

You can copy your recalculated data and your revised sparkline with benchmark all the way down your table. If some cells don't have a benchmark line, it's likely because the dataset doesn't get close to the benchmark data value of 85. In this case, go back into the *sparkline axis* menu and adjust the *maximum value* so that it is inclusive of your target value.

A comparison line—in some form—gives that necessary context that massively increases the interpretive power of the data display. And think of other ways you could use this line, such as for targets, averages, national standards—yes keep dreaming!

EXERCISES

Scout out some of the public data visualizations (such as in the Wall Street Journal or the New York Times) and look for different ways that people show comparison to a benchmark—sometimes it's a dashed line, sometimes it is one consistent brand color, and sometimes it is a simple x on the graph. Find three different ways that others have shown comparisons to a target or benchmark.

If you tried to add the benchmark line to the sparkline in that last example, you probably noticed that you can't format the benchmark line to make it a different color. Or so you think! This is where code comes in handy, as discussed in Chapter 3. Grab code (with gratitude) from this site at **http://msdn.microsoft.com/en-us/library/office/ff197606%28v=office.15%29.aspx** and test out different colors!

Believe it or not, some pretty amazing people have developed plug-ins for Excel that make bullet chart development a relative breeze. Some are free and some cost a bit. Search "bullet chart Excel plug in" to find them. But, be a little careful. My plug-in worked fine in Excel 2010, but didn't work at all when I upgraded to Excel 2013. They can break. They won't operate for someone else who gets your file with your lovely bullet graphs. For those reasons, I prefer to rely on what Excel contains on its own. Even so, it's worth it to take a look around at the plug-ins available. Pick one and plug it in to Excel. Make a bullet graph and then see if you can reverse engineer it. Try to explain how the plug-in is maximizing different parts of Excel to craft the graph.

RESOURCES

There's more to the story of my dashboard for the Walton Family Foundation. They took it a step further. Read my blog post at http://stephanieevergreen.com/dashboard-conversation/ to see what happened next.

I coedited a special issue of a journal where we focused on data visualization. One of those chapters discusses the process of making data dashboards in a clear and articulate way. If this discussion on bullet graphs has you dreaming about dashboarding, check out the 2013 article by Veronica Smith referenced below.

Jorge Cameos has a great site, which includes a blog and a set of courses you can take to learn to build a dashboard in Excel. Check him out at http://www.excelcharts.com/blog/data-visualization-courses/

REFERENCES

Few, S. (2013). *Bullet graph design specifications.* Retrieved from http://www.perceptualedge.com/articles/misc/Bullet_Graph_Design_Spec.pdf .

Smith, V. S. (2013). Data dashboard as evaluation and research communication tool. *New Directions for Evaluation,* 21–45.

5

WHAT THE SURVEY SAYS

SHOWING LIKERT, RANKING, CHECK-ALL-THAT-APPLY, AND MORE

LEARNING OBJECTIVES

After reading this chapter you will be able to

Modify traditional graphs and create potential alternatives

Differentiate between graph types appropriate for sequential versus Likert-type questions

Handle the *Not Applicable* data category

Use error bars to actually increase readability of a graph

Visualize branching questions in several ways

This chapter shares a menu of options for displaying survey data, including ranking, rating, and check-all-that-apply questions. I'll show you common visualization options, point out what the critics say about them, and offer possible solutions and alternatives that might better meet your communication needs. Our goal here is to present survey data so that readers can better understand survey respondents and effectively use the data to take more informed action.

Rating scales are usually shown in a stacked bar graph, which poses some significant obstacles to being seen as reader friendly. However, there are some options: design it thoughtfully with an intentional color scheme and order, or convert the data to another graph type.

A diverging stacked bar graph repositions Likert scale data so that it diverges around a central point, with the positive affect falling out to one side and the negative affect falling out to the other. It handles some of the criticisms of the regular stacked bar graph by making it easier to compare the middle values in your rating scale.

Breaking the data out into small multiples is another possibility that is particularly useful when one really wants to compare each of the response options in a rating scale. Each response option will essentially appear on its own baseline, making comparisons a snap.

Even though a rating scale might have an obnoxious nine response options that doesn't mean we have to report on all of them. Often, our audience doesn't care about the difference between "agree" and "somewhat agree." If we aggregate the similar responses and graph those larger groups, then the traditional stacked bar doesn't appear so cumbersome.

One of these alternatives will fit your rating data; but, ranking data is a different story.

The simplest way to show ranking data is through a column or bar chart, ordered by frequency from greatest to least. These charts work just fine, most of the time. When do they fall short? Well, when the values in your dataset are all high, such as in the 80% to 90% range (out of 100%). Then, a chart with a set of tall columns can be visually aggressive. In that case, try a lollipop graph, which looks like its name—a dot for the value, that sits on top of a stick, connecting the dot to an axis.

Another way to handle ranking data is to isolate the top three or five items with the highest ranking and assign an icon or picture to each item. The p Pair the icon with the corresponding percentage in a large, interesting font and you could be all set.

Branching questions are a whole different animal because their structures are questions, within questions, within questions. For shallow branching, you can get away with an annotation inside another graph. For deeper branching, try a nested map that visualizes a whole series of branched questions, one inside the other.

Finally, this chapter addresses the three ways to visually handle *not applicable* data:

1. If the missing data are small and consistent, just note this in the subtitle.
2. If the missing data are large and consistent, add the sample size to your data labels.
3. If the missing data are large and inconsistent, graph them off to the side.

This is one hefty chapter and by the end your ninja skills are going to be off the charts (or, literally, *on* the charts).

WHAT STORIES CAN BE TOLD ABOUT WHAT THE SURVEY SAYS?

Goodness knows, it seems as if every other phone call on a landline is someone with a survey. This type of call is so widespread because a survey remains one of the best ways to systematically discover the opinions of representatives of a group. Surveys have been conducted on every topic imaginable, so stories can include these variations:

- Respondents said Option A was most favorable
- Most of the respondents had a negative view of our service

CHAPTER 5 • WHAT THE SURVEY SAYS   103

- Of the options we gave, respondents liked X, H, and O best
- Customers said our top three services are resume coaching, mentor matching, and job skills training
- Polls showed that 47% of the students knew a Hispanic/Latino who dropped out of school
- Citizens believe A & J will be good candidates

Survey data tell the story of what people think, feel, do, or believe.

HOW CAN I VISUALIZE WHAT THE SURVEY SAYS?

So much of the decision making in the chapter leans on the survey question type. We walk through options for ranking, rating, and branching question types. Be sure to check out the resources at the end of this chapter for color, which is very important in our examples, and some visualization support for specialized question types, such as network analysis.

RATING

Rating questions come in two basic forms: those that have sequential response options (think Poor to Excellent) and those that are diverging (such as Strongly Disagree to Strongly Agree and other Likert-types). We can use similar graph types to visualize these two kinds of questions, with minor tweaks for better emphasis.

STACKED BAR

A stacked bar graph can be a reliable friend. Most of the time, when reporting on percentages that make up a whole, stacked bars can be trusted to come through for you. But, sometimes just like your best friends, stacked bars show up to the party loud and confused, wearing a little too much makeup. Let's look at how to tame them into being supportive of your rating dataset.

Default stacked bar graphs often look like Figure 5.1.

Sit down and drink some water, default stacked bar. What's going right is that it is easy to see that all of the yes, sorta, and no responses add up to 100%. Good! It's easy to see that we asked seven questions in this section of the survey. I don't really know if that's important. But, I'm working hard to pull out anything good from this visual. The stacked bar as a graph type isn't all that bad, it just needs some formatting help.

The common criticism about stacked bars is that they can be hard to interpret. Let's say you were mostly curious about the students in the middle of this stacked bar, those who said "sorta." While we are good at judging the length of bars, it can be hard to compare the sorta responses for each survey question because they don't share a common baseline. In the example, do you think there are more students who reported sorta on "I see leadership opportunities for Latino/Hispanic youth" or for "My close friends have volunteered in the past 12 months"? It's even harder to tell because the default color scheme assigned by Excel doesn't distinguish the segments from one another all that well. On top of that, we have a disconnected legend that does little to help us understand what each segment represents (especially in black and white, right?).

FIGURE 5.1   Default stacked bars can be hard to read.

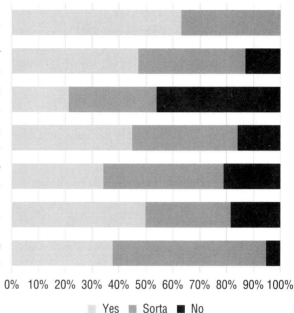

While we can't completely eliminate all of those problems with the stacked bar, the suggestions in this section can address the ones that are the most offensive.

One way to handle these issues is to rock the formatting of the traditional stacked bar. Same data, better told.

EXCEL NINJA LEVEL: 4

Tweak 1: Sort the questions from greatest to least on the category that matters the most to your audience. In this case, we are assuming that is the *yes* data. Others would be more likely to focus on the *no* data, especially in business and sales. Sorting the data makes it easier for readers to quickly assess what was most often reported and least often reported in this dataset. The typical stacked bar has no intentional sort order—it's commonly the order that the questions were asked on the survey. The thing is, readers don't care about the order of the questions on the survey! If you sort your data table from smallest to greatest on your category of interest, Excel will graph your data greatest to least.

Tweak 2: Apply a sequential color scheme. Recolor each segment of the stack from darkest to lightest shades of one color. I usually apply lightest color to the category of least importance (the no data, in this case). Matching a sequential color scheme to sequential data makes sense to readers and can help them mentally group the *yes* data and the *sorta* data if they want to. It also holds up better when reprinted in black and white.

FIGURE 5.2 Slight tweaks make the standard stacked bar chart easier to interpret.

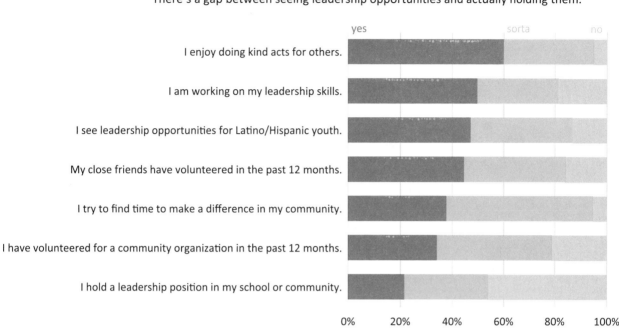

Students volunteer more than they hold actual leadership positions.
There's a gap between seeing leadership opportunities and actually holding them.

Tweak 3: Reposition the legend. When the bar segments are horizontal, but the default legend is vertical, it makes the readers volley through a bunch of mental gymnastics to connect the information and interpret the graph. In this case, I just deleted the legend and inserted textboxes above each segment in the stacked bar. I linked the textboxes to the corresponding cells in my table. Remember how to do that?

Insert a textbox. It will have a dashed line border and a blinking cursor (Figure 5.3), waiting for your words. Click on the border of the textbox so the dashed lines become solid (Figure 5.4).

Then go straight to the formula bar in Excel and type in an equals sign (Figure 5.5).

Then head to the cell in your table with the label you want to insert. In this case, it's the label that says yes. Click inside that cell. Excel will add that cell's location to the formula bar, right after your equals sign.

Hit Enter and your textbox will populate with the label. From there, you should change the color of the word yes so that it matches the color of the yes segments in the stacked bar below it. You can reposition the textbox as needed, too. That kind of flexibility doesn't come with a default legend. So, if the legend isn't working for you to maximize your graph, try linked textboxes instead.

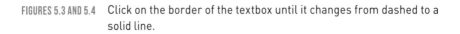

FIGURES 5.3 AND 5.4   Click on the border of the textbox until it changes from dashed to a
solid line.

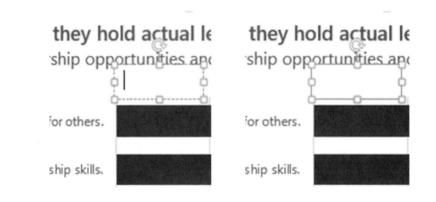

FIGURE 5.5   Type an equals sign in the formula bar.

FIGURE 5.6   Click in the cell you want as your label.

Those tweaks go a long way in making the default stacked bar work its best for your sequential data. The same strategies can help diverging response options, too. The only extra consideration involves the color-coding tweak. For diverging datasets, use a diverging color scheme. You'll need two shades of two colors and a neutral color for neutral.

One end of the response set is cast in blues, with the darker blue on the outside and the lighter blue on the inside. The other end of the stacked bar gets two shades of another color (see Figure 5.7). Neutral is in a light gray. This works even better with culturally associated color schemes. In the United States, reds and oranges are viewed as more negative, so use them on the disagree side of the data. Blues tend to be seen as more positive.

FIGURE 5.7   Apply the darkest colors of each shade to the more strongly felt sentiments.

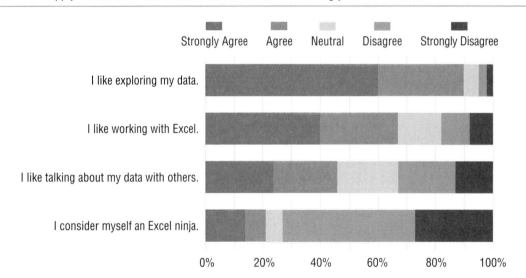

I pulled the color schemes for several of the graphs in this section from **ColorBrewer2 .com.** It is a website developed by Cynthia Brewer's team, designed for cartographers (mapmakers!) who deal with situations where they need several colors to be distinguishable when placed right up next to one another. The examples in this chapter don't have anything to do with maps, but we can use the same tools because our data segments also touch each other. ColorBrewer has color schemes for both sequential and for diverging datasets. The website gives you the full color scheme, along with the RGB (Red, Green, Blue) color codes you need to customize your graph inside Excel.

SMALL MULTIPLES

The previous tweaks get us further away from the loud and obnoxious default stacked bar, but I'm still unsettled because they don't entirely solve the problem of the difficulty comparing those middle values. This example and the next can give you a lift here. Let's start with small multiples and apply it to the yes/sorta/no data from earlier. We are going to use ninja skills to break up the stacked bar into three sets of regular bars, all in the same graph.

We could simply make three separate bar graphs, one for the *yes* data, one for the *sorta* data, and one for the *no* data. That could be totally fine if that's all the ninja skill you are up for today. The downside to that situation is the fidgeting you have to do to align all the graphs and labels and the care with which you must copy and paste them so they hang together as one visual. This next method takes a little more behind the scenes work, but it keeps the visuals in one tidy place.

We are going to use secret buffer columns. My table is in Figure 5.8.

EXCEL NINJA LEVEL: 9

FIGURE 5.8   Insert a column next to each actual data column in your table.

	Yes	Yes Buffer	Sorta	Sorta Buffe	No	No Buffer
I hold a leadership position in my school or	22%		32%		46%	
I have volunteered for a community org in th	34%		45%		21%	
I try to find time to make a difference in my c	38%		57%		5%	
My close friends have volunteered in the pa	45%		39%		16%	
I see leadership opportunities for Latino/His	47%		39%		13%	
I am working on my leadership skills.	50%		32%		18%	
I enjoy doing kind acts for others.	60%		35%		5%	

My actual data are separated by a column I inserted next to each. Those inserted columns are for my secret ninja buffer data. Each actual data column gets its own buffer buddy next door. Together, the data column and its buffer buddy need to add up to 100%.

See how the yes data and the yes Buffer data add up to 100% for each survey question (see Figure 5.9)? Compute this for each data and buffer duo.

FIGURE 5.9   Subtract 100% from each value in your actual data column and put the remainder in the buffer column.

	Yes	Yes Buffer	Sorta	Sorta Buffe	No	No Buffer
I hold a leadership position in my school or	22%	78%	32%		46%	
I have volunteered for a community org in th	34%	66%	45%		21%	
I try to find time to make a difference in my c	38%	62%	57%		5%	
My close friends have volunteered in the pa	45%	55%	39%		16%	
I see leadership opportunities for Latino/His	47%	53%	39%		13%	
I am working on my leadership skills.	50%	50%	32%		18%	
I enjoy doing kind acts for others.	60%	40%	35%		5%	

Now select all the data, even the headings, and insert a 100% stacked bar graph. I modified my earlier stacked bar to include the buffer data and it looks like Figure 5.10.

FIGURE 5.10   Select the whole table and insert a 100% stacked bar. It will look loud and obnoxious.

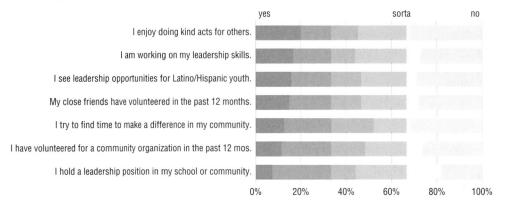

Students volunteer more than they hold actual leadership positions.
There's a gap between seeing leadership opportunities and actually holding them.

Not much left to do to make this chart look amazing. Inside the graph, right click on each of the buffer segments and change their color to *No Fill* (Figure 5.11). Choose *Format Data Series* and look for the paint bucket icon or the *Fill* menu.

FIGURE 5.11   Each buffer segment should not be filled with any color.

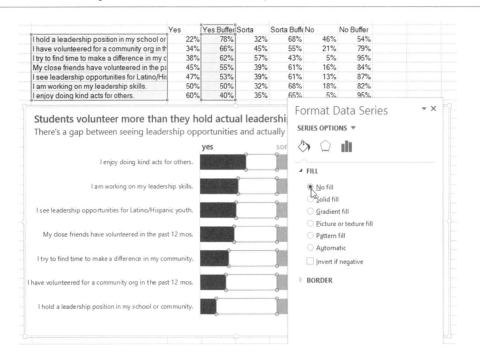

	Yes	Yes Buffer	Sorta	Sorta Buffer	No	No Buffer
I hold a leadership position in my school or	22%	78%	32%	68%	46%	54%
I have volunteered for a community org in th	34%	66%	45%	55%	21%	79%
I try to find time to make a difference in my c	38%	62%	57%	43%	5%	95%
My close friends have volunteered in the pa	45%	55%	39%	61%	16%	84%
I see leadership opportunities for Latino/His	47%	53%	39%	61%	13%	87%
I am working on my leadership skills.	50%	50%	32%	68%	18%	82%
I enjoy doing kind acts for others.	60%	40%	35%	65%	5%	95%

You should already see the three separate bars in one graph! Don't stop, keep whipping this graph into shape by deleting the x-axis and gridlines, since they no longer make much sense. You'll want to replace this with data labels inside the base of each actual data segment of the stacked bar. Next, reposition the legend labels over their corresponding bars (Figure 5.12).

Now we can tell whether the sorta responses are different for those two survey questions I mentioned earlier (they aren't). Yes, the data labels are there to tell us, but even if the labels were gone, we can compare the lengths of those sorta bars because they now share a common baseline. It's also true that we don't necessarily need to have different colors on each set of bars, since they no longer touch one another. Make them all the same color if you aren't trying to emphasize one set of response options over another.

Super cool ninja trick, isn't it? These secret buffer zones are going to keep coming in handy. It's all about mastering the software and what it can do in order to make the best possible visualizations for your data.

FIGURE 5.12   Small multiples of regular bars in the same graph make it easier to compare values that were in the middle of the stacked bar.

Students volunteer more than they hold actual leadership positions.
There's a gap between seeing leadership opportunities and actually holding them.

	yes	sorta	no
I enjoy doing kind acts for others.	60%	35%	5%
I am working on my leadership skills.	50%	32%	18%
I see leadership opportunities for Latino/Hispanic youth.	47%	39%	13%
My close friends have volunteered in the past 12 mos.	45%	39%	16%
I try to find time to make a difference in my community.	38%	57%	5%
I have volunteered for a community organization in the past 12 months.	34%	45%	21%
I hold a leadership position in my school or community.	22%	32%	46%

DIVERGING STACKED BAR

Diverging stacked bar charts are great for showing the spread of negative and positive values, such as Strongly Disagree to Strongly Agree, and because they align to each other around the midpoint, they can handle some of the criticism directed at regular stacked bar charts, which is that it is difficult to compare the values of the categories in the middle of the stack (Heiberger & Robbins, 2014; Talbot, Setlur, & Anand, 2014). Making a diverging stacked bar was approximately 8 billion times easier than I expected; it just takes a little ninja skill.

The secret again is hidden buffer values at either end of the bars. I told you they'd come in handy!

Figure 5.13 is what my data table looks like after adding the buffer values.

FIGURE 5.13   I added some notes to the table to help you conceptualize how this is going to work.

Buffer		Strongly Agree	Agree		Disagree		Strongly Disagree	Buffer	
<------------------------------------ Add to 100%					Add to 100% -->				
	15%	50%	35%		8%		7%		85%
	20%	70%	10%		10%		10%		80%
	25%	45%	30%		15%		10%		75%
^turn bars white								turn bars white^	

Let's walk through it a bit. In the middle, in the dark text, are my actual data values, what I ultimately want to show the audience. On either side I have Buffer columns. These are the secret columns! In gray you can see my notes. So here's the plan. Within each row, all values from "Disagree" over to the right need to add up to 100%. Just mentally sum your Disagree and Strongly Disagree values and type the remainder in the Buffer column (or make a formula if you need to flex more Excel muscle). Same thing for Agree over to the left.

Then select all the headings and values, from Buffer to Buffer, and insert a 100% stacked bar graph. Mine looked like Figure 5.14 at first.

FIGURE 5.14   Excel made six stacked bars instead of three.

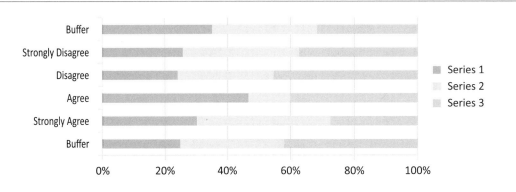

Not cool. I should see six segments in the stacked bar, not six bars. So right-click on the graph, choose *Select Data,* and click on *Switch Row/Column.* Now, it looks like Figure 5.15.

FIGURE 5.15   Each of the three stacked bars has six segments.

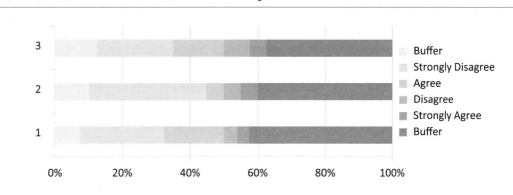

Bingo! So now it's time to make the two Buffer categories white. Just right-click directly on the Buffer bars and select the white fill color. When you're done it should look like Figure 5.16.

Look at that! Now the only bars with color are the ones that encode our values. Still, it doesn't look that great, right? So, delete the legend (we'll add it back in later), delete the gridlines, and delete the y-axis. Delete the x-axis, too . . . BUT FIRST! We want more of the chart area taken up by our actual values. Right now, the stacked bars are squished together because Excel set the maximum of the x-axis to accommodate our Buffer zones. Right-click on the x-axis, select *Format Axis,* and in that dialogue box, pick a new max that it is nearer to the end of the bar segments you want showing. I chose 70%.

FIGURE 5.16   The Buffer bars become white so they essentially disappear—they are really only there to support the structure of the data visualization.

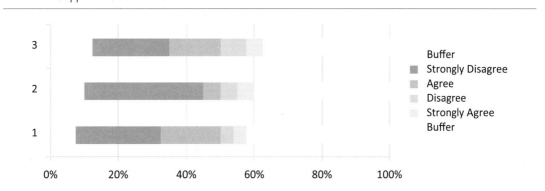

I also added data labels and changed the colors so that the positive values were bluer and the negative values were redder, to reflect what I discussed about colors in the last section (see Figure 5.17).

FIGURE 5.17   Use shades of two colors to help the audience mentally group each half of the diverging stacked bar.

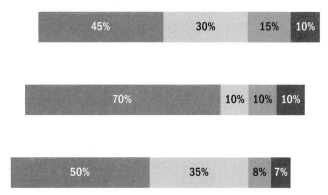

I find it helpful to add a line down the middle so that readers really can see how the segments diverge. To do that, click on the *Insert* tab. Look in the *Illustrations* group and you should see an icon that looks like a group of shapes. Open it and click on the line (Figure 5.18). You've probably done this plenty of times in PowerPoint or Word! Then click to draw the line on top of the graph.

FIGURE 5.18   Insert a line down the midpoint of the graph.

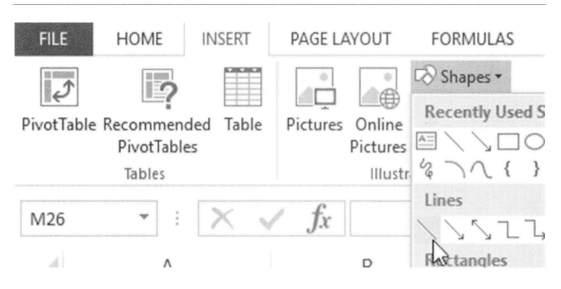

To finish it off, I just need to add back my legend (across the top, using linked text-boxes), give it a descriptive chart title, and add in my survey questions as data labels (also using linked textboxes) as in Figure 5.19. I ultimately added a white border to each segment of the bar, too.

FIGURE 5.19   The diverging stacked bar makes it easier to compare all positive responses to all negative responses.

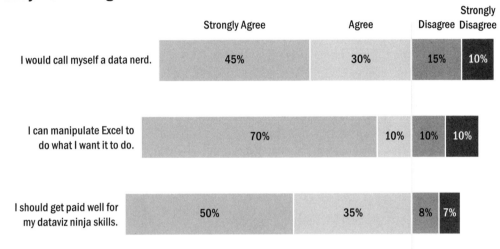

POW! That's right! It takes just a little forethought with some basic math to better represent diverging survey data and circumvent some of the issues of a basic stacked bar.

WHAT ABOUT NEUTRAL?

Can I still use the diverging stacked bar chart if I have a neutral category (i.e. a five point scale instead of a four point scale)?

—Meredith

Yes, Meredith, you can! Go back to the table and insert two columns in the middle of the table. Now, divide your neutral value by two and type that number to each column such that half of neutral belongs with your positive values and half with your negative. This keeps the neutral category aligned to the middle, sort of straddling the midline. It does get a little tricky to add data labels to each segment, though, because Excel wants to label each half. You'll want to insert a textbox and type in your total neutral value. You may also decide that the line isn't as impactful or necessary. Personally, I don't think it has quite the same effect, but try it out and let me know your take on the neutral situation!

You can turn a sequential response set into a diverging set by choosing a place in your response options where you want the divergence to occur. For example, if the response options are Poor, Fair, Good, and Excellent, then you might decide that these options split between Fair and Good. Or, your group might have really high standards and the split falls between Good and Excellent. However, because that divergence choice is largely up to the subjective opinion of the graph maker, sequential response options don't naturally feel as well-suited to a diverging bar graph. But hey, I'm not going to hold you back. It might be just the perfect visualization for your particular sequential data.

AGGREGATED STACKED BAR

Probably the most common way of visualizing rating survey data is via a stacked bar chart, just like the one below (Figure 5.20) created by the team at The Hole in the Wall Gang Camp. (Long sidenote: Have you ever heard of this place? It's a camp, started by Paul Newman [swoon], for children with severe illnesses, such as cancer, hemophilia, sickle cell, and other terrible things that should never happen to children. Just reading their latest data report made me cry. Then, thinking about their data report later made me cry again. Just a little something in my eye right now, must be an eyelash.)

Their basic stacked bar chart reports on Camper Appreciation and the team already wisely ordered the bars from greatest to least on Strongly Agree and made the title into a takeaway sentence. However, when looking at Figure 5.20 you can probably see a few

FIGURE 5.20   The typical stacked bar gets a bit hard to read.

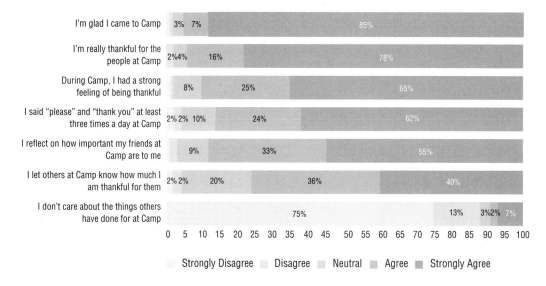

89% of campers agreed or strongly agreed they felt appreciation at Camp.

things that aren't really working. The labels in the skinny parts are scrunched. The x-axis is labeled in 5% increments, which is overkill. And just overall, it feels like a lot to mentally process. What do we do?

My strategy was to first find out what they really wanted to say about their data.

Ann Gillard, Director of Research and Evaluation, said, "We were fortunate to see such strong positive outcomes and want to celebrate this as we share the story of Hole in the Wall with potential campers, families, funders, and friends."

Lucky for us, they neatly encapsulated it in their title. Notice how they are grouping "agreed and strongly agreed" with their words? They are doing a bit of digestion for their readers by collapsing those categories into a number that's more meaningful.

And Ann knew it. She said, "We have found that our readers like to see percentages of people rather than numbers of responses, and that readers want to know what people agree with rather than reading about averages. So, we moved away from reporting means in these charts and put the means into an appendix for the other data nerds to view." Ann is on the right track, plus she called them data nerds so now she is my best friend.

I followed their lead and aggregated those categories in the graph by summing their values in the Excel spreadsheet. This equals the Aggregated Stacked Bar seen in Figure 5.21.

You'll also notice I reversed their categories. Since they are emphasizing the positive responses in their messaging, I put those bar segments on the left, so they share a common baseline that's easier for the audience to read. I only put number labels

EXCEL NINJA LEVEL: 2

FIGURE 5.21   If the difference between Agree and Strongly Agree doesn't matter much to your readers, aggregate those categories in the graph.

Campers were overwhelmingly thankful for their Camp experience.

Note that last question is intentionally negatively worded.

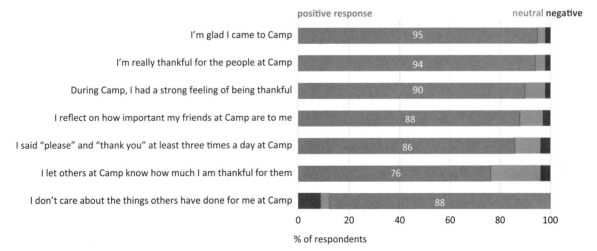

on those positive responses. I also used their Hole in the Wall Gang brand color there (it's green) and grayed out the rest to add further emphasis where they want it. Notice that I followed this pattern even for the last question, which was reverse-coded, where answering negatively is a good thing. I reduced the number of increments on the x-axis and color-coded the title a little more.

With those tweaks, the amazing things happening at Hole in the Wall Gang are even clearer to their readers (i.e., future campers, donors, etc.). Aggregated stacked bars are a really good visualization choice when the level of detail in a Likert-type scale is unnecessary.

CHANGING THE WORDING OF THE SURVEY

When you have one item that needs to be reverse-coded would you consider rewording the question when you present the data? (I would probably have tried to word the question in a different way in the survey to avoid this, but there are certainly times where the question needs to be worded as it is).

Sheila

Hi Sheila, I definitely wrestled with how to handle this reverse-scored question. One thing I might consider for the future is rewording this question in the chart / report with an asterisk explaining how this was originally reverse-worded and scored.

Ann Gillard

I'll just chime in to say I do think researchers tend to be a little too loyal to the survey when it may not be ideal for the audience. I support changing the wording on the graph, carefully, and with a note, as Ann mentions. While we don't want to mislead anyone about the questions asked, no matter what, reverse-coded questions are a little confusing and there's no perfect way to handle their presentation, but I think slightly altering the wording in the graph probably does the least damage.

Stephanie

I'm sure you have the hang of this by now, but it is also totally possible to collapse sequential categories into aggregate bars. Perhaps Poor and Fair combine on one side and Good and Excellent combine on the other. As long as it makes sense to your readers and you feel you are fairly representing the survey respondents, collapse away!

RANKING

Ranking questions are the kind of survey questions where you allow the respondents to select more than one answer. It could be that they can check all that apply. It could be that you are asking them to rate each answer option on its own scale. It could be that you ask respondents to rank a given set of answers from Best to Worst. Whichever way, there are a couple of right ways and tons of wrong ways to visualize ranking data.

COLUMN GRAPH

Let's say you want to poll your clients about which social justice topics are most important to them. You craft a survey with the question "Which social justice topics are most important to you? (Check all that apply)" and your survey lists 20 options plus an "other" fill in the blank option. Because respondents can pick more than one option, there's no way these responses will add up to 100%. No. Way. Take a look at Figure 5.22 for the table of data.

But, often when people see a set of percentages that belong to one survey item, they are too quick to pull the pie chart trigger. Such errors of assumption produce visualizations that look like Figure 5.23.

Excel shouldn't even allow pie charts to be made from check-all-that-apply data. It's all too easy to insert one and think the job is done. But, this is how visualizations end up making the rounds on Twitter as jokes among the slightly savvy crowd or end up on wtfviz.com. The values do not add up to 100%, so a pie chart is the wrong visualization.

FIGURE 5.22 A quick sum of these values shows they add to 1,119%.

Africa/Pan Africa/African Americans	34%
Asian/Asian Americans	25%
Caribbean/Caribbean Americans	67%
Disability Advocacy	49%
European/European Americans	52%
Gender Equity	34%
International Students	87%
Interngenerational/Generational	21%
Jewish Heritage/Observance	85%
Latino/Latina	69%
LBGTQ/Ally	79%
Middle Eastern Heritages and Traditions	73%
Mixed Race	80%
Muslim Observance	29%
Non-Traditional Students	61%
Other	9%
Pacific Islander/Pacific Islander Americans	59%
Religious Equity	64%
South Asian/South Asian Americans	12%
Trans-racial Adoptee/Parent	76%
Veteran	54%

FIGURE 5.23 A pie chart is not the right visualization for this data.

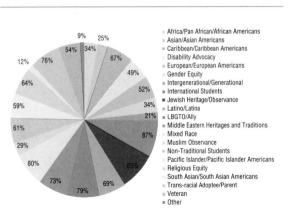

- Africa/Pan African/African Americans
- Asian/Asian Americans
- Caribbean/Caribbean Americans
- Disability Advocacy
- European/European Americans
- Gender Equity
- Intergenerational/Generational
- International Students
- Jewish Heritage/Observance
- Latino/Latina
- LBGTO/Ally
- Middle Eastern Heritages and Traditions
- Mixed Race
- Muslim Observance
- Non-Traditional Students
- Pacific Islander/Pacific Islander Americans
- Religious Equity
- South Asian/South Asian Americans
- Trans-racial Adoptee/Parent
- Veteran
- Other

It makes much more sense to graph this data as a simple bar chart, and it makes much MUCH more sense to order those bars from greatest to least as in Figure 5.24.

Remember back in Chapter 1 when we discussed how humans are pretty decent at comparing the lengths of things? Bar charts encode data by length, so it is less onerous for viewers to read a bar chart. But, we can make it even easier by ordering the bars by greatest to least values (or least to greatest; I could hear arguments either direction). This way, readers can quickly scan the graph and see what was most popular and what was least popular.

FIGURE 5.24   A bar chart is a better fit for check-all-that-apply data.

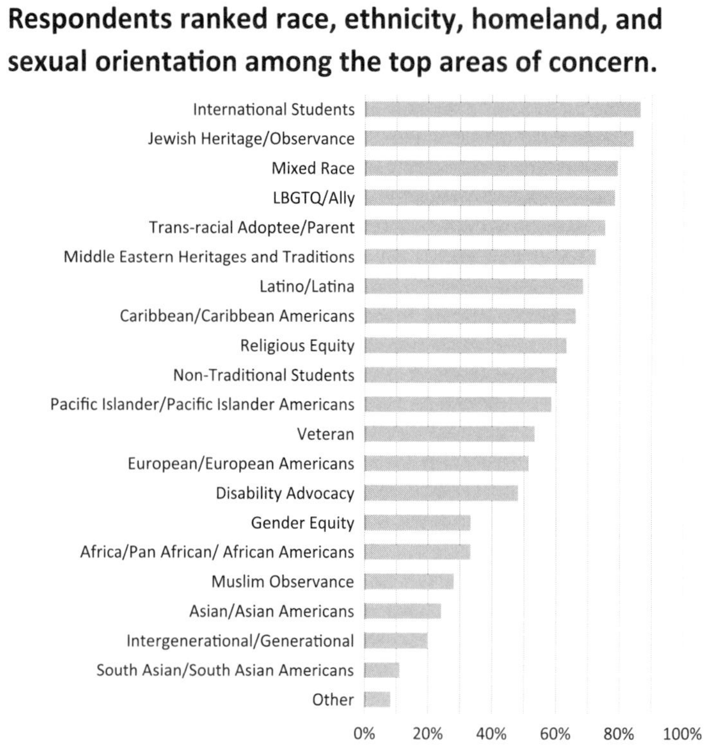

Respondents ranked race, ethnicity, homeland, and sexual orientation among the top areas of concern.

International Students	
Jewish Heritage/Observance	
Mixed Race	
LBGTQ/Ally	
Trans-racial Adoptee/Parent	
Middle Eastern Heritages and Traditions	
Latino/Latina	
Caribbean/Caribbean Americans	
Religious Equity	
Non-Traditional Students	
Pacific Islander/Pacific Islander Americans	
Veteran	
European/European Americans	
Disability Advocacy	
Gender Equity	
Africa/Pan African/ African Americans	
Muslim Observance	
Asian/Asian Americans	
Intergenerational/Generational	
South Asian/South Asian Americans	
Other	

0%   20%   40%   60%   80%   100%

And on that note, it's entirely possible that people really only care about the most popular (or the least). This long list of possible areas of concern could very well be overkill. Sure, we need to provide a fairly exhaustive list of response options on the survey, but that doesn't mean we have to visualize all of those options for the reader. It may be more effective to limit the reporting to the top three or five concerns. Focusing the visual in this way can help readers hone in on what is most important, make the visualization less overwhelming, and more quickly compel action (see Figure 5.25).

FIGURE 5.25   Zoom in on a handful of items that are the most frequently checked in a check-all-that-apply survey question.

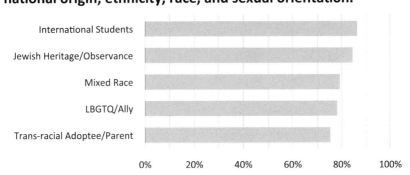

The top five areas of concern were broad—including national origin, ethnicity, race, and sexual orientation.

THE LOLLIPOP VARIATION

Another way to make the lengthy bar chart less visually overwhelming is to remove even more ink. We've already come a long way—we deleted tick marks, lightened gridlines, and removed an axis line. What else is left to remove? Well, what's left is all that ink making up each bar. I know it sounds ridiculous to think we could remove any of that ink because it is what encodes our data. But, really all we care about on those bars is the very end, where it stops, since that's what tells us the value. Instead of an ink-heavy bar chart, we are going to make an ink-friendly lollipop graph.

The backbone of the lollipop graph is a scatterplot, which means we will need x-values and y-values. The x-values are easy—those are my survey responses. The y-values are going to be faked, just inserted to make each lollipop equidistant from each other. So Figure 5.26 shows the new data table, with my actual survey responses and a new column next door where I typed in placeholder data, from 1 to 21.

EXCEL NINJA LEVEL: 8

FIGURE 5.26   Add a column of data that will serve as your y-values—no one will ever see it.

	A	B	C
1			Lollipop spacing
2	Other	9%	1
3	South Asian/South Asian Americans	12%	2
4	Interngenerational/Generational	21%	3
5	Asian/Asian Americans	25%	4
6	Muslim Observance	29%	5
7	Africa/Pan Africa/African Americans	34%	6
8	Gender Equity	34%	7
9	Disability Advocacy	49%	8
10	European/European Americans	52%	9
11	Veteran	54%	10
12	Pacific Islander/Pacific Islander Americans	59%	11
13	Non-Traditional Students	61%	12
14	Religious Equity	64%	13
15	Caribbean/Caribbean Americans	67%	14
16	Latino/Latina	69%	15
17	Middle Eastern Heritages and Traditions	73%	16
18	Trans-racial Adoptee/Parent	76%	17
19	LBGTQ/Ally	79%	18
20	Mixed Race	80%	19
21	Jewish Heritage/Observance	85%	20
22	International Students	87%	21

FIGURE 5.27   Your graph should be a series of dots.

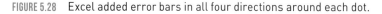

FIGURE 5.27   Your graph should be a series of dots.

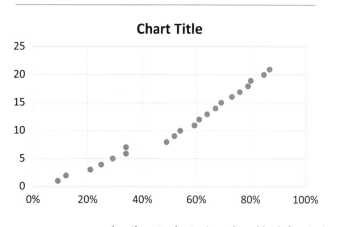

Now highlight both columns with numbers and insert a simple scatterplot (Figure 5.27). Don't highlight the data labels or the header row, or else the graph won't work out properly.

The scatterplot process created dots—these are the lollipops! It is basically visualizing just the end of the bars in the bar graph. Right now, I suggest you click on the horizontal gridlines and delete them. They can confuse things if we keep them in place any longer.

It's time to make the stick of the lollipop. We are going to create these using error bars. In Excel 2013, navigate up to the *Chart Tools>Design* tab and look for the button that says *Add Chart Element.* Click the drop-down arrow there, hover down to *Error Bars,* hover on it's arrow to open another menu, and finally click on *More Error Bars Options.* In Excel 2010, you should just see a button in the *Chart Tools* ribbon for *Error Bars.*

As soon as I clicked on *More Error Bars Options,* my graph went wacky (see Figure 5.28).

We do not need the vertical error bars at all. So, in the dialogue box that opened, change the number in the *Fixed value box* to zero and the figure now looks like Figure 5.29.

FIGURE 5.28   Excel added error bars in all four directions around each dot.

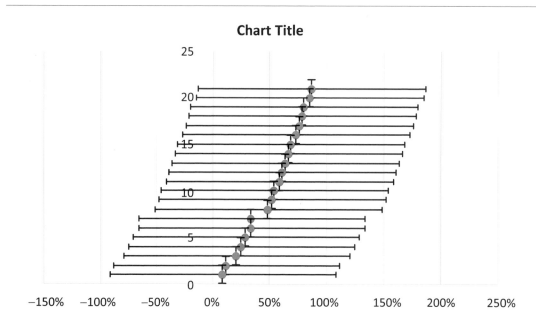

FIGURE 5.29   Adjust the *fixed value* under the *Error Amount.*

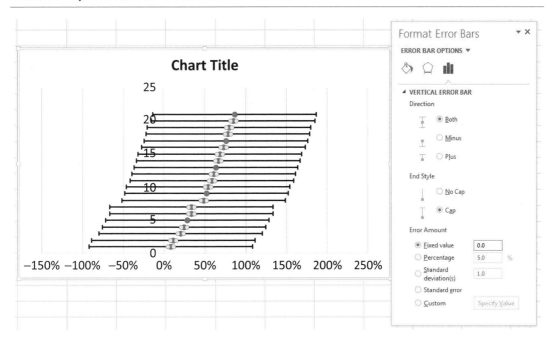

This action eliminated one set of error bars. To get to the other set, click on the little arrow next to *Error Bar Options* and then switch from *Series 1 Y Error Bars* to *Series 1 X Error Bars* (Figure 5.30).

FIGURE 5.30   Switch between graph elements through the drop-down menu at the top of the dialogue box.

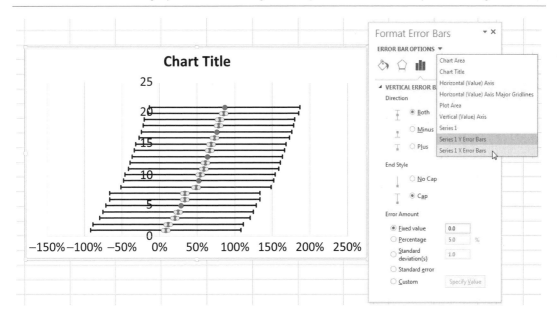

FIGURE 5.31   Horizontal error bars can be adjusted to meet the axis line and look like sticks for your lollipops.

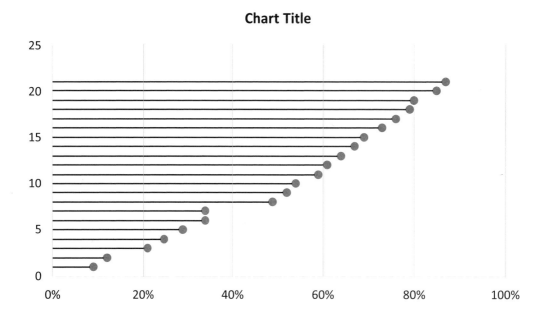

You'll see the same basic options, now just for the horizontal set of error bars. Here is where the magic happens. You'll want to adjust every bit of this dialogue box. To make our lollipops, we really only want the error bars that shoot out to the left, so in the *Direction* area, switch from *Both* to *Minus* (Figure 5.31).

In *End Style,* get rid of the cap. In *Error Amount,* click the radio button by Percentage and type in 100% (Figure 5.31). This will fix your x-axis so it starts at 0%, just as it should, and will extend the lollipop stick from the lollipop head to the y-axis (Figure 5.32).

Give yourself a fist pump because that was awesome.

Next up, let's fix that y-axis, shall we? Right-click on it and adjust the maximum to 22—that is one more than the highest number we listed in our fake data. If, in doing so, Excel then adjusts your minimum, just change it back to zero. Now you can delete the y-axis labels altogether.

Let's get the data labels in place now, so we know which lollipop represents what. We are going to insert another series of fake data so that we can use its labels. Since we are still working with a scatterplot, the y-values for the data are already here—we will use the same y-values in

FIGURE 5.32   The essential pieces of the lollipop graph are in place.

Chart Title

the Lollipop spacing column. But, the x-values that we are adding will be new. So, add another column of data and this time just fill it up with zeroes. This way, the new series of data will be a set of dots all the way over on the left side of the graph and the labels we eventually put there will look like regular, standard, proper labels for the lollipops. The table will now look like Figure 5.33.

Right-click on the graph and click *Select Data*. In the dialogue box that opens, click on *Add* in the *Legend Entries* section. Use the cell picker icons in the new box to select Label holders as your series name, all those zeroes as the Series X values, and all the numbers underneath Lollipop spacing as your Series Y values as shown in Figure 5.34.

FIGURE 5.33 Add another column of data, full of zeroes, to act as label placeholders.

	A	B	C	D
1			Lollipop spacing	Label holders
2	Other	9%	1	0
3	South Asian/South Asian Americans	12%	2	0
4	Interngenerational/Generational	21%	3	0
5	Asian/Asian Americans	25%	4	0
6	Muslim Observance	29%	5	0
7	Africa/Pan Africa/African Americans	34%	6	0
8	Gender Equity	34%	7	0
9	Disability Advocacy	49%	8	0
10	European/European Americans	52%	9	0
11	Veteran	54%	10	0
12	Pacific Islander/Pacific Islander Americans	59%	11	0
13	Non-Traditional Students	61%	12	0
14	Religious Equity	64%	13	0
15	Caribbean/Caribbean Americans	67%	14	0
16	Latino/Latina	69%	15	0
17	Middle Eastern Heritages and Traditions	73%	16	0
18	Trans-racial Adoptee/Parent	76%	17	0
19	LBGTQ/Ally	79%	18	0
20	Mixed Race	80%	19	0
21	Jewish Heritage/Observance	85%	20	0
22	International Students	87%	21	0

FIGURE 5.34 Add another series of data, composed of the data for Label holders and Lollipop spacing.

	A	B	C	D
1			Lollipop spacing	Label holders
2	Other	9%	1	0
3	South Asian/South Asian Americans	12%	2	0
4	Interngenerational/Generational	21%	3	0
5	Asian/Asian Americans	25%	4	0
6	Muslim Observance	29%	5	0
7	Africa/Pan Africa/African Americans	34%	6	0
8	Gender Equity	34%	7	0
9	Disability Advocacy	49%	8	0
10	European/European Americans	52%	9	0
11	Veteran	54%	10	0
12	Pacific Islander/Pacific Islander Americans	59%	11	0
13	Non-Traditional Students	61%	12	0
14	Religious Equity	64%	13	0
15	Caribbean/Caribbean Americans	67%	14	0
16	Latino/Latina	69%	15	0
17	Middle Eastern Heritages and Traditions	73%	16	0
18	Trans-racial Adoptee/Parent	76%	17	0
19	LBGTQ/Ally	79%	18	0
20	Mixed Race	80%	19	0
21	Jewish Heritage/Observance	85%	20	0
22	International Students	87%	21	0

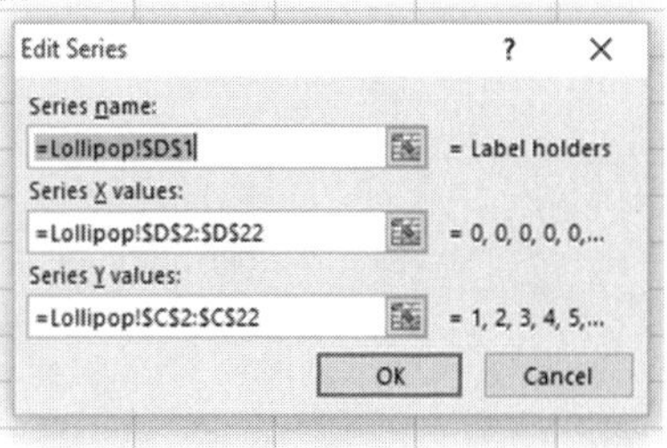

Click OK and your graph now has a second set of dots going up the left side of the graph. Sweet! We are going to add data labels to the dots! But, there's no room for the data labels yet. So, click inside the graph, on the white background (Excel calls this the plot area). Its border will become active and you should see a little square white box on the left, in the midst of your new series of dots. Click on that baby and drag it over to the right so that you are shrinking the plot area and making room for your labels (Figure 5.35).

FIGURE 5.35   Drag the side handle over to the right so you have space for the labels.

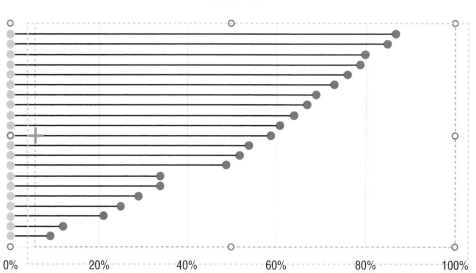

Now that there's room to breathe, right-click on the new set of dots and select *Add data labels*. Excel is going to give you the y-axis values, which are a secret. But, click on each one and link it to the cell with the label you desire using the linked textbox trick we discussed elsewhere in this book. Be sure you select the *Left* label position. You may need to readjust your plot area here or enlarge your entire graph to make room for all those labels (I did both).

Labels are in place, lollipop and stick are ready to go. It's time to get rid of the second set of dots that our labels are attached to. Right-click on those dots and select *Format Data Series*. In the *Marker Options* window, select *None* to eliminate the marker dots altogether.

The last step now is to add an awesome title and make any color adjustments (Figure 5.36).

Go ahead and compare this lollipop graph (Figure 5.36) to the original bar graph of the same data a few pages back (Figure 5.24). Less visually demanding, isn't it? Even though it took us several more steps to make the lollipop chart, we put in that elbow grease in order to make life easier for our readers. Plus you learned about the secret power of error bars in this process!

FIGURE 5.36   The lollipop graph is less visually overwhelming than a traditional bar graph.

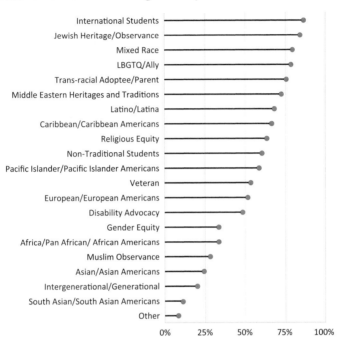

Respondents ranked race, ethnicity, homeland, and sexual orientation among the top areas of concern.

EXCEL NINJA LEVEL: 3

Lollipops can also be vertical and thankfully that doesn't take as much work. We are talking about Excel Ninja Level 3 here. You'll simply highlight your actual data values and insert a line graph with markers (instead of a scatterplot—so also no need for extra columns of fake data [I hear you cheering].). Then delete the line. Add error bars to the markers the same way we just did (only you'll notice half as many error bars to deal with). I usually like to increase the size of the markers to something really big, like 20, and position my data labels smack in the center (see Figure 5.37).

Yummy enough to eat, I know! Just be thoughtful here because the size of the marker technically spans a

FIGURE 5.37   Lollipop graphs can replace column graphs too.

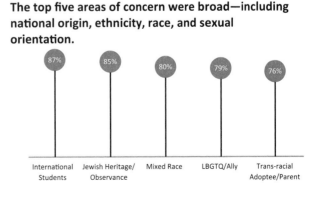

The top five areas of concern were broad—including national origin, ethnicity, race, and sexual orientation.

range of values, not just the one in its label. This kind of a lollipop is a little less visually accurate, but has all kinds of appeal for its simplicity.

Lollipop charts are decent alternatives to standard bar and column charts any time, for any kind of data that would work in a bar or column, not just for check-all-that-apply data. They are especially helpful when the visualization is overpowering due to its massive ink because the lollipop focuses attention at the value.

LARGE NUMBER WITH ICON

I saw this next example in a magazine (Figure 5.38) and thought of you.

We don't have the survey question that Consumer Reports asked, but it was probably something like "When you tried to negotiate a better bundle package, which of these deals did you receive? (Check-all-that-apply)." The clue that the respondents could check multiple answers is that the five answers we can see here add to more than 100%. Rather than try any sort of graph, Consumer Reports chose to display the five answers using large numbers paired with a simple icon.

The most tedious part of developing a graphic like this is simply finding the icons that match your underlying category. Most of us have probably spent hours searching through websites trying to find suitable images. Add to that task the challenge of finding a set of images that all look like they belong together! Let me rescue your afternoon with two very helpful websites:

EXCEL NINJA LEVEL: 0
(USE POWERPOINT)

The Noun Project—accessed at https://thenounproject.com/ was started by folks who dreamed of having an icon for everything. It's a super exhaustive site with a power-house search system that makes finding icons an easy task. The icons generally have a similar look and feel to them, too—meaning they mostly look like they were drawn by the same hand (or hand on a mouse). The icons come in black and white for easy recoloring. Many are free or at most they cost $1.00 USD.

Flat Icon—accessed at http://www.flaticon.com/. The awesomeness of Flat Icon can be summed up in two words: Free. Vector. Vector means that you can resize the image as large as you'd like and it won't blur or fuzz on you. The icon you create for your graphic in your report can also appear on your slides in a much larger and visible form and it

FIGURE 5.38   Try combining a single large number with an icon that represents that category.

will still look crisp and clean. The icons on this site are no charge, but many do require attribution, in that you need to give the icon designer credit somewhere in your report or on your site, wherever the icon appears.

Alternatively, you could simply make your own icons. It wouldn't be all that difficult or time consuming to construct the icon for Nothing (though maybe think a little harder about something more effective than a circle with a line through Thing). To construct an entire graphic like this one, use any kind of blank canvas software—even PowerPoint would do the trick. You just insert textboxes and icons and be happy.

I wouldn't want to see a report full of the large number with icon visuals, but it can work well in limited doses for check-all-that-apply data.

BRANCHING

Branching questions are the type of question where if a respondent answers one way, then he or she is given an additional set of questions that branch out from the first answer. Anytime you hear someone talking about data, and describing the survey responses this way " . . . and of those, 45% said . . ." then he or she is talking about subsets of respondents who were given particular questions based on their answers to previous questions. For example, when the survey says "if you said *Yes,* proceed to question 32," the path through the survey branched. Sure, you could just graph those answers with one of the other options presented in this chapter. But, it isn't likely that your readers will quickly grasp that you have isolated a subset of respondents for examination. Let's look at a few other visualizations that make it clearer.

Of this 88%, **65%** love you

ANNOTATED GRAPH

If your branches don't extend very far or the data you need to report is limited, consider the simplest charting method: add an annotation inside another graph. The annotated note provides just a little extra explanation—the data from your branch.

EXCEL NINJA LEVEL: 2

The data here in Figure 5.39 came from a survey where young adults with autism were asked whether they work part time or full time. The survey branched from there, probing about hourly pay, benefits, and promotions, depending on which side of the branch the respondent followed. Both groups were asked about hourly pay at some point and it was this extra data that we wanted to display for both groups.

FIGURE 5.39   Embed extra data from down the branch into the original graph to give it more impact.

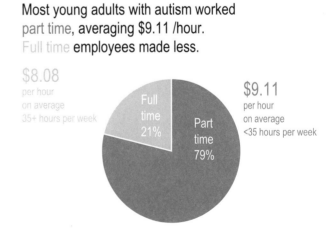

Most young adults with autism worked part time, **averaging $9.11 /hour.** Full time **employees made less.**

$8.08
per hour
on average
35+ hours per week

Full time 21%

Part time 79%

$9.11
per hour
on average
<35 hours per week

SOURCE: Roux, Anne M., Shattuck, Paul T., Rast, Jessica E. ,Rava Julianna A., and Anderson, Kristy A. *National Autism Indicators Report: Transition into Young Adulthood.* Philadelphia, PA: Life Course Outcomes Research Program, A. J. Drexel Autism Institute. Drexel University, 2015. Used with permission.

The annotated graph strategy can be applied to any kind of graph type, but a pie chart works here because we only have two slices. Each slice has an annotation, detailing the average hourly pay for full-time and part-time workers, including a note that defines full- and part-time hours. The annotations were inserted with textboxes—and several of them. I inserted one text box for the hourly dollar amount and linked it to the cell in the table so that when those numbers change with next year's data, the textbox will update. I inserted a second textbox below each hourly rate and typed in the text "per hour on average" and the definition.

Clearly, there's only so much extra text we can pack into one data visualization, so the annotated graph strategy for branching data can handle limited depth down the branch.

NESTED AREA GRAPH

Figure 5.40, my friends, is a nested area graph.

See how it works? In this case, 25% of the survey respondents said no (and they skipped to the next section). 75% of the respondents said yes, they visualize data. The people who do visualize data were of most interest in this study, so they were given an extra set of questions. Of that 75% who visualize data, 81% reported "daily." This software company is only curious about primary users, those who visualize daily, so those folks saw even more questions pop up in their survey window. And of those who visualize data daily, 64%

FIGURE 5.40   The inner rectangles represent the subsets of respondents.

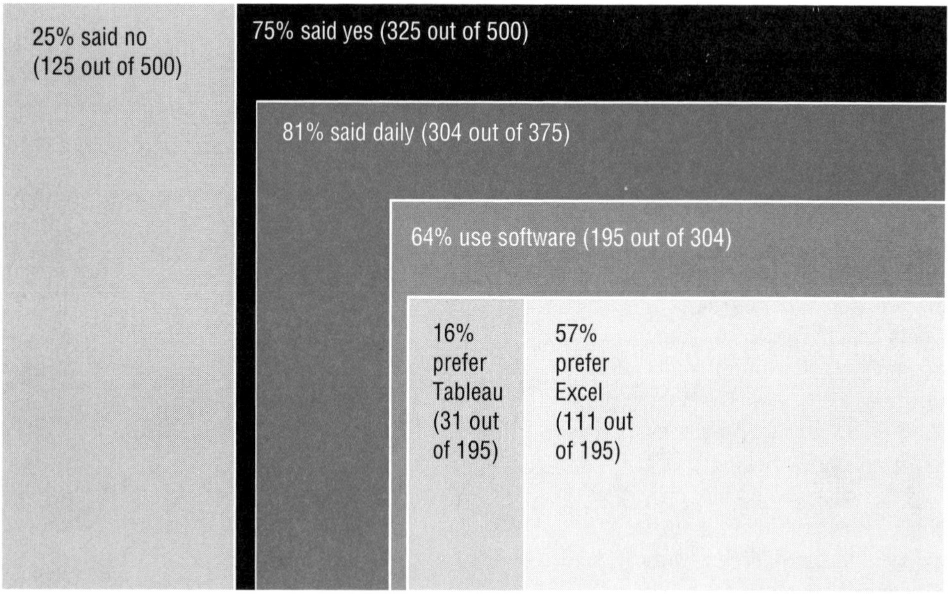

said they use software. You get it? It's a pretty intuitive visualization. Nested area graphs can handle more levels of branching than the pie chart plus large number example.

This is graphing by area—which is tricky. Remember how Chapter 1 pointed out that humans are bad at interpreting area? Turns out the difficulty with judging area isn't any different if the area is in a circle (like a bubble graph) or a square (um . . . that's a nested area graph) (Heer & Bostock, 2010). Therefore, the rule is that the area must be proportionate to the data it's representing—a reader should be able to put down a ruler and calculate the area of the "daily" square and it had better be 81% of the area of the "yes" square. And it is.

I made this diagram in PowerPoint. I started by calculating the total rectangle area by just throwing out some dimensions that would be easy to work with. Area is height times width (oh, high school geometry class). I said 6 inches by 10 inches, or 60 square inches, would be the area to represent all 500 respondents. The dark blue yes rectangle had to be 75% of that size, or .75 multiplied by 60 square inches, which is 45 square inches. I wanted the yes rectangle to be the same height as the overall rectangle, which was 6 inches. So, I divided 45 square inches by the 6" height and got 7.5" for my width. So far I've just been using a calculator. Now it's time to actually visualize! Insert a rectangle in PowerPoint (see Figure 5.41).

EXCEL NINJA LEVEL: 0
(MAKE IT IN
POWERPOINT)

FIGURE 5.41   Over in the right of the *Drawing Tools* section, you'll see where to enter the height and width dimensions you calculated.

Look in the orange *Drawing Tools* section, inside the *Format* tab, for the *Size* area where you can punch in those dimensions you just calculated.

To get to the blue daily rectangle, I calculated 81% of the size of the yes rectangle, which you'll recall was 45 square inches. The product is 36.45 square inches. I wanted it to nest inside the yes rectangle, so the height needed to be smaller than 6″. I chose to lay this out with 5″ in height, which leaves a width of 7.29″. So, I inserted another rectangle and sized it up properly. And so on.

Sounds complicated, but it really isn't too hard. You just pick an area to start with for your total set of respondents and divide it up in proportion to the data it needs to represent.

What makes the nested area graph seen in Figure 5.40 work best: Listing the n's alongside the main heading in each rectangle. This will help people who are having a hard time wrapping their brains around the visualization because they can see how the n's carry down into each section, such that the numerator for the parent rectangle becomes the denominator for the child. Main headings can be inserted with textboxes.

What doesn't work: Using PowerPoint's Scale Height and Scale Width features. You might have started exploring PowerPoint and noticed that if you right-click on the rectangle, you see a menu option called *Size and Position*. If you open it, you'll see a place to enter height and width, just as we've been doing. You'll also see spots that say *Scale Height* and *Scale Width,* where PowerPoint offers the ability to scale the rectangle by a specific percentage. You may be tempted to shortcut the above process and simply copy one rectangle and type 81% into the *Scale Height* and *Scale Width* boxes. At first, it may even appear to work, but once we get down to the inner rectangles of the nested area graph, it becomes clear that the scale option is a little wonky. Try it if you don't believe me. The surefire way to make a proportionally representative nested area graph is to break out the calculator and crunch those numbers by hand.

VISUALIZING NOT APPLICABLE OR MISSING DATA

Yes, I know the jig is up. All of my examples in this chapter so far have been pretty tidy, as if every response option was addressed by every single respondent. The truth is that life and data collection are messy. How can we show that different questions have different sample sizes? The most appropriate visualization method will depend on the severity and inconsistency of your problem.

NOTE SMALL CONSISTENT MISSING DATA

The easiest solution when data is acting like a tiny, but equal opportunity absentee for every response option is to just make a note of it somewhere in the graph. My preferred location is in a subheading, underneath the main takeaway point of the visualization. Make it smaller (in a report, like 9-point font) and gray (see Figure 5.42).

If the data is missing consistently it is good to note, but not a super critical issue. This treatment marks the issue, but relegates its importance to a background matter.

FIGURE 5.42   Add a subtitle to the graph to explain the missing or removed data, if it is consistent across all categories.

SBIRT increased across all races and ethnicities between 2013 **and** 2014**.**
Gray dots represent 2011. Data missing for 10.3% of respondents. Each race category excludes Hispanic/Latino.

SOURCE: Stephanie Evergreen (2015). "SBIRT Graph." Oregon Health Authority Office of Health Analytics. Used with permission.

ADD SAMPLE SIZE FOR LARGE CONSISTENT MISSING DATA

EXCEL NINJA LEVEL: 1

Here's everyone's favorite nightmare: You sent your reliable research assistants out to collect data with some paper and pencil surveys . . . only one page of the survey was missing. It'll be OK because you have more data, but what to do with those questions that have many fewer responses? The answer: Note the sample size in the data label.

To do this in Excel, you can add the sample size to each data label cell in your table. Make a line break within a cell (on a PC) by holding down the Alt key while you hit Enter.

In the formula bar, the data appear broken onto two lines (Figure 5.43).

FIGURE 5.43   Type Alt+Enter at the end of a line to create a line break within a cell.

Do you have health coverage of any kind for yourself?
n=487

In the graph, the "missing" data show up as part of your data label, under its corresponding question. In this case, the prenatal question was asked on a different page, but it was grouped with other healthcare data from the missing page for reporting purposes. The data label makes it clear that the sizes are inconsistent among the questions in this graph (Figure 5.44).

FIGURE 5.44   Add the sample size for each question when there is significant missing data.

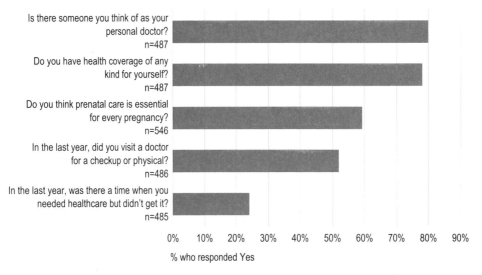

While many report having a primary doctor, most didn't see the doctor for regular checkups and one quarter didn't even get care when it was needed.

The same strategy can be used for large amounts of Not Applicable data. You can delete it from the graph, but the remaining data labels need to note the sample size. Again, the strategy here is to note the absence in a clear but diminished way.

EXCEL NINJA LEVEL: 9

ADD A GRAPH ON THE SIDE FOR LARGE INCONSISTENT MISSING DATA

The messiest data to deal with are those cases when lots of respondents skipped questions that weren't applicable to them. The most accurate way to handle such data is to be super honest that it is gone and show it in the graph—just off to the side.

To do this in Excel, we are going to combine two graph methods we already discussed in this chapter: diverging stacked bars and small multiples.

The left portion of this table should remind you of the way we set up the diverging stacked bar table. We add secret hush-hush buffer zones to either end of the Likert scale so that both halves add to 100%. Not Applicable answers are way over to the right, followed by a secret buffer column that pairs up with the Not Applicable data to also add to 100%. Adding across each row here should total 300% (see Figure 5.45). I know it goes against your survey methodologist instincts, but see this through.

FIGURE 5.45   Add secret buffer columns for the negative responses, the positive responses, and the Not Applicable responses.

Please rate your overall experience with:

	Bad Buffer	Poor	Fair	Good	Excellent	Good Buff	Not Applic	N/A Buffer
Room service	100%	0%	0%	6%	8%	86%	86%	14%
Spa	100%	0%	0%	2%	22%	76%	76%	24%
Valet	73%	6%	21%	40%	16%	44%	17%	83%
Concierge	97%	1%	2%	26%	30%	44%	41%	59%
Housekeeping	81%	5%	14%	42%	37%	21%	2%	98%
Fitness center	98%	1%	1%	63%	22%	15%	13%	87%
Front desk staff	88%	5%	7%	52%	36%	12%	0%	100%

Graph everything—the whole table, including the headings—as a 100% stacked bar graph. As with the other secret buffer graphs, you'll mark the secret buffer bars as *No Fill,* and you should have three of those buffer values represented in each stack. You have now created a diverging stacked bar graph illustrating your main responses and a separate graph to the right with your Not Applicable responses (see Figure 5.46).

FIGURE 5.46   Turn the buffer segments *No Fill* and you are almost there.

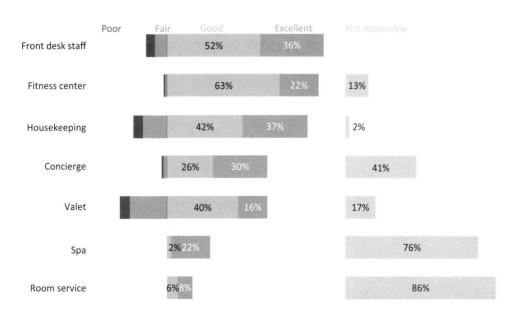

Front desk staff had the most positive responses but also the most guest complaints.
Room service and the spa had no negative responses, but very few people made use of them.

If you have forgotten any of the steps, review the sections that discuss Diverging Stacked Bar and Small Multiples graphs. But, really it's just formatting from here, folks. I used strong color coding and inserted linked textboxes for labels at the top of each response option.

The title here is important because it needs to explain why both graphs are included and necessary for proper interpretation. It's a complicated concept. If it becomes difficult to encapsulate both graphs in a single title, it's probably a good sign that you are trying to convey too much information and that perhaps the Not Applicable data should be dropped and mentioned in another way. If you do drop the Not Applicable data, then go back to the previous section and be sure to add the sample size to each label.

The overarching point of this section is that you should treat the missing or Not Applicable data differently from the main data you collected. Your primary data need to be seen in its own light.

EXERCISES

Head over to ColorBrewer2.com and snag a color scheme for your favorite rating data. Look for one that is close to your organizational color scheme, or one that makes semantic sense to you (as in reds for Strongly Disagree). If you don't see the RGB color codes right away, look for a drop-down menu that may be set to HEX (those are web codes). Select RGB to get the codes you need for Excel. The numbers are listed in order so that the first one is for R, the second for G, and the third for B.

Look up wtfviz at http://viz.wtf/ and have a hearty chuckle at the illogical data visualizations that actually made it to print and screen. Then pick one that you laugh at the hardest and remake it so that it's better. You will likely need to rethink the graph type and review the formatting in terms of color and legend. Sketch it first on paper and then try to remake your redesign on a computer.

Network diagrams stem from specific types of surveys, where you essentially research the strength of the networks within a group of people. Try this: Make a list of all the students in your class and distribute that list to everyone in class, asking them to mark the students with whom they've had at least two previous classes together. Collect all the data by tallying responses. This data would be visualized in a network diagram.

I'll illustrate this by using an example from my colleague, John Burnett, who runs Haiku Analytics, which is located at http://haikuanalytics.com/. John was working with a senior center who wanted to get their seniors together to regularly interact for bridge or cribbage or gin and tonics or whatever to reduce isolation and improve their fun and quality of life. The smart launch of any program should be preceded by a little fact-finding mission. I mean, who's to say the seniors aren't already connected and whooping it up? There should be some data to drive the decision to fund a new social program. John ran a small study similar to the one I'm asking you to do in this exercise.

Analyzing these connections takes a specialized software program: NodeXL is a handy one because it is free, acts as a plug-in for Excel, and allows plenty of visual customization. It visualizes the data

(Contined)

FIGURE 5.47   The diagram visualized four main groups in the senior network.

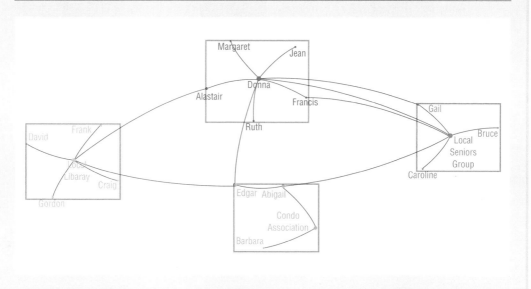

SOURCE: John Burrett (2015). "Senior Social Network." Haiku Analytics. Used with permission.

by assigning each person in the survey list as a dot (or node) and draws connections between the people in the network via lines, where the thickness of the line represents more connections. The network diagram also groups together those who report hanging together. John's senior center network diagram shows four main groups.

The interpretations able to be made off of a network diagram are glorious. First, we can clearly see that the seniors are fractured into four groups, which don't even all gather in the same place. So, yes we can confirm that a senior social program is necessary. We can also see that in order to get everyone to buy-in to the program, the staff will need to develop a strategy around each group's kingpin, like Donna. We can also see connections between groups, so we know that if the staff can convince Donna, it's likely that Edgar and the others at the condo association will be game. The visualization drives strategy and action.

Use pencil and paper or try out NodeXL (can be accessed at **https://nodexl.codeplex.com/**) or another software program and visualize your class survey data. Check out the Resources section at the end of this chapter for more extensive training on social network diagrams. Even with their potential to get a bit complex, network diagrams are becoming more popular as a concise way to show many interconnections with specific check-all-that-apply data.

RESOURCES

Visualizing social network diagrams can be clunky using some traditional analysis programs. The most elegant network diagrams are often made through specialized software and perhaps some programming skills. For a great overview of the software available for network diagramming, check out Andy Kirk's collection of resources, which can be retrieved from http://www.visualisingdata.com/index.php/resources/

The nested area graph example first came in front of my eyes via Innovation Network's State of Evaluation Report. It's an amazing, visual forward report and even if you have no interest in its subject matter, you'll want to click through it to stare in awe at the thoughtful (and proportionate) data visualizations. Go to http://www.innonet.org/client_docs/innonet-state-of-evaluation-2012.pdf

REFERENCES

Heer, J., & Bostock, M. (2010). Crowdsourcing graphical perception: Using mechanical turk to assess visualization design. *Proceedings of the SIGCHI Conference on Human Factors in Computing Systems* (pp. 203–212). New York, NY.

Heiberger, R. M., & Robbins, N. B. (2014). Design of diverging stacked bar charts for Likert scales and other applications. *Journal of Statistical Software, 57*, 1–32.

Talbot, J., Setlur, V., & Anand, A. (2014). Four experiments on the perception of bar charts. *IEEE Transactions on Visualization and Computer Graphics, 20*(12), 2152–2160.

WHEN THERE ARE PARTS
OF A WHOLE

VISUALIZING BEYOND THE PIE CHART

LEARNING OBJECTIVES

After reading this chapter you will be able to

List options other than pie charts for showing parts of a whole

Articulate a reason why you might not need visualization

Break down parts of a whole by location in several ways

Construct the best possible pie chart when you choose to use one

This chapter will share methods for visualizing parts of a whole, particularly demographic survey questions, and introduce visuals not previously discussed, such as mapping and pie charts. Yes, we will review when pie charts are appropriate. This chapter features demographic datasets a lot and I placed it further back in this book on purpose. Demographic data are usually gathered for context so that researchers can understand their respondents. However, the data are often asked first on the survey and thus reported first during dissemination (usually with a visual for every demographic question). This chapter argues that visualizations are powerful, so we should only visualize that which is most important to the study and the readers—which means that sometimes the visuals for demographics should appear at the end of a report, and sometimes the demographic data shouldn't be visualized at all.

When parts of a whole are necessary for reporting, this chapter outlines many possible visualizations.

Contrary to cutting-edge belief, pie charts do have a place in visualizing parts of a whole. The visual works best under this condition: when you can remove the percentage signs and the reader is still able to interpret the angle slices accurately, or at least understand the point made through estimation. The largest slice should start at noon and the slices should then run clockwise in descending order.

When there are many slices, I usually unwrap the pie, so to speak, so that the reader is in a position of judging by length rather than judging by angle. One way to do this is to cast the data into a single stacked bar.

Technically, part-to-whole data that are represented in binned quantitative values should be shown as a histogram. These charts are not the sexiest of the bunch, but if you want to be proper, this is your solution, and again its interpretation is by length.

Treemaps are also a decent way to show part-to-whole data, even though they visualize by area. They are particularly powerful for showing hierarchical or nested relationships.

Part-to-whole data that is location-based is best charted on a map. In this chapter, I'll introduce you to several methods inside and outside of Excel that make mapping a breeze.

Go ahead and keep pie charts in your data visualization arsenal, but you're wise to broaden your spectrum so that you have the most appropriate visual to represent your part-to-whole data.

WHAT STORIES CAN BE TOLD WHEN THERE ARE PARTS OF A WHOLE?

Anytime that you are trying to show that the things you are talking about add up to 100%, you are telling a story about parts of a whole. Whenever you need to describe the proportionate components of a group, this is a story about parts of a whole. When you are illustrating the descriptive characteristics of your research subjects, you are talking about parts of a whole. Specific stories can include

- Most students persisted to graduation, but some dropped out and some had incomplete attendance
- Our employees are mainly female
- Our newest phone already has 5% of the market share
- The student body composition is 75% Free and Reduced Lunch and 25% paid lunch
- Here are the income groups into which our survey respondents fell
- This map shows the percentage of our users who come from each state in the United States
- The majority of our visitors are ages 10 and younger and 56 and older
- Market data show we have three main profiles of customers

While these stories primarily focus on demographic topics, parts of a whole charts are also in play when reporting survey responses, so be sure to check out other chapters for options built around Likert scales and check-all-that-apply questions.

HOW CAN I VISUALIZE THE PARTS OF A WHOLE?

Even though we typically show parts of a whole as a pie chart, other options can be stronger at showcasing different stories within our data.

DON'T VISUALIZE AT ALL

EXCEL NINJA LEVEL: 0

Probably not what you expected to see in a book about visualization, right? This option is a necessary part of our toolkit because oftentimes researchers visualize every single demographic question when it isn't important to do so. The urge is there, I believe, because researchers are compelled to graph all questions on the survey, regardless of whether they are relevant to the story in the data; automatically graphing every question is just the way things have typically been done "around here."

The problem with such a mode of operation is that it dilutes the power of the visual. People are vision driven. Our eyes are drawn to pictures, graphics, and visualizations first. They grab our attention (Stenberg, 2006). So, when we overload our reporting with graphs for every survey question, we visually exhaust our readers. This isn't to say that too many graphs are detrimental to attention spans. It is to say that when we graph things that aren't important we confuse our readers and make them question what point the graph has or why we deemed it important enough to place it in the report.

My position here is that most of the time the demographic questions aren't important enough to visualize. While they may be valuable data to collect for the researcher, in order to look for correlations or to generally disaggregate and identify patterns, unless that investigation turns up something really interesting to the reader, the demographic questions stop carrying much value. They often don't convey much of a point or tell a compelling story on their own. Consider tucking them in the appendix, or in some tables online for super interested readers rather than casting them into a visualization.

PIE CHARTS DONE RIGHT

We all have heard that pie charts are bad, but why is that so? Remember Chapter 1? Humans are not great at judging angles.

Take a look at the typical pie chart as shown in Figure 6.1. I've labeled the wedges for us. Which wedge is bigger, two or five? You might be able to see that wedge three is slightly bigger than wedge four, but is one bigger than six?

Even if we ordered these wedges from greatest to least, it would still be hard to answer those questions. And this is why researchers add value labels to each wedge. While it is easier to see that wedge five is bigger than wedge two, and that,

EXCEL NINJA LEVEL: 1

FIGURE 6.1   Angle is hard to compare.

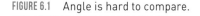

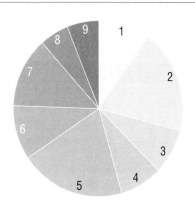

FIGURE 6.2   Labels help identify quantity, but then what's the purpose of the visualization?

FIGURE 6.3   With a limited number of wedges and a clear point, the pie chart is an acceptable visualization.

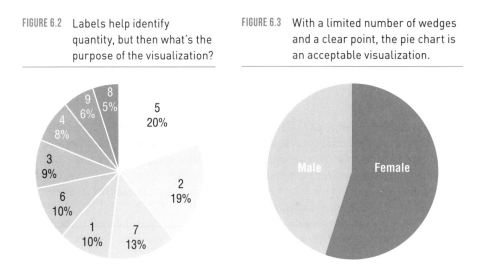

in fact, wedges one and six are the same, we are making that judgement using the value labels, not the pie wedges themselves. The visualization doesn't support any extra interpretation at this point.

As Stephen Few (2009) said, for all intents and purposes, this might as well be a table. And I would add, especially if it is just to illustrate a demographic question that has no larger story.

Pies don't necessarily aid comprehension over a table of numbers, but Schonlau and Peters (2012) found that they didn't impair comprehension either, so they could end up being the right visual to emphasize your parts-of-a-whole story. The true test of whether a pie chart can successfully tell your data story is whether you can pull something meaningful out of it without any number labels. For example, Figure 6.3 needs no percentages for you to quickly assess what I'm trying to say. This is a totally appropriate use of a pie chart.

In Excel 2013, the default pie chart option includes white borders around each wedge, which you can see in Figures 6.1 and 6.2. But, research shows that readers can "read into" these white borders and get a sense that the group making the data is disjointed or disconnected. To get rid of those white borders, right-click on any wedge, select *Format Data Series,* and change the border color to *No Border.*

Keeping that rule of thumb in mind, pie charts work best when you have roughly four or fewer wedges and the wedges are either really different from one another in angle or are really similar to each other. A circle sliced into quarters is easy to visually recognize; and Muscatello, Searles, Macdonald, and Jorm (2006) found that when the differences were distinct, pie charts performed just as well as bar charts. We tend to read pie charts in a clockwise order (in Western cultures), so start the largest slice at noon and arrange the wedges such that they run greatest to least.

100% STACKED BAR

The pie chart rules are helpful, but if you have more than four categories in your dataset, you'll need other options. Many in the data visualization community would probably suggest you swap the pie for a bar chart (Figure 6.4).

Humans can compare and assess lengths better than angles, so a bar chart looks like a good alternative to a pie chart. However, it seems harder to detect that these categories are parts of a whole, that they add up to 100%, that they account for all campus salaries.

One option would be to just say something like "These values represent 100% of campus salaries" in the subtitle of the graph. If it is important to you to visualize that these are parts of a whole, another option is to unwrap the pie chart, so to speak, such that it is a rectangle showing length rather than a circle. Replace the pie chart with a 100% stacked bar (Figure 6.5).

FIGURE 6.4   A bar chart renders quantity by length.

FIGURE 6.5   Unwrap a pie graph by making a 100% stacked bar.

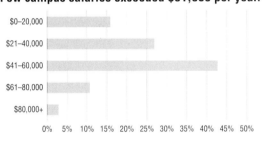

Few campus salaries exceeded $61,000 per year.

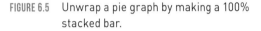
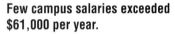
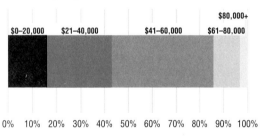

Few campus salaries exceeded $61,000 per year.

Usually we see stacked bars in a set, representing a chunk of survey questions. They can also be useful in isolation, as a single stacked bar, to reflect a single demographic question.

In this case, the categories have a natural order so the values are not running greatest to least. The table of data is set up according to the ordinal ordering of the income categories.

Highlight all of the data in the table and insert a 100% stacked bar chart. It is the third option in the top row of the bar chart family (Figure 6.6).

Initially, the graph does not look as it should. We need all five segments of data in one stack rather than five stacks of just one segment each. Look in the *Design* tab and click the button that says *Switch Row/Column* (see Figure 6.7).

EXCEL NINJA LEVEL: 2

Finishing off the graph is just formatting from here. To get to the end product shown in Figure 6.5, I chose a different font (Open Sans Condensed) and recolored the segments dark to light shades within one color, which make them easier to distinguish when reproduced in black and white. I added the data labels with textboxes and positioned them above each segment. You'll notice the segment on the far right is way too skinny to handle the full label sitting directly on top of it. So, I repositioned that label higher in the graph and inserted a line to connect the segment to its label.

While a standard bar chart is certainly an option for showing parts of a whole with many categories, a 100% stacked bar makes it more obvious that the values add up to

FIGURE 6.6   Choose the third option in the top row of bar charts.

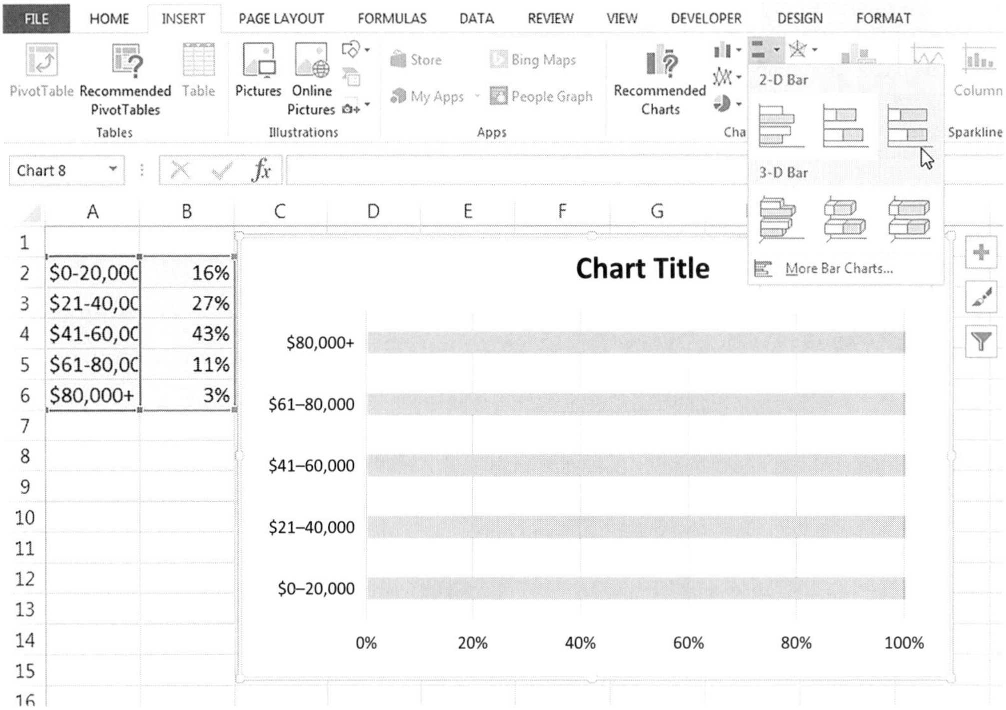

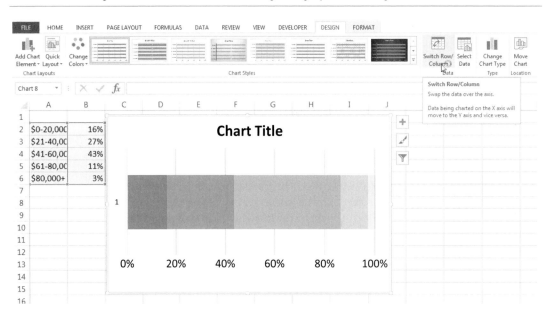

FIGURE 6.7   Switching the row and column will rearrange the graph into the right visualization.

100%. That said, it may still be harder to compare the values of each category to one another, because they don't share a baseline. If proportion of the whole is the story you need to tell, choose a 100% stacked bar. If you actually need your audience to compare the parts, a standard bar chart is a better option.

HISTOGRAM

I tend to shun histograms because they feel clunky to me. But, that's my personal preference, not backed by any kind of research. So, I will introduce you to histograms anyway. They are technically the proper way to visualize binned quantitative values. In other words, when the categories are ranges of numbers . . . in other words, the income graph above (Figure 6.5) should have been a histogram.

FIGURE 6.8   Histograms show binned quantitative values.

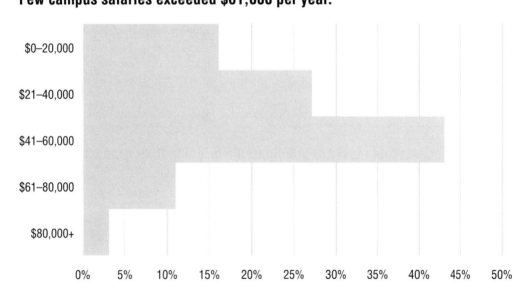

Figure 6.8 (using the dataset from Figures 6.4 to 6.7) is not the prettiest thing I've ever seen, yet still this may come in handy.

A histogram is nothing more than a standard bar or column chart, with absolutely no space between the bars or columns. They give a good picture of the overall shape of the dataset.

The data we are working with in this next example (Figure 6.9) is museum visitorship by age bracket. The age brackets are the clue that we are dealing with binned quantitative values.

First, insert a basic column chart.

Then right-click on any of the columns and select *Format Data Series*.

In the menu box that opens, you'll see a setting called *Gap Width* with a slider next to it. The default is probably 219% (Figure 6.9). This is the size of the gap between the columns. You want to shrink that gap to 0%. Just drag the slider all the way to the left and your gaps will disappear.

EXCEL NINJA LEVEL: 2

FIGURE 6.9   The x-axis categories are age brackets, suggesting a histogram may be the right visualization.

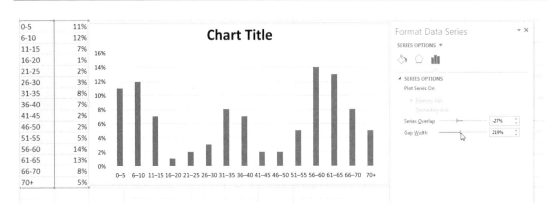

In a histogram, however, each column is still individually represented, allowing you to change the color of certain columns to bring attention to those portions of the visual if you want (see Figure 6.10).

FIGURE 6.10   Change the fill color of individual columns within the histogram to support your story.

Visitor age suggests that most are grandparents bringing their grandchildren.

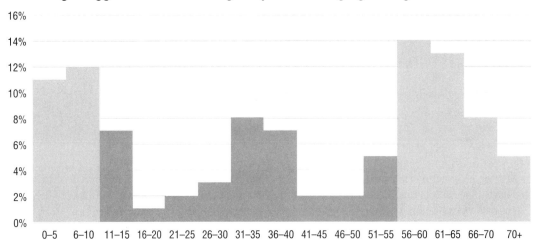

Eliminating the white space between the columns of a typical column graph can accentuate the overall shape of the dataset, particularly when the variables are continuous, but grouped or binned.

TREEMAP

Treemaps are square or rectangle shapes that represent parts, all positioned inside a larger square or rectangle that represents a whole. I hope your critical thinking alarm is sounding off because this is essentially plotting parts of a whole as area—and we aren't so great at judging area. So, why do people prefer treemaps over pie charts, when angle is better for us than area (though both aren't great)? It's because treemaps let us visualize a hierarchy, too.

Check out how this display tells us that Peter oversees Kori and Mary, and that Kori and Mary both oversee two other employees. The sizes of the boxes represent sales so that we can see that Kori's group has higher sales than Mary's group (Figure 6.11).

Within each group, we can see how individual employees fared. Treemaps also let us layer in an additional piece of data using color. Here color represents the growth in sales over the previous year. Darker colors mark more extreme growth (positive or negative).

As of this moment, when I'm typing these words, treemaps are not a default chart option in Excel 2013 or earlier versions. It has been included by default in Excel 2016, but I understand there are still some bugs at the time of this writing. In Excel 2013, you can access a treemap app in the App Store, but it is seriously flawed. I've discussed the flaws

FIGURE 6.11   Treemaps show nested parts of a whole.

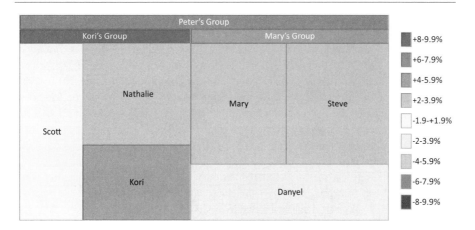

FIGURE 6.12   Enter your overall dimensions and your data to generate your treemap specs.

Enter the height and width of the area you want the treemap to occupy
Height: 7 Width: 10

Enter the values (from largest to smallest) that you want the treemap to show.
Enter at least four values and leave blank any values you aren't using.

Largest:	20%
Second:	15%
Third:	10%
Fourth:	8%
Fifth:	5%
Sixth:	
Seventh:	
Eighth:	
Ninth:	
Tenth:	

Results

Use the exact height and width values below
to create the reactangles for the treemap in PowerPoint

	Height	Width
Largest:	7.000	3.448
Second:	2.763	6.552
Third:	1.842	6.552
Fourth:	2.395	4.032
Fifth:	2.395	2.520
Sixth:	NA	NA
Seventh:	NA	NA
Eighth:	NA	NA
Ninth:	NA	NA
Tenth:	NA	NA

Calculator

at length with the programmers and we designed a sweet update to the app, but it is still unclear when it will be released, if ever.

So, in the meantime make your treemap by hand inside PowerPoint. You will want to make sure that each shape of the treemap is proportionally accurate, in that it matches the data it's representing (just as we discussed when making the nested area graph from Chapter 5). And fortunately, my friend and presentation expert Dave Paradi has a treemap calculator on his website at **http://www.thinkoutsidetheslide.com/simple-treemap-calculator/** that you can use to generate the heights and widths you'll need for each piece of your treemap.

The calculator is embedded right on Dave's site (Figure 6.12).

You'll start by entering the size you want the total treemap to consume. I said 7" by 10." Then you'll begin typing the values each piece of the treemap should represent. I typed in 20%, 15%, and 10%. It doesn't matter if you enter percentages or whole numbers, as long as you are consistent. As I enter the values, the data in the lowest part of the calculator starts to change. Dave has helped us figure out the heights and widths we need to use in PowerPoint.

EXCEL NINJA LEVEL: 0
(MADE IN POWERPOINT,
UNLESS YOU HAVE EXCEL
2016 ALREADY, YOU
LUCKY DOG)

Open PowerPoint and look for the *Shapes* button. It's in the *Insert* tab. Click the *Shapes* button to see all the shapes you can insert. Pick the rectangle, then move your cursor onto the slide and drag your mouse to make a rectangle. It doesn't matter how big it is. Once you have drawn the rectangle, you'll see an orange *Drawing Tools* tab open up. Way over on the left you'll see the height and width. Simply change these numbers to match the calculations generated from Dave's calculator (Figure 6.13).

Repeat this process for the other pieces of the treemap, matching the size to the calculated dimensions.

With just a handful of pieces, it's pretty obvious where each piece should go to fit into a solid, completed treemap (and Dave's calculator has a limit on the number of pieces it can calculate anyway). But, I could see that my pieces were not totally aligned. So I held down the Control key while I selected the ones on the bottom. Then I let go of the Control key and clicked inside the orange *Drawing Tools* tab, on the button called *Align*. In that menu, I selected *Align Bottom*. I'll need to check that all pieces of the treemap are aligned to one another so that it looks perfect.

To finish it off, I'll add color to show growth (Dave suggests white borders) and text-boxes to label each piece of the treemap (Figure 6.14).

FIGURE 6.13   Adjust the height and width of inserted rectangles to make the treemap.

FIGURE 6.14   Create your own growth legend and add textboxes to finish the treemap.

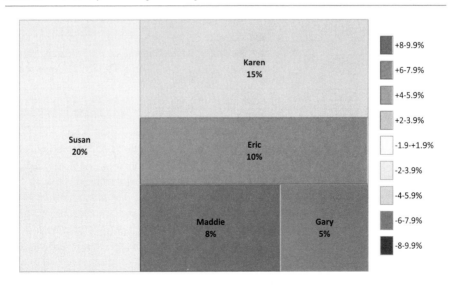

While Dave's calculator does not nest treemaps, as I show back at the start of this section, you can still create one with the calculator by inputting the values for each nest independently. For example, let's say I wanted to show that Susan, Karen, Eric, Maddie, and Gary were all a part of Carla's group and that Carla's group had 60% of the department sales while Milena's group had 40%. I would begin by entering the total size of the treemap and then only calculate Carla (60%) and Milena (40%). Then I'd start a new calculator and its total size would only be the dimensions I just calculated for Carla. Get it? You can make it work—and surprisingly fast.

MAP

Increasingly, our social sciences understand the importance of geolocation when studying outcomes. How respondents or constituents are spread over location can reveal patterns and insights that can't be seen any other way. While early mapping software has been available to the highly specialized in our fields, basic mapping is now accessible for researchers like you and me.

Mapping and Excel have never really been mentioned together in a positive light. It seems like they aren't compatible. Most people don't know that with Excel 2013, we have some (very limited) mapping options. When those options aren't sufficient, I'll leave you with further possibilities.

Both of these Excel-based options require that you tap into the Office app store, newly available in Excel 2013. You will need Internet access to use these mapping options. Click on the *Insert* tab and then look for the area called *Apps*. You'll click on the *Store* button, with the little red shopping bag icon.

You will see mapping apps you can download—some for a cost and some for free (Figure 6.15). Here we explore two of the free options.

Let's look at Geographic Heat Maps and Bing Maps. To use either of these, click on the listing and then click on the *Trust It* button. It will now appear in the *My Apps* area of your Excel toolbar for future use—though you'll still always need an Internet connection to use it.

FIGURE 6.15   Apps let you extend what Excel can do.

Geographic Heat Maps

Let's be super clear upfront: This heat map only contains a United States map and can only visualize at the state level. So, if that's your game, this map app might work for you. It's incredibly easy to use. You simply list your states in one column and your data in the next. In Figure 6.16, I show Midwest region website users.

To insert the map, click in your *My Apps* area and then click on the *Geographic Heat Map* app. A nice chart area will appear in your spreadsheet. Click on the gear in the upper left to select your data.

Click inside the *Select Data* box and then highlight your entire table. Excel should pick up which column is states and which is full of numbers, but if not, adjust it in step two of the dialogue box. Then pick a color scheme. This is the part that makes

EXCEL NINJA
LEVEL: 2

FIGURE 6.16   This map can handle one column of states and one associated column of data.

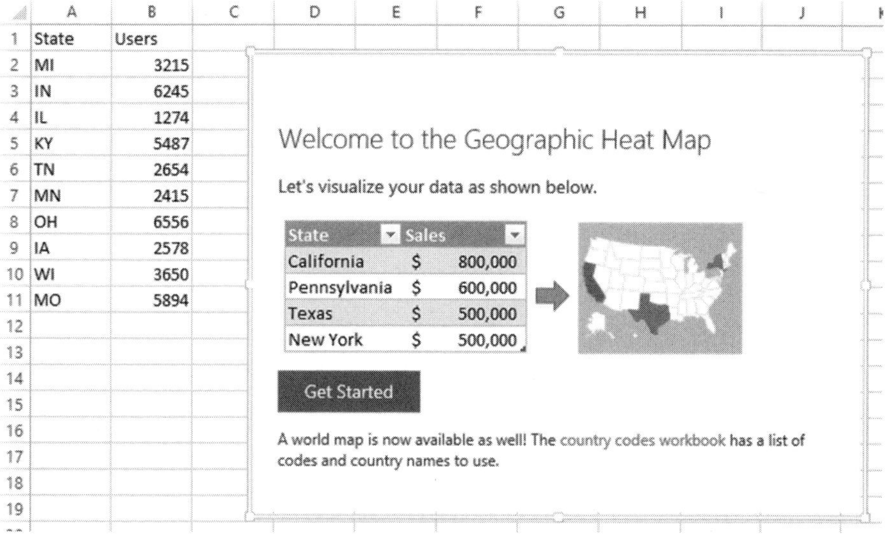

me really sad. Red-green is not a good color combination. It doesn't hold up well when reprinted in black and white, and red-green is the most common form of colorblindness, such that people with that affliction would only see a bunch of browns. So, I work with grayscale. Enter a title if you want (you can always go back and add this later if you need to visualize the data in order to know the point of the graph). Then click *Save* (Figure 6.17).

FIGURE 6.17   Choose from the limited color scheme.

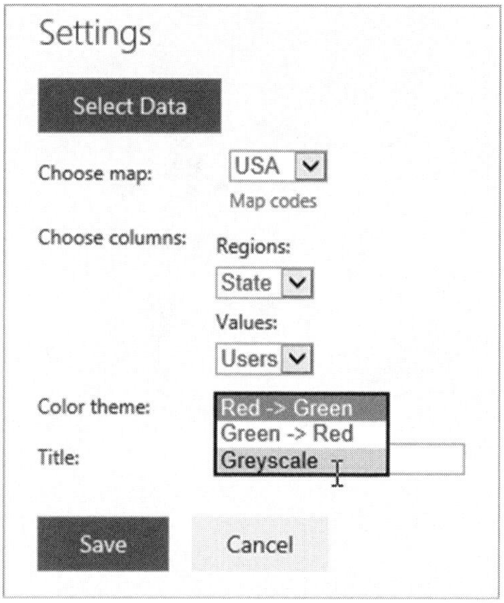

The map initially shows the entire United States, but you can easily zoom in on your area of interest. The app has rendered a visualization (Figure 6.18) where each state is color-coded by quantity. If you hover over any state, you'll see a pop-up box that details the exact quantity for that state.

However, there are some downsides: the grayscale option may have been the best of the bunch, but with gray as a background and white for states that aren't in the dataset, the grayscale color scheme makes the states in my dataset a bit camouflaged. Further, the assignment of the gray shade to each state is decided within the app and can't be changed. The formula the app uses to determine each value's corresponding shade isn't clear. And finally, the app provides little formatting flexibility, such as moving the title to the upper left of the graph.

Even with those drawbacks, this map may work well for you because it is super simple to use and the final display is fairly clutter free. Keep this last point in mind.

FIGURE 6.18   The final product uses color-coding to indicate quantity.

Bing Maps

If you need to map your demographic data on a more granular scale, you can also try the Bing Maps app in Excel 2013. Rather than filling a bounded area with a color, Bing Maps visualizes by points on a map. Take a look at my table in Figure 6.19—it lists cities in Michigan. Bing can produce circles or pie charts (your only two options) at each city's point on the map. Note also that while I want to show percentage male and female, the app can't handle percentages. The values need to be whole numbers.

EXCEL NINJA
LEVEL: 2"

Once the table is formatted the way you want it, click the *Bing Maps* button in the *Apps* area. It will insert a map charting area into your spreadsheet (Figure 6.19).

FIGURE 6.19   Insert a Bing Map, highlight your table, and then click the pointy circle icon to visualize your data.

The app will drop pie charts onto each city, reflecting your data (Figure 6.20). If things aren't looking quite right, you can make limited adjustments in the settings. Click on the gear icon to open the settings options.

Figure 6.20 shows how you can choose the colors for your data (though you can't customize the colors to your own branding, but you can probably get close). You can also choose whether you want circles (one data point) or pie charts (two data points). You will have to insert a textbox for your map title.

FIGURE 6.20   Choose your colors, your graph type, and your map type in the Settings window.

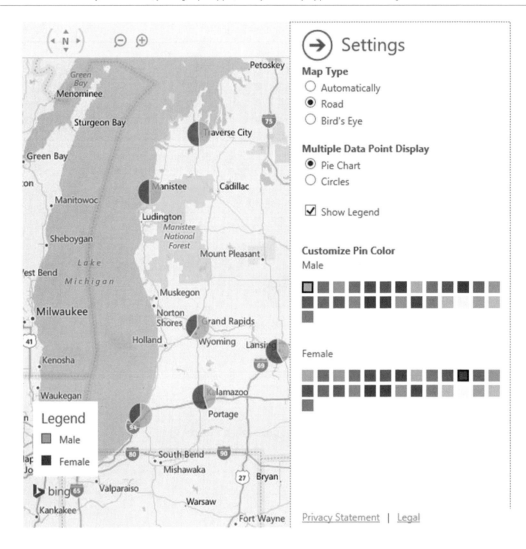

This seems great, but hopefully since you read Chapter 1, you recognize the downsides to using this app. Comparing pie charts (angle) or circles (area) are both difficult for our brains.

Moreover, you'll notice in the settings window in Figure 6.20 that you can choose different map types. None of them are great. This is the other part about Bing maps that makes me sad. No matter the map type, the ultimate display shows too much detail. My map shows cities that aren't in my dataset, state boundary lines, thick purple highway lines and large highway labels. It's too much clutter that makes it ever harder to just see the data I am trying to display.

FIGURE 6.21   Clicking on any pie chart reveals a pop-up box with more details.

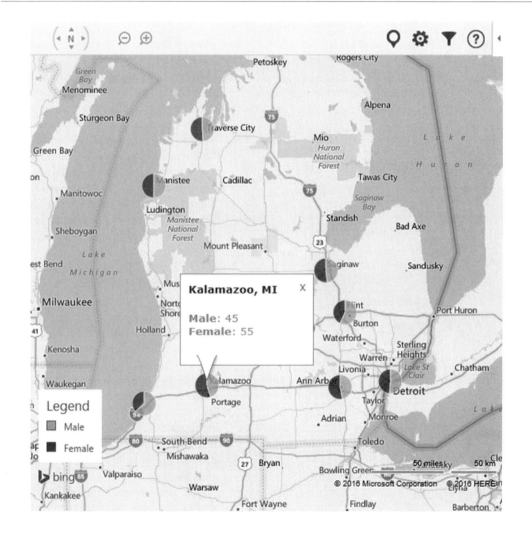

And this level of detail is often present in other fee-based software, such as ArcGIS or Tableau. While the precision of the visual is topnotch, the default display is overly cluttered.

On the bright side, the larger geographic area that you work with, the fewer unnecessary details in the display. Bing maps can handle global data and can operate with latitude and longitude coordinates, and even zip code-level data.

Both of these mapping options support limited interactivity and work with Excel Online, for web display. But, both have considerable drawbacks. So, let me show you how to get around these issues—it kind of involves cheating.

Editable Maps

We are now venturing out of Excel territory . . . all the way over to PowerPoint. Editable map files are not housed in any kind of geographic software. They are illustrations, based on real maps. These illustrations have muted the extraneous details, such as highways and green sections representing forests. You simply download the file—usually as a PowerPoint or possibly a PDF that you can convert to Powerpoint—and work with each piece of the illustration. Here's an example in Figure 6.22.

EXCEL NINJA LEVEL: 0

FIGURE 6.22   This editable map of India from Presentation Magazine renders each state or union territory as its own shape.

India—States and Union Territories

In this example, I downloaded an editable map of India from Presentation Magazine. It comes as a PowerPoint file. On the slide, each portion of the map is an independent shape. Ultimately I'll be able to use this to create a heat map, like the one based in Excel that I mentioned earlier, only this way I can customize the ranges and colors.

First, I'll create a legend based on my data. In this case, I'm trying to visualize the percentage of textile factories located throughout India. I decided what ranges would be appropriate for my data and then created a legend here by inserting squares and textboxes (Figure 6.23).

Click into the *Insert* tab in PowerPoint. Locate the *Shapes* button and click the arrow next to it. Then click on the rectangle shape and draw a rectangle somewhere in your slide. Change the fill color for the rectangle by clicking on it so that it is highlighted. Then look in the orange *Drawing Tools* tab, in the *Format* options, and locate the *Shape Fill* button (Figure 6.24). Click it open and you'll see loads of options for changing the fill color of your rectangle.

You can choose one of the default options, or click on *More Colors* to customize

FIGURE 6.23 Create a legend based on reasonable ranges for your data.

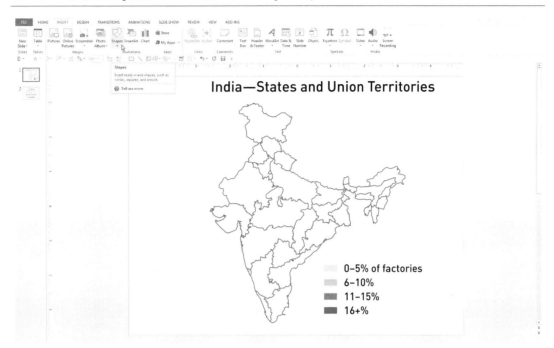

your choices. Given that the ranges here are increasing in steps, it makes sense to choose a set of colors for the legend that run light to dark. Keep this *Shape Fill* button in mind because we will return to it in just a moment.

Also in the *Insert* tab, locate the *Text Box* button, click it, and insert a textbox where you can type in the range that corresponds to each rectangle color in the legend.

Now that the legend is established, it's time to color-code the map. Since each state or union territory is its own shape, I'll just hold down the Shift key on my keyboard so that I can select multiple items, and click on the states that fall into the same range (Figure 6.25).

With the right shapes selected, I'll return to that *Shape Fill* menu and pick the color from my legend that corresponds to the data for these shapes (Figure 6.26).

We have several advantages here over using the Excel-based heat map: Editable maps are available for many parts of the world. I can customize the ranges for my data that make the most sense to me. I can choose

FIGURE 6.24 Choose a fill color for the rectangles in your legend.

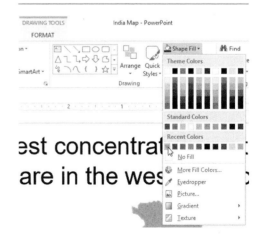

FIGURE 6.25 Select multiple shapes at once by holding down the Shift key and clicking on each shape.

FIGURE 6.26   The geographic heat map is constructed by establishing a legend and changing fill colors.

India—States and Union Territories

The highest concentrations of textile factories are in the west and south of india.

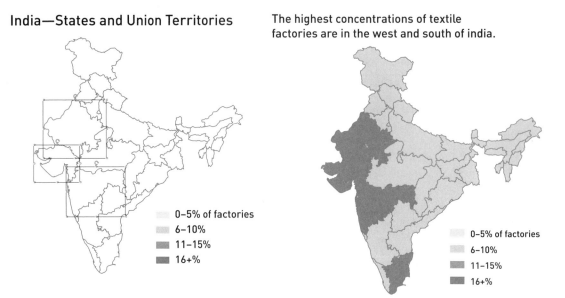

0–5% of factories
6–10%
11–15%
16+%

0–5% of factories
6–10%
11–15%
16+%

color schemes beyond red/green and grayscale. It also visualizes cleaner than the Bing Map app option—no highways, no lakes, no forests.

At Presentation Magazine's website, where I obtained this file, you can find editable maps for some continents—at the country level—and the United States map, at the state level, for free. If you need a more detailed map, you can easily find U.S. county-level online for around $40 USD. Search on "editable map" or "vector map" plus your search terms. If you are handy with programs like Illustrator, you can buy county-level maps from the major stock photo sites and carry out some quick color changes. To get maps that are more fine-grained than county-level, such as school district or Census block maps, check with your local government offices. Many have editable maps files that you can turn into heat maps for your specific demographic or part-to-whole data.

A quick word of caution: Using color to communicate data on a map invariably brings more attention to states with a larger geographic area (Montana) even if other states have a higher population (New Jersey). If this area bias is a concern for you, consider inserting equally sized circles over each state and color-coding those to represent your data (Atz et al., 2014) or replace each state shape with a square or hexagon to make them equally sized (see Figures 6.27 and 6.28). I'm currently Team Hexagon.

The hexagon map was made in PowerPoint, by inserting hexagons and then changing the fill color of the shapes. While the modified map doesn't achieve perfect geographic fidelity (i.e., Utah has a coast), it does give balance to the states and it includes the District of Columbia, which is often left out of traditional maps.

FIGURES 6.27 AND 6.28   The hexagon map gives equal visual weight to each state.

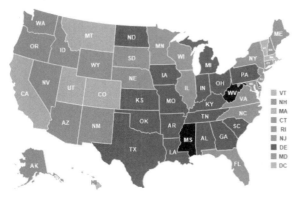

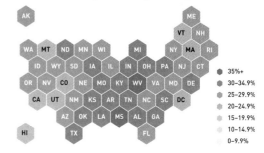

EXERCISES

Gather some materials (paper, pencil, computer, banana peels) and visualize 75% and 25% with them in as many ways as you can in 2 minutes. Come back when time is up. How many ways did you visualize those two percentages? Perhaps you sketched a quick pie chart—and this is a fine time to do so. Maybe you made a stacked bar chart—also OK. Maybe you put four quarters on the table and turned one upside down. I ran this activity once and someone in the audience drew a cow with one leg cut off. With just two percentages to visualize, you have many options to work with, a spectrum of the typical to the . . . weird. Your choice should be determined by the story you need to tell and the audience you are talking with (one of these will speak more to a group of teenage punk fans).

Head over to The Top Ten Worst Graphs. This collection of data visualization from scientific literature includes a 3D pie chart. Remake it into something more interpretable. It can be found at **www.biostat.wisc.edu/~kbroman/topten_worstgraphs/**

Grab your favorite Census data which can be retrieved at **http://www.census.gov/topics.html** and a map template from Presentation Magazine at **http://www.presentationmagazine.com/editable-maps**. Create your own legend to fit your selected Census data and format the map template to visualize your data.

RESOURCES

Try out Tableau Public at **https://public.tableau.com/s/** for mapping at a hyper local-level. You'll need zip code or latitude and longitude information. It plots points, just like Bing Maps, but has the most nonoffensive level of extraneous detail I've seen yet. The only hitch is that for the free public version of Tableau, your data must be available for anyone's eyes.

Check out the square and hexagon state shape maps that attempt to remedy the area bias found in actual state shaped maps. The New York Times outlines their alternatives and shares an example map showing sexual orientation data at the website **http://blog.apps.npr.org/2015/05/11/hex-tile-maps.html**

You should see what else Dave Paradi has on his site! He has calculators for all kinds of visuals, slide makeover examples, and results from his biannual survey of what makes PowerPoint annoying (my favorite). Check it out at **http://www.thinkoutsidetheslide .com/simple-treemap-calculator/** Use his diverging stacked bar calculator to compare to my method from Chapter 3.

REFERENCES

Atz, U., Heath, T., Heil, M., Hardinges, J., Fawcett, J., Lee, Y., Leitner, P., & Smith, A. (2014). *Best practice visualisation, dashboard and key figures report.* European Commission, OpenDataMonitor Project. Report FP7-ICT 611988.

Few, S. (2009). *Now you see it.* Oakland, CA: Analytics Press.

Kong, N., Heer, J., & Agrawala, M. (2010). Perceptual guidelines for creating rectangular tree maps. Visualization and Computer Graphics, *IEEE Transactions, 16*(6), 990–998.

Muscatello, D. J., Searles, A., Macdonald, R., & Jorm, L. (2006). Communicating population health statistics through graphs: A randomized controlled trial of graph design interventions. *BMC medicine, 4*(1), 33.

Schonlau, M., & Peters, E. (2012). Comprehension of graphs and tables depend on the task: Empirical evidence from two web-based studies. *Statistics, Politics, and Policy, 3*(2).

Stenberg, G. (2006). Conceptual and perceptual factors in the picture superiority effect. *European Journal of Cognitive Psychology, 18*, 813–847.

HOW THIS THING CHANGES
WHEN THAT THING DOES

COMMUNICATING CORRELATION
AND REGRESSION

LEARNING OBJECTIVES

After reading this chapter you will be able to

Identify the limited options for visualizing regression

Match option to audience sophistication

Use words to communicate regression to a mainstream audience

egression and correlation are actually fairly straightforward ideas when we spell out our findings in a complete sentence, telling a story about how two things change in relation to each other (romantic, eh?). However, explaining the thinking behind regression or showing the data in a visual can often introduce confusion. Let's discuss our options here. This is going to be a short chapter.

Scatterplots are the most common method for showing regression or correlation. The typical scatterplot can be enhanced with careful attention paid to the text in the graph. This is probably best suited for highly data literate audiences who won't struggle much with interpreting this complicated visual.

Moderately data friendly audiences may respond better to a diagram in which the relationships between variables have been drawn out. This kind of audience understands the basics of regression and correlation without necessarily knowing how to calculate either.

Audiences who would be intimidated by the words "regression" or "correlation" would probably appreciate no visual at all, just a simple sentence that tells them the relationship discovered through analysis.

WHAT STORIES CAN BE TOLD ABOUT HOW THIS THING CHANGES WHEN THAT THING DOES?

Whenever we are trying to describe how to things change in relationship to each other, we are telling a correlation or regression story. Yours might sound like one of these:

- Every time we adjust one thing, another thing changes
- When children eat a nutritional breakfast 5 days a week, test scores increase by three points
- These two things are totally interrelated
- Based on the current pattern, we predict moderate growth over the next quarter
- The more I exercise, the better I feel
- These outliers don't fit the pattern and may be worth investigating

Stories about things that correlate are so cool and so insightful. So, why do we often use statistical equations to talk about them? Perhaps this is the biggest challenge we nerds face—taking the most complicated things we learned to calculate in graduate school and making them understandable for our audiences.

HOW CAN I VISUALIZE HOW THIS THING CHANGES WHEN THAT THING DOES?

To begin, we punch up a basic scatterplot and then try two other non-Excel methods for communicating regression and correlation.

SCATTERPLOT

Exploring for cool datasets, I found Radical Math, an awesome website at http://www.radicalmath.org/ that provides social justice-based data and lessons for high school math teachers. It's pretty sweet. The scatterplot seen in Figure 7.1 was included in one lesson (and occasionally someone says to me that they'd rather have the axes switched, but you'll have to take that up with Radical Math).

EXCEL NINJA LEVEL: 3

It shows the number of military recruits per 100,000 people versus the percentage of people of color in different New York City boroughs. Impactful data to display. Creating this in Excel is pretty straightforward. You simply highlight your two series of data in your spreadsheet and then click on the *Insert* tab and select the very first scatterplot option (Figure 7.2).

But, the current display isn't doing much to convey anything interpretable for many people.

FIGURE 7.1   The original scatterplot visualizes two continuous variables, one on each axis.

FIGURE 7.2   The very first scatterplot charting option is the one for you.

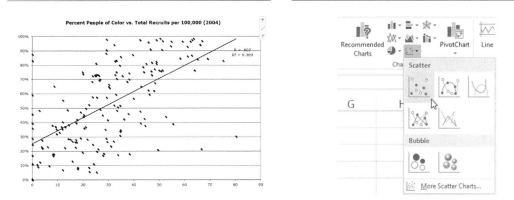

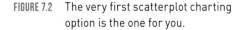

SOURCE: Jonathan Osler (2004). "Military Before." Radical Math. Used with permission.

To boost a basic scatterplot, I add a title that states the relationship I'm seeking to show—in other words, how when this thing changes, so does that thing (Figure 7.3).

FIGURE 7.3   Declarative titles are the easiest way to add clarity to the visualization.

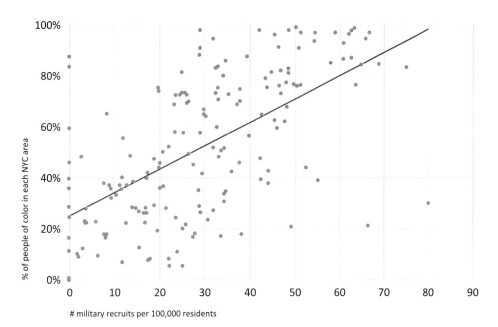

The more people of color living in an area of NYC, the more military recruits.

Graph is based on 2004 data. Analysis shows a strong correlation (R = .607)

I also added a subtitle that gives pretty important information, such as the fact that these data are from 2004. If you think the R value is important, put it here, though many readers won't know what it means. Wouldn't it be helpful to have axis labels? In this case, I think so too.

This visual is fine enough, but it's going to lead to questions. Readers are going to want to know which locations are on the trend line. They'll want to know about those outliers. They'll want to know, for example, what location has nearly 90% people of color and absolutely zero military recruits. So, I added labels (right-click, *Add Data Label*) to selective markers. But, the label is likely to be interrupted by a gridline or another marker. To maintain the label's legibility, I gave it a semitransparent fill.

Click on the label and then open the *Drawing Tools* tab. Click on the *Shape Fill* dropdown arrow and select *More Colors* (Figure 7.4).

In that *More Colors* box, I chose white for the solid fill color, but I increased the transparency to 50%. This gives the text some solid backing so that it can be seen, but still allows one to detect a marker that is hanging out in the background (Figure 7.5). Selective labeling is powerful because it answers that next set of questions that people will have when they look at the data.

Oh, it's Riker's Island that has loads of people of color and no military recruits. That's a jail. Makes sense. So, a simple scatterplot can be strengthened by paying careful attention to the text of the graph—the title, subtitle, axis labels, and annotations. Of course, if you made this scatterplot online, a user could hover over any dot to reveal a pop-up box with the details about that point. But, please for the love of Pete don't add labels to every dot or your audience will call for your head. If it's necessary to provide a bit more information about each dot, check out the References at the end of this chapter and read up on Cleveland and McGill's (1984) suggestions for ways to visually code each point, such as color or shape changes, or replacing the dot with a symbol or representative letter.

To show the relationship among several variables, researchers usually use a set of small multiples to arrange the different scatterplots into a matrix.

Even still, there's good reason to take pause and consider whether this visualization is going to be digestible for your readers. For decades we've known that scatterplots are not always easy to interpret. Loh (1987) showed four different scatterplots, all rotations of the same set of data, which should have had the same correlation—yet the correlation coefficient was different for each.

Li, Martens, and van Wijk (2010) compared interpretation of scatterplots and what they called "parallel coordinate plots." Parallel coordinate plots are essentially slopegraphs. Though they had a relatively small sample of people, those few people tended to overestimate the correlation when looking at the data in the parallel coordinate plots. The estimations were more accurate when looking at the scatterplots. But, even still they note, trying to read correlation off of a scatterplot tends to be faulty, and that, in fact, the cognitive load increases when the correlational relationship is

FIGURE 7.4   Add a semisolid background to the label so the text is visible against a noisy scatterplot.

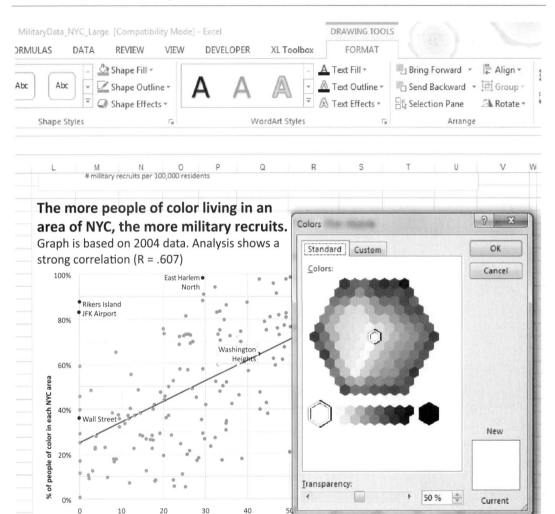

moderate. But, hey at least Rensink and Baldridge (2010) found that we are consistently off in our erroneous estimates. Plain and simple, scatterplots can be confusing to interpret. Even though the points are dots on a line, which is the easiest thing for us to interpret, it's the relationship being depicted that causes the trouble, not the individual points.

FIGURE 7.5   A standard scatterplot is more digestible with careful crafting of all possible text.

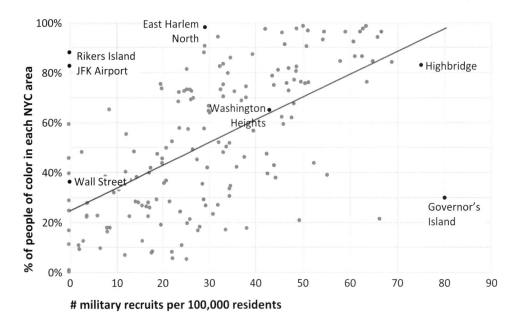

The more people of color living in an area of NYC, the more military recruits.

Graph based on 2004 data. Analysis shows a strong correlation (R = .607)

DIAGRAM

If it's a relationship we really need to communicate, we have heaps of possibilities at our disposal. Why not just diagram the relationship using some basic shapes as seen in Figure 7.6?

In this case, I'm assigning circles to variables and communicating the strength of their relationship with different arrow designs. A solid arrow means a strong correlation, a dashed arrow indicates a weak correlation, and no arrow signals no relationship.

Crack open PowerPoint (or your favorite blank canvas software) to begin diagraming. Inside PowerPoint, click in the *Insert* tab and then look for the family called *Illustrations*. Click on the *Shapes* button and you'll see a whole menu of shapes to insert. I chose the oval and made it into a circle (Figure 7.7).

The cursor changes to a plus sign, indicating it's time to hold down a mouse button and drag your cursor on the canvas to draw the circle. It doesn't really matter at this point if it is a perfect circle, just drag and make something. When you let go of the mouse button, you'll see a brand new orange tab called *Drawing Tools*. Click it.

EXCEL NINJA LEVEL: 0
(DRAW IT IN POWERPOINT)

FIGURE 7.6   Drawing the variables and their relationships might be the most understandable way to visualize the data.

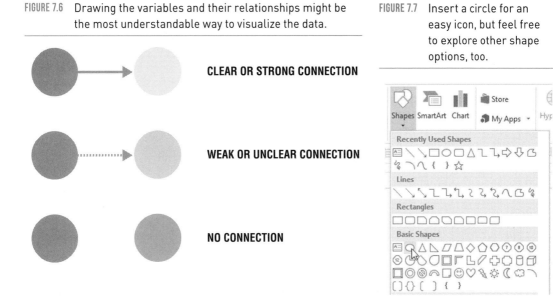

CLEAR OR STRONG CONNECTION

WEAK OR UNCLEAR CONNECTION

NO CONNECTION

FIGURE 7.7   Insert a circle for an easy icon, but feel free to explore other shape options, too.

Look over on the right and you'll see a place to change the object's size. The height and width should match to construct a perfect circle. I can see I need to click on the up arrow next to the width to make the object I inserted completely round (Figure 7.8).

Right-click on the circle and select *Copy*. Right-click again and select *Paste* to make another circle. Drag the second one over to the right a bit, since it will represent the dependent variable.

Connect the two circles with an arrow. Go into the same shapes menu and choose an arrow from the list of options. Hold down your mouse key while you drag your cursor to insert the arrow onto the canvas. When you release the mouse button, you should be able to drag the start and end of the arrow to the edge of the circle such that the arrow sticks to the circle because PowerPoint is smart and realizes you probably want to connect these shapes. The points on either end of the arrow turn green when they are connected to the circle.

To change the arrow from a solid line, right click on it and select *Format Shape*. The *Format Shape* menu provides all sorts of ways to change the look of the arrow. In the *Dash type* options, pick one of the choices that makes you the happiest and click it to change the arrow and show a moderate correlation (Figure 7.9).

FIGURE 7.8   Clicking the up arrow increases the size to the next tenth of a point.

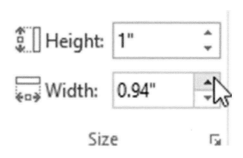

FIGURE 7.9   The Dash type menu supplies dash pattern options for your line.

Now, how do we know what these circles stand for? What a great opportunity to use simple icons that reflect each variable. I visited FlatIcon at http://www.flaticon.com/ and searched on my variables' keywords and downloaded four icons. FlatIcon is free, but you need to provide attribution. Therefore: The icons in Figure 7.10 are made by Freepik from FlatIcon and are licensed by Creative Commons BY 3.0.

FIGURE 7.10   Simple icons can stand in for your larger conceptual variables.

EARLY CHILDHOOD

GPA

LANGUAGE ARTS

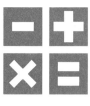

MATH

The icons come from FlatIcon as picture files. When you click the download button on the site, the image file will download to your computer. Open the file, copy the picture (right-click, select *Copy*) and paste it into Excel, PowerPoint, or whatever program you are using.

I inserted the icons into the diagram and placed them over the top of each circle. The thing is, the icons are black and my circles are a pretty dark color and so none of this is contrasting all that well. PowerPoint loves you and so it's really easy to do a simple color change right here, without moving into a fancy graphic design software.

When you insert the icon, you'll get a new purple tab called *Picture Tools*. Open it. Over on the left is a button called *Color,* just waiting to be clicked. When you satisfy its urges, you'll see a dozen or so preset color changes, one of which will swap out the black fill color for gray—a "washout," as illustrated in Figure 7.11.

FIGURE 7.11   Preset color adjustments in PowerPoint make color changes easy.

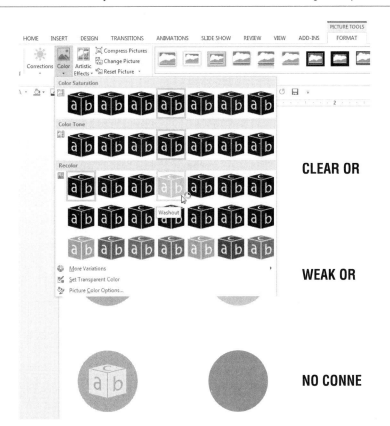

Gray usually works for me, but if you really want the icon color to be white, after you have washed out to gray, look at the button next door called *Artistic Effects*. In there (Figure 7.12), you'll see a style called *Photocopy* that will turn that gray to stark white.

FIGURE 7.12   After Washout, select Photocopy to make the icon white.

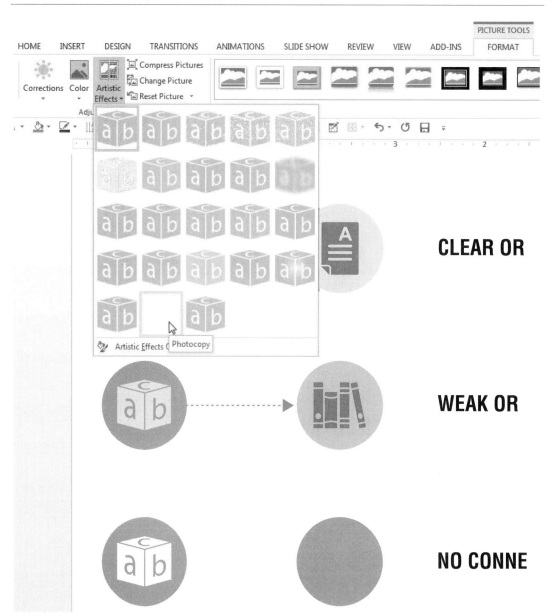

This story could be extended a bit further with a well-placed textbox that supplies a tiny bit of extra information. Particular audiences may want to know one level of detail underneath the major correlative relationship, such as how much one variable impacts the other. This is just the sort of question that can be answered with an annotation. Insert a textbox above the arrow and type in a few extra words that add detail (Figure 7.13).

FIGURE 7.13   Click on the Textbox button to draw a textbox on your canvas.

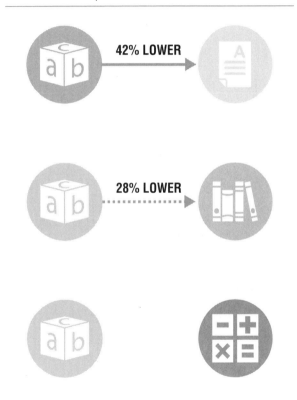

Your cursor will turn into an upside down cross. Move the cursor near the arrow, hold down the mouse button, and drag to draw a textbox on the canvas.

Together these graphic elements depict the story of the correlation without an actual graph type that can seem intimidating.

You are creative and I'm sure you'll think up several variations on my example shown in Figure 7.14. Perhaps shape or color or some other eye-catching attribute can be used to designate significance. The big idea is that we can draw out the correlation in a diagram that may make it more approachable for mainstream audiences who would otherwise struggle with a scatterplot.

DON'T VISUALIZE IT AT ALL

Of course, even easy diagrams need some explanation, don't they?

The pictograms I created in the last section (Figure 7.14) still can't stand on their own. Someone (*ahem* me) needs to spell out the exact relationship between these variables. So my title for the final Figure 7.14 needs to be something like "By the time they reached 6th grade, those who had participated in the early childhood program

FIGURE 7.14   This fairly simple diagram is going to speak to some audiences who would be put off by a scatterplot.

as youngsters had 28% lower reading scores than those who didn't participate, even when we controlled for previous GPA, attendance, and demographics." That sounds wordy, I know (and probably surprising! The early childhood program actually did lead to lower scores later on). Coming up with a concise sentence is challenging, but that's our job—to put in the effort to make our research understandable to the people who need to use it. So, work toward something like "During 3rd grade, those who had been in our preschool program attended three more days, on average, than those who were not in our program," or even "Students who did not attend our program missed three extra days of school."

EXCEL NINJA LEVEL: 0

FIGURE 7.15   A well-worded sentence cast in an interesting design can be all you need to talk about your regression.

Students who did **NOT** **ATTEND** our program missed **3** extra days of school.

Visualizations should aid the understanding of the data. If a single sentence can summarize and clarify the point that needs to be made and the visual doesn't bring additional enlightenment, perhaps don't visualize at all.

With all of the research suggesting that scatterplots actually contribute confusion, your best bet might be to carefully craft a sentence that captures your point and format it similar to the way that I suggested back in Chapter 1, for showcasing a single number. If you look back, you'll see that I just inserted several textboxes, varied the font size of the words in the phrase, and positioned the textboxes near each other.

Wow, are we already at the end of this chapter? It's a short one! But, now you have three options for visualizing regression or correlation. In my view, your choice here is pretty audience-driven. More sophisticated groups can handle a scatterplot. Groups that are tuned in to data, but never took an advanced statistics course will be able to interpret a diagram. People who are scared of data altogether will still grasp the main findings of your analysis when it is expressed as a single sentence.

EXERCISES

All three of these options can be carried out using the same dataset. If you don't have a suitable dataset, grab one from the resources below and make the three visualizations I've suggested in this chapter. Then show all three to three people you know: a data nerd, a data friend, and a data novice. Get feedback on which one they like best and why.

Download Cleveland and McGill's 1984 paper on *The Many Faces of a Scatterplot* (see References, below). Read through why they suggest a sunflower to handle some common scatterplot issues. Then open Excel and explore the *Marker Type* options and think of a way you could manually change the marker types to visualize data the way that Cleveland and McGill recommend.

RESOURCES

We all know by now that correlation does not equal causation. Just typing that sentence made me tired because this concept is repeated so often. To add some levity to the situation, see Tyler Vigen's work around spurious correlations at **http://www.tylervigen.com/spurious-correlations**. It will give you something interesting to talk about at your next cocktail party when the smart guy in the room starts repeating "correlation does not equal causation."

This fantastic Radical Math website at http://www.radicalmath.org/ has tons of data and lessons, albeit some of it dated, for middle and high school teachers to use, all focused on social justice issues.

Are you still feeling that the scatterplot axes need to be swapped or wondering why others would care so much? Custom normally calls for the dependent variable to be on the y-axis. Read more on that at http://mathbench.umd.edu/modules/visualization_graph/page02.htm and then decide how much it matters to you.

REFERENCES

Cleveland, W. S., & McGill, R. (1984). The many faces of a scatterplot. *Journal of the American Statistical Association, 79*(388), 807–822.

Li, J., Martens, J.-B., and Van Wijk, J. J. (2010). Judging correlation from scatterplots and parallel coordinate plots. *Information Visualization, 9*(1), 13–30.

Loh, W. Y. (1987). Does the correlation coefficient really measure the degree of clustering around a line?. *Journal of Educational and Behavioral Statistics, 12*(3), 235–239.

Rensink, R. A., & Baldridge, G. (2010, June). The perception of correlation in scatterplots. In *Computer Graphics Forum, 29*(3), 1203–1210.

8

WHEN THE WORDS HAVE THE MEANING

VISUALIZING QUALITATIVE DATA

LEARNING OBJECTIVES

After reading this chapter you'll be able to

Consider new ways to visualize qualitative data

Format a simple quote for a bigger impact

Lists strengths and weaknesses of word clouds

Identify three ways to use photographs to visualize what people said when you talked to them

While qualitative data visualization has not developed anywhere close to the extent of quantitative visualization, this chapter will give a sampling of the best options out there today.

Of course, we must discuss word clouds. They are popular because they are one of the few visualization options to emerge for qualitative data. Word clouds have limited depth, but they gain power when the user can drill down to see quotes that contain the word, a video of that person speaking, or related information.

Pictures are one of the easiest ways to represent qualitative data. Photographs humanize abstract concepts. They can convey more information in a snapshot of a full scene than an entire narrative report. Pictures are a great fit for quotes, for representing cluster analysis, and for showing before and after changes to a location.

Heat maps are another option, if you are comfortable doing some light quantifying of qualitative information, especially at the individual interviewee level. They cram some succinct interpretation into a tiny spot, but tend to be less visually engaging than some of the other options.

Finally, we will depart from Microsoft all together and look at how Prezi can be used to show an entire qualitative research project. With Prezi's open canvas layout and ability to drill down into details, it makes a fine platform for visualizing how qualitative concepts fit together.

I'll continue to hope that by the time this chapter is published, the world will have even more ways to show qualitative data.

WHAT STORIES CAN BE TOLD WHEN THE WORDS HAVE THE MEANING?

Even though visualization of qualitative data is a tiny list of options, the actual field of qualitative data is large—everything from open-ended survey comments to reports of community-wide well-being. Therefore, the stories we can tell are nuanced.

- This quote illustrates our quantitative findings
- Listen to the story of this person who represents most of our clients
- Look at how this street corner changed after our project
- Our interview research found two main themes among staff and residents
- Survey respondents generally had four suggestions for improvement
- This person is a profile composite of one segment of your consumer group
- Focus group participants saw college prep connected to parent education

Qualitative data are sometimes the result of engaging in interviews, case studies, focus groups, and collecting open-ended comments on a survey. It is also sometimes the result of pulling a lot of data together, such as a community-wide intervention or a cluster analysis of demographic profiles. You can always quantify the qualitative: count up the number of times something was said and graph it using one of the choices from another chapter. Our goal here is to stay as firmly as possible in the qualitative camp and add to your toolbox of visualization methods.

If you are involved in qualitative analysis at all, you probably know that there are several more visualization options available than the ones I describe here. There are choices like phrase nets and phrase trees and other dynamic ways of showing connected ideas from qualitative research. My colleague Stuart Henderson includes these in his chapter of my coedited volume of *New Directions for Evaluation* (2013). Stuart inspired several of the visualizations in this chapter as well. He's one to watch. However, many of the visualizations I'm talking about in this paragraph are more appropriate for the analysis phase of research. They work well while exploring the data and looking for patterns and meaning, and visualization certainly has a role there. But, these kinds of visuals are totally inappropriate for communication to those outside of the research team because they tend to be nonsensical without a great deal of additional context, and are laborious to use. I'm picking and choosing from the broad universe of qualitative visualizations to highlight those that support engagement and interpretation for the masses.

HOW CAN I VISUALIZE WHEN THE WORDS HAVE THE MEANING?

After we tackle common methods for visualizing, we will progress to more engaging visualizations.

WORD CLOUDS

My friend Humphrey Costello referred to word clouds as "dog vomit." Others have called them the mullet of the Internet. Ha, ha, ha . . . gross! How is it that something can be so hated, and yet be so common? I think it's because people want to use word clouds more seriously than they were intended. Word clouds are a visual display of the most frequently used words in a given set of data, with a fun font and some eye candy color scheme.

EXCEL NINJA LEVEL: 0 (NOT IN EXCEL, AND AN EASY COPY/PASTE)

Here in Figure 8.1, I pasted all the tweets in my feed from the last five hours into Wordle, the most common word cloud platform. Knowing Twitter, what do you think are the most common words I'll see?

Of course, the most common words that appear are "retweet," "reply," "favorite," "hours," and "ago" since these are words that appear with every single tweet. There's

FIGURE 8.1   A word cloud visualizes most frequently used words.

no way this is an accurate representation of what was happening in my Twitter feed, and this is why people get upset. However, with Wordle (a free word cloud program), you can remove selected words from the word cloud. Right-click on any word and ask for its removal (see Figure 8.2).

FIGURE 8.2   Right-click to remove any unwanted words, such as "permalink" and "view."

Each time I clean up an extra unnecessary word, the word cloud reconfigures to show a new display of most frequent words. The second menu bar also lets me choose from a select list of fonts and color schemes.

It's eye-catching, isn't it? People put this type of art on their office walls because it's pretty. But, what can we discern from this cloud? I see the first and last names of the people who tweet a lot. This I already knew because they are all up in my feed. Beyond that, I see words like "media" "data" "News" "foundation" "business" "Graphics" and "work." This probably tells you a little bit about what a nerd I am. Beyond that, it doesn't give much insight into the discussions in my community, and this is the second problem people have with word clouds—the lack of insight.

FIGURE 8.3   What does the final version of the word cloud tell you?

It's important to keep in mind that the purpose of a word cloud is not really to generate insight. It is to display the most frequently used words. We ever hopeful analysts are the ones wishing to squeeze insight out of it. The tool isn't the problem, entirely. If we can accept word clouds for the limits of what they can do, we may be better positioned to use them appropriately. They are best for showing the gist of the data—a holistic view (Bletzer, 2015; Rivadeneira, Gruen, Muller, & Millen, 2007).

Can you spot the word "smug" in that word cloud? Wouldn't I love to know who said that! And that is another limitation of traditional word clouds. It would be more helpful if we could click on a single word and get more details, such as excerpts from the tweet, or interview transcript, or open-ended survey comment where this word occurred.

I know of one resource that gives us that drill-down capability—WordyUp. It is a word cloud generator that groups words into clusters if they appeared together, a nice upgrade from the Wordle word cloud. WordyUp has a subscription fee, but you can test out how it works with 500 words or less (Figure 8.4).

FIGURE 8.4   Word cloud generators that group words that appeared together in the transcript are better.

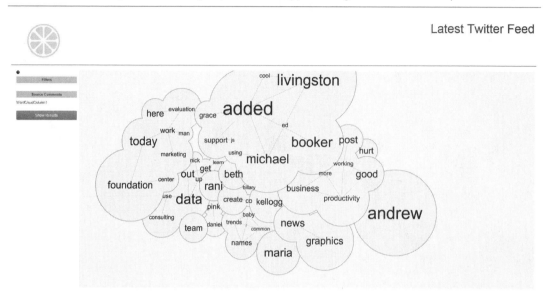

There's also a different selection of words, even though I used the same tweets in WordyUp that I popped into Wordle. The opacity of the algorithms is another solid critique. From here we can see that there was something in the news about common baby names, something about business productivity, something about marketing evaluation foundation work, and something about data use consulting, to name a few things that stick out to me.

If I want to know more about any of these words, I can click on a word to reveal the transcript where it appeared.

For example, clicking on "foundation" shows me the one tweet where the word occurred and the actual foundations that have been tweeting in the last few hours (Figure 8.5).

You'll also see the ability to hide a word, so I can eliminate "added" and "ed."

If I click *Drill Down,* I get a whole new view that places the word in the center of its own word cloud (Figure 8.6).

The drill-down view shows me details about other concepts and words related to the target word. This flexibility is a necessary step to make word clouds more useful for analysis and interpretation.

Several qualitative analysis software programs can now generate something similar to this level of interactivity. The best ones support moving the word cloud online for others to access. Keep in mind that the largest words will be remembered the most (kinda the point), but so will words in the upper left quadrant, whether or not those are most germane to your findings (Rivadeneira, Gruen, Muller, & Millen, 2007).

FIGURE 8.5   Click to drill down to the transcript/tweet level.

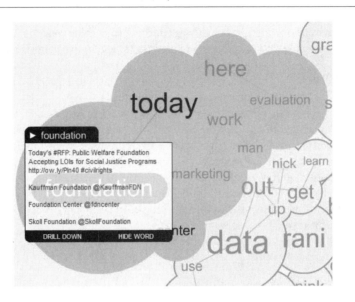

FIGURE 8.6   Drilling down to the next level recasts a specific word in the spotlight.

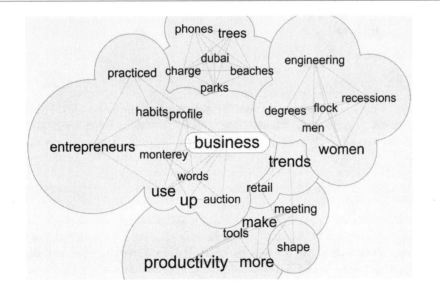

PICTURES

Qualitative visualizations can feel complicated, but sometimes the best way to convey this kind of data is by using a picture: Something you draw, something you snap, or something you buy. We have at least three ways to use pictures for qualitative data visualization.

EXCEL NINJA SKILL LEVEL: 0,
NONE OF THIS HAPPENS IN EXCEL

Pictures Humanize a Quote

Heaven help us, Figure 8.7 is how quotes are usually shown.

Usually, there are lots of quotations, italicized, in a row. The reader is expected to slog through each quote and pull out the parts most pertinent to the point that the author is trying to convey. It isn't clear which part of the quote is most important, especially if there are several quotes strung together.

In a slideshow, quotes usually appear alone, still italicized, shown while the presenter reads the full quote from the slide. Quotes are tough—the presenter needs to read the full thing because it fits in with the talk, but the audience is compelled to read the whole thing as well because we like reading words.

Figure 8.8 illustrates a definite improvement.

FIGURE 8.7   The typical quote style doesn't do much to engage the reader.

"To invent, you need a good imagination and a pile of junk." — Thomas A. Edison

FIGURE 8.8   Use selective color and line breaks to help the reader along.

"To **invent**,
you need a
good imagination
and a
pile of **junk**."
— Thomas A. Edison

Here, I made a bunch of tiny changes that better convey the quote. First, I made line breaks at naturally occurring points, so that each line ends up being a logical chunk, kind of like a poem. Each line also takes less actual "reading" because the eye can pick up an entire line at a time. If I was presenting this in a slideshow, I'd use animation to make each line show up one at a time, just as the speaker speaks it.

I also used a condensed font so that the text is less spread out. Yes, I'm attempting to design it so that the reader doesn't have to make much eye movement to read. Sounds trivial, but eye movement takes work and cognition, and we want this quote understood at a glance. Condensed fonts help us reduce the amount of eye movement required.

Then I added color on key words in the quote. It depends on what you want people to pay attention to, of course. If I was focusing on use of imagination in the workplace, I'd have put my color on imagination instead. Two things to remember: (1) Color really has to be selective—use only one or two key words. Too much color kills the point of emphasis, and (2) the rest of the text is in a shade of gray to help the color pop out more.

I kicked this up one more notch by bringing in a photo of the person being quoted—with consent, of course! It might not do much here (though isn't he cute?), but think about adding pictures of interviewees of program participants to their respective quotes in your report. Get permission, of course. It's just that adding pictures is a powerful way to elicit some emotion out of the reader and help drive the quote home even more. Imagine this picture/quote combo (Figure 8.9) in your report sidebar—much more impactful and memorable than a string of italicized text.

FIGURE 8.9 Show the face behind the quote so that the reader can connect on an emotional level.

"To **invent**, you need a good imagination and a pile of **junk**."
— Thomas A. Edison

Pictures Represent Client Segments

Stock photos also have their place in qualitative reporting, especially when your data are pulled together to create a composite demographic. Smart businesses use cluster analysis (a specific data analysis that mixes quantitative and qualitative data) to figure out the three or five main customer types that solicit their business. They generate demographic profiles of these customer types: how much money they earn, how much money they spend, how often they shop, their race and gender, their main business-related needs. How smart! Because now the business can target advertisements or cater the shopping experience to speak to these specific demographic profiles using a deeper understanding of who they are and thus better resonating with their clients.

Behind the scenes, I often recommend visual profiles of the client groups (Figure 8.10).

Adding a photograph, even if it is a stock photo, to a list of characteristics gives those characteristics some life, something tangible that people can relate to when using the profiles to become a better business.

Beyond cluster analysis, stock photos can be used to add depth to survey responses. When your analysis shows significant differences by certain demographic variables, it's a perfect time to add photographs of the main respondent groups to your reporting.

A word of consideration: The stock photos are meant to protect individual identities of your actual clients or respondents, but you must still take care to ensure that the stock photo subject matches your target group pretty closely.

For example, I was running a workshop in New Zealand and discussing stock photo sites where photos could be obtained for free. I showed them this screenshot of USA.gov, which has a section with free imagery (Figure 8.11). The Kiwis said they could immediately tell these were photos from the United States and they were not New Zealand children. If you are looking for, say, New Zealand-specific stock photos, include the country as a keyword when you search.

FIGURE 8.10 Use real or stock photos to represent client profiles and help internal teams hone their efforts (Figure 8.10).

Susan
Licensed Architect
Uses BSA Space for continuing education classes & networking

Chris
Emerging Professional
Uses BSA Space to find the right employer

1/3 of our clients are active 5 days a week

FIGURE 8.11   Be sure the stock photos maintain similarity to your actual respondent group.

PICTURES ARE WORTH $1,000

Funny thing about the use of pictures to accompany main ideas or quotes: the picture makes a difference. While this research might not transfer to all study and reporting scenarios, how interesting that researchers found that pictures of just one charity recipient garnered significantly more donations than photographs of several recipients (Västfjäll, Slovic, Mayorga, & Peters, 2014). They postulate that this may be because people feel their donation is more spread out if they see several people in the appeal picture. You may not be working in a charitable situation, but it is still a good reminder to be thoughtful and intentional about the photographs you choose.

Before   **After**

Pictures as the Story of Change

Wow, Stephanie, life at your homestead must be so different after that terrible house next to you was bulldozed by the city! What's changed?

Well, I could write up many pages of the details, but the answer is clearer and faster if I show you two pictures (Figure 8.12)—what it looked like before and after the bulldoze.

Before, you can see a shabby house. After, you can see that where there was a house, there is now a hammock, a clubhouse for my kid, an umbrella at a picnic table, chairs

FIGURE 8.12   Pictures reveal differences that are immediately interpretable.

| BEFORE | AFTER |

(around a fire pit), and a garden. There's a quality of life difference evident. Sure, it could be described in words, but if you place your hand over the photos and just read my previous sentences, it isn't quite the same. You can't quite understand the stark change without the photo.

Photographs are the rock star tool for visualizing a location, especially before and after some kind of intervention has occurred. The nonprofit that organized a roadside cleanup will best show its impact through pictures of a littered road and a grassy one. The charitable organization that provides cows to rural villagers is going to have the most compelling story of impact with pictures of the receiving families at their homes before and one year after the cows arrive. You get the picture?

The great part of this is that you really need nothing more than your smartphone or even one of those disposable cameras to make this kind of visualization. The trick is to try to get as near as possible to the same shot. Stand in the same place on the same kind of day. Take notes of your position when you take your before photo so that you can replicate it at your second shoot.

If you have the skills and financial resources, you don't have to stop at photographs. Illustrate the before and after. World Vision is completely spot on with the animated story in Figure 8.13 of their community intervention.

In 1998, when World Vision started work in the Nkoma community, development was pretty low. World Vision painted the picture. The teardrop markers with the pluses inside

FIGURE 8.13   Note the slider set to 1998. This is how the Nkoma community looked before World Vision intervened.

show places where a user can click for more details. Drag the slider toward 2013 and the picture changes (Figure 8.14) to represent the community transformation.

FIGURE 8.14   The after illustration shows significant development.

The designers embedded additional qualitative data within the picture by adding videos and photographs. Way more effective than an appeal letter, this visual engages the user in the impact story, connecting donors to the people in the Nkoma community and spurring donations.

Whether you use a software program or your phone, pictures of the scene can be a smart way to show qualitative information and communicate that the words hold the meaning in the study.

HEAT MAP

In that last section, we traveled from visuals that show an individual quote all the way to full-scale pictures of community change. Let's get back down to the research study environment with interviewees and transcripts. A heat map isn't actually a stunning illustration, but it is a nice way to summarize your interview data into one visual.

Completely inspired by my aforementioned qualitative guru friend, Stuart Henderson, I created a heat map for a recent set of interviews I conducted with board members for a nonprofit organization. The nonprofit had been trying to build board member capacity by holding a 30-minute professional development training session at the end of every board meeting designed around a set of topics. How was board capacity altered as a result of the trainings? Which trainings were most helpful? The heat map diagrams the sentiments of the board members.

In Figure 8.15, the columns each represent an individual interviewee (*Int* stands for interviewee, but you can really make that say whatever you want). The rows are the different training topics. I created a simple 3-point scale of usefulness and assigned each point a color. Then I analyzed the interview transcripts, made judgements about each interviewees' attitude toward the training topics, and changed the color of their intersecting cells as appropriate.

FIGURE 8.15   Heat maps indicate interviewees' sentiments around different themes that emerged from a qualitative study.

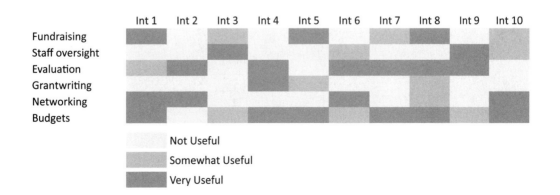

We can read this heat map horizontally and see that Budgets and Evaluation were widely viewed as useful topics to the board members. Grantwriting, not so much. Reading vertically we can see that everyone found some use in something, a good indication that the board members are all engaged in their role. No one reported that "nothing" was useful.

Making this heat map in Excel is a breeze. You type one interviewee per cell in Row 1 and then one theme per cell in Column A. You set up a legend by changing the fill color of individual cells (Figure 8.16).

Click inside the cell that you want to color change and then look for the paint bucket button in the *Home* tab. Click that button and select a color from the drop-down menu or click on *More Colors* and customize your own palette.

EXCEL NINJA LEVEL: 1 (YES, WE ACTUALLY MAKE SOMETHING IN EXCEL!)

FIGURE 8.16   Adjust the fill color from the Home tab.

It made the most sense to me to make the category *Not Useful* white, so it wouldn't stand out when I was looking at the heat map. But, I still wanted to indicate that the color in the legend was white, so it didn't look like I just forgot to put a color there.

The way to do that is to add a border to the cell. The border button is directly to the left of the fill color button in the *Home* tab (Figure 8.17).

Be sure your mouse is in the cell that needs the border and then click on the *Borders* button. In that menu, you will see an *All Borders* option, which will put black borders on all four sides of the cell. I find black lines to be too harsh and distracting, so just as I show you in Figure 8.17, I clicked on the last option, *More Borders.*

From here, I can choose a softer gray from the color menu (Figure 8.18).

Once the legend is established, you'll simply change the fill color of the cell to match the corresponding legend entry. Note that though you see gridlines around cells when in Excel, they won't show up when you print or PDF the image. If you want the heat map itself to have borders around the *Not Useful* cells, you'll need to manually add borders to each.

A stark contrast to the interactive website, I know, but heat maps are a really concise way to summarize individual-level interview data and maintain interpretability.

FIGURE 8.17 Click on All Borders or customize the look through More Borders.

FIGURE 8.18 Adjust the color and thickness of the borders in the Format Cells Border menu.

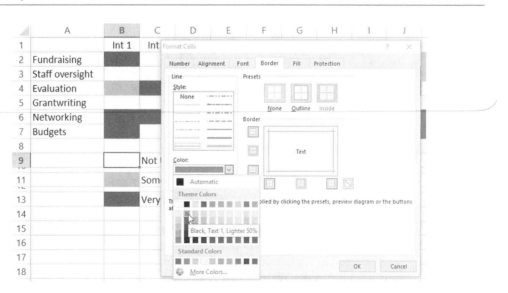

PREZI

Yes, this Office fangirl is going to talk about Prezi. Have you heard of it?

Prezi is a software marketed as a contrast to PowerPoint, an alternative way to present information that is not the linear Slide 1 to Slide 2 method. Prezi is a big open canvas that lets you draw out concepts and express ideas that are interrelated rather than linear. Prezi is free if you don't mind your work being publicly accessible and reusable. The paid version offers privacy, image editing, and support.

Another feature of Prezi is that it allows you to zoom in and out of specific points on the canvas, so you can swap between big picture and tiny detail really easily. The only trouble is that the zooming in and out can get out of hand. People get excited about adding it in to their presentation so they go nuts and the end result is that the audience begins to feel motion sickness.

I tend to stay away from it—UNLESS the whole open canvas interconnected idea big picture and tiny detail features truly fit my needs. And boy does it ever fit qualitative data!

I made the Prezi visual seen in Figure 8.19 from a research study conducted by Stuart Henderson (I may have mentioned him once or twice). The study interviewed clients and counselors at a substance abuse clinic.

In this view of the Prezi, you can see the overall structure: There were two big ideas that emerged from the study, each with associated research questions. The answers to the questions spin out into greater detail. This kind of diagramming isn't as easy in PowerPoint.

FIGURE 8.19   Prezi lets you visualize the whole study as a diagram.

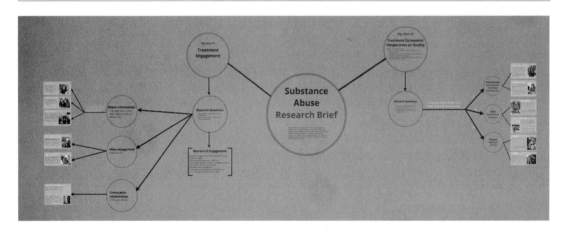

When I want to show the detail (Figure 8.20), I can zoom in (carefully).

In this figure, we can still see some extra markings in the upper left—a circle and part of a line. These extra bits could easily be a distraction, but I think they serve the purpose of helping the viewer keep track of how all these pieces connect together.

From here I could choose to dive deeper into any of the gray squares to the right, which contain an individual quote and a stock photo picture that relates to it (a technique discussed earlier in this chapter). Or, I could choose to zoom back out to a bigger picture and explore another aspect of the study.

FIGURE 8.20   Zoom in to any level of detail for a closer look.

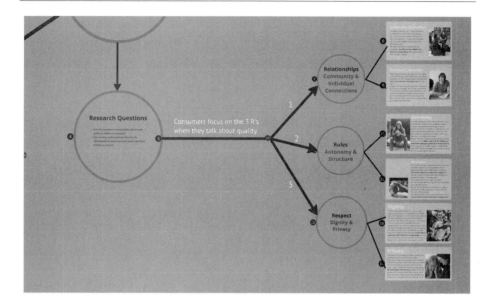

Making a Prezi takes some time (set aside a full day or more) and practice, but it is remarkably user-friendly.

The circles and squares you see in my Prezi are called "layouts," which you locate through the ever helpful *Insert* menu, top center of the screen. You can just click and drag any of the layouts onto the canvas (Figure 8.21).

FIGURE 8.21   Open a new canvas and begin by inserting a layout.

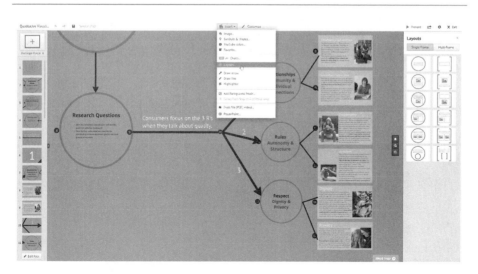

Once you pop the layout onto your canvas somewhere, Prezi will ask you to add text and replace the picture (Figure 8.22). Any of the components in the layout can be moved or deleted. You'll return to that Insert menu to add arrows or more layouts until your diagram is complete.

Each time you add a layout to the canvas, Prezi will tack it onto the end of the list running down the left side of the screen (see Figure 8.21). Every one of these is going to be a stop on the journey through the Prezi—a place you can zoom in to—unless you click *Edit Path* to adjust it. You can always zoom in or out on something specific and add that view to the path list, too.

In this way, you structure the experience of the data by guiding people through your story. I have yet to see a better way of showing the complex relationships among themes and topics in qualitative research, while also being able to drill down to the individual quote level. This is Prezi done right. And I'm sure you can do even better.

As with many visual processes, it will be a billion times easier to sketch your idea out on paper before whipping open your laptop. With a solid plan in mind for your diagram, visualizing your qualitative data should be a breeze.

FIGURE 8.22   Prezi will prompt you to add content to the layout.

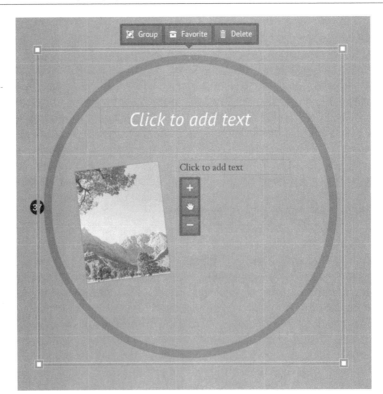

I hope that someday this chapter is a whole book of its own. Qualitative data visualization has plenty of room to grow. We covered a broad range of options, but really only touched on one or two options for different data collection and analysis methods. Qualitative visualization requires a bit more license to be creative than the material covered in the other chapters because it demands that we think in pictures. My experience is that we all have that creative light in us, we just need to give it permission to come out.

EXERCISES

Go to the Prezi that I created based on the substance abuse qualitative research project and explore it at http://prezi.com/iu-h-wgiimte/?utm_campaign=share&utm_medium=copy. Make lists of the things you like about it and the things you would change. Come up with at least three points on each list.

Head to Wordy Up at https://www.wordyup.com/, and using the free trial on their home page, paste in the latest posts from one of your social networks, keeping in mind that there's a 500 word limit to the free test, so you'll probably want to clean up the posts first. Hit *Generate* and see if the resulting word cloud tells you anything insightful. Paste the same text into the more static word cloud generator, Wordle at http://www.wordle.net/create, and compare the usefulness of the two word clouds.

Interview 10 people in class about what they did last weekend and how much fun they had doing each activity. Pull out the main themes and make a matrix heat map where you plot the main themes as rows and use levels of fun for the shades of gray. Write a summary paragraph that captures the overall interpretations gleaned from the visual.

RESOURCES

Read what Humphrey said about word clouds here at http://stephanieevergreen.com/word-cloud-dog-vomit/

The world is full of great stock photo sites. One of my favorites is Getty Images at http://www.gettyimages.com/ simply because of the search filters. You can ask the site to only show you photographs that have a single individual—or a group. You can even specify the general age range of the people in the photograph and what ethnicities you'd like to represent.

Explore the World Vision infographic at https://www.worldvision.org.nz/portal/ourwork/community-Nkoma.aspx both to learn about their work and to see how they visualized their data. Thanks to my friend Kate McKegg for pointing me to this awesome example.

I interviewed Drew Banks from Prezi for my Rad Presenters Podcast. I drilled him with my hard questions about the common Prezi issues, and he promised that most, if not all of them, are user issues: Prezi can be done right. He shared his list of well-done Prezis for your scrutiny at http://www.radpresenters.com/episode-20-with-drew-banks-from-prezi/

REFERENCES

Bletzer, K. V. (2015). Visualizing the qualitative: Making sense of written comments from an evaluative satisfaction survey. *Journal of educational evaluation for health professions, 12.*

Henderson, S., & Segal, E. H. (2013). Visualizing qualitative data in evaluation research. *New Directions for Evaluation, 139,* 53–71.

Rivadeneira, A. W., Gruen, D. M., Muller, M. J., & Millen, D. R. (2007, April). Getting our head in the clouds: Toward evaluation studies of tagclouds. In *Proceedings of the SIGCHI conference on Human factors in computing systems,* 995–998. San Jose, CA.

Västfjäll, D., Slovic, P., Mayorga, M., & Peters, E. (2014). Compassion fade: Affect and charity are greatest for a single child in need. *PloS one, 9*(6).

HOW THINGS CHANGED OVER TIME

DEPICTING TRENDS

LEARNING OBJECTIVES

After reading this chapter, you will be able to

Choose the best chart type based on the story you need to highlight around change over time

Record a macro to streamline future visualizations

Decide when truncating the y-axis is and isn't appropriate

This chapter will discuss

- Line graphs, your old friend
- Area charts, which show trends over time that add up to 100%
- Stacked bars, a great alternative to area charts when your data add to 100%, you only have a few categories, and one of the categories is very small
- Deviation bars, perfect when you just need to talk about the change that has occurred

- Slopegraphs appear again, to show change from start to end, though this time you'll make one using a macro
- Dot plots are also back to depict how things changed over time, again made with a macro
- Sankey diagrams, a new visualization type, which are best for showing flow

Traditionally, people only use line graphs to visualize change over time, but the chapter shows other effective ways and provides convincing reasons why variations on the line graph are needed. We'll also review some current thinking on when it is acceptable to tweak the traditional line graph's layout to tell the proper story.

WHAT STORIES CAN BE TOLD ABOUT HOW THINGS CHANGED OVER TIME?

Data are usually tracked over time to monitor how things did or didn't change after some kind of intervention has occurred. We can essentially tell many of the same stories from previous chapters, but with the added twists and turns that happen when the years pass. Some possibilities for stories include:

- Things changed/didn't change
- After is so much better/worse/the same as before
- We started this intervention and the outcome improved as a result
- When the legislation took effect, we saw peaks in services for several years
- Sales increased 0.5% over the last quarter
- Maternal services have steadily increased their proportion of hospital use
- Here's how much change occurred on this measure in the last decade
- Hispanics have increased their health profile more than any other group in the last two years
- The funds came in through 4 different grants and flowed through several buckets before dispersion to programs and beneficiaries

If you are a Super Academic, like me, you might not have been trained to speak in stories written this way. You are probably more familiar with (proud) geek terminology like "time series," "pre-posttest," or, if you are of a certain ilk, "retrospective pre-test." Any of those analyses are suitable for churning out stories about how things changed over time.

HOW CAN I VISUALIZE HOW THINGS CHANGED OVER TIME?

Let's start with getting the simplest visualization just right and work our way up to the most complex graph types with the promise that everything along this spectrum will knock your socks off.

YOUR OLD FRIEND, THE LINE GRAPH

We are all so used to seeing change over time expressed as a line graph that my elementary-age kid knows how to read these graphs, where time runs along the x-axis.

Zacks and Tversky (1999) tried to put discrete data on a line graph and change over time in a bar graph, and wow were people confused. We see lines as trends over time. We should still devote some space and give them some love because even though they are quite familiar to most of us, they can often end up looking like my tangled strings of Christmas lights.

The 2010 American Psychological Association (APA) Style Guide (another old friend) recommends no more than 4 lines per line graph. This is a handy rule of thumb to keep us from graph overload. In some cases,
feel free to bend this rule. For example, when the lines also represent parts of a whole, it isn't likely that the lines will crisscross too much, and so fitting in a fifth or sixth line on Figure 9.1 would probably be just fine.

What concerns me, though, is that the lines suggest continuous measurement, do they not? The lines are implying values that are associated with points in between those labeled on the x-axis when the reality is that we probably only measured this stuff once

FIGURE 9.1   Line graphs are the most common way to depict trends over time.

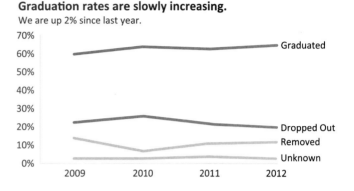

Graduation rates are slowly increasing.
We are up 2% since last year.

FIGURE 9.2   The markers on the line indicate actual measurement or reporting points.

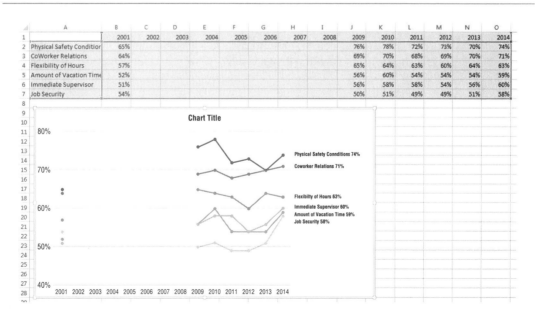

a year. I think people are so accustomed to seeing change over time represented this way that we are probably fine not keeping ourselves up at night worrying about this, but it does give us reason to think through some alternatives.

One way to handle this would be to add markers to the lines where data collection occurred (Figure 9.2). This is especially useful if data collection did not happen at regular intervals or if I'm only concerned about particular points in the data.

EXCEL NINJA LEVEL: 2

The presence of the marker on the line communicates on our behalf, showing when data collection actually took place. Making this happen in Excel is all about how you set up your data table. As you can see in Figure 9.2, I simply added empty columns for the years that I don't want to report. However when I inserted the line graph with markers, it did not connect the lonely marker for 2001 with the others. To fix this, right-click on the graph and choose *Select Data*. In that pop-up box, you'll see a button in the lower left that is called *Hidden and Empty Cells* (Figure 9.3). Click it.

FIGURE 9.3   Tell Excel to connect the points surrounding the empty cells.

Hidden and Empty Cell Settings   ?   ✕
Show empty cells as: ○ Gaps
○ Zero
⦿ Connect data points with line
☐ Show data in hidden rows and columns
OK   Cancel

Select the radio button that tells Excel to show the empty cells by connecting the data points with a line (Figure 9.3).

If we are interested in predicting where satisfaction will be on these variables, let's say by 2017, we can add the projection to the graph by expanding the data table. It will be important to visualize this data differently, since it is not (yet) real. And this is one of the only times that I recommend changing the line from solid to a pattern. I typically use the dash. To change just one line segment, click on the last point of the line twice so that it is the only point highlighted. Then right-click on it and select *Format Data Point*. In the *Format* menu, look for the *Line* features and change the *Dash type* from solid to a dash pattern (Figure 9.4). This will alter the line segment that precedes the point.

You're probably noticing that the lines are getting pretty crowded by 2017. And I'm actually only visualizing about half of the survey questions related to employee satisfaction. If we throw them all in the graph, things are going to get complicated. Javed, McDonnel, and Elmqvist (2010) tested this very situation to understand how people can best interpret and compare change over time when the line graph gets complicated. What do you think they found? Remember the solution for when things get complicated? Break these out into small multiples (see Figure 9.5).

Some tips for creating small multiples line graphs.

1. Make the first one perfect, then copy/paste and select new data

2. Be sure that the axes are all the same—new data may lead Excel to change the scale

3. Shorten the x-axis labels and consider labeling every other year to fit them into the narrower space

FIGURE 9.4   Change the appearance of data that should not be interpreted the same as the rest.

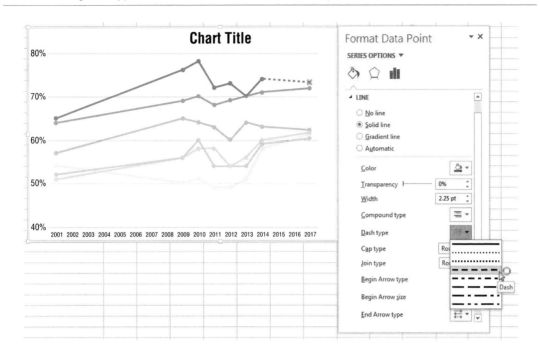

FIGURE 9.5   Placing each line on its own graph makes them easier to see.

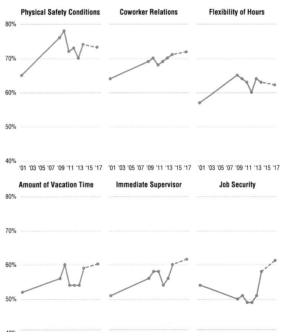

AREA GRAPH

EXCEL NINJA LEVEL: 2

I sure can't say that I love area graphs, but sometimes there's no better way to show trends that make up 100%, over time. An area graph is essentially a line graph, with each segment stacked on top of one another. In this way, it shows parts of a whole.

A regular line graph doesn't make it obvious that these categories represent portions of an entire group (Figure 9.6).

A line graph can be problematic here. We have a propensity to show parts of a whole as a pie chart, but comparing these over time is also quite a challenge (see Figure 9.7).

FIGURE 9.6   How do you determine that these categories are parts of a whole?

FIGURE 9.7   Now we can see that these are parts of a whole, but comparison is hard.

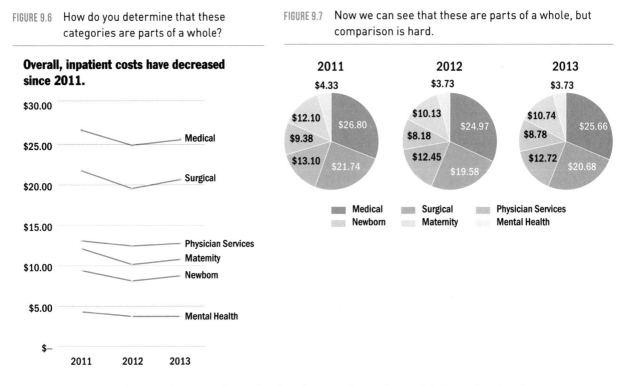

Area graphs are an alternative that show trend over time and indicate that the pieces make up an entire unit (Figure 9.8). One of my clients called these a "square pie."

Making this kind of graph in Excel is very easy. Area graphs are a default chart option.

In Figure 9.9, I selected the second area graph option here, where the segments all stack one on top of the other. This is a good choice when graphing raw data (rather than percentages). The third option in this row is the 100% stacked area graph and you should use this when graphing percentages and parts of a whole that add to 100%. The first option is probably the chart used the least—the segments are positioned in front of one another.

While the area graph can seem like a logical chart choice for this circumstance, we still encounter some drawbacks. Note how in Figure 9.8 we can see that the top of the chart drops significantly in 2012. Where did those cost savings occur? In which segment? Well, we can see that it probably wasn't Medical, the stack on the bottom. And this is easy for us to determine because the Medical segment has a level baseline from which we can judge the slopes at the top

FIGURE 9.8   The area graph addresses the flaws of the two previous graphs.

FIGURE 9.9   Area graphs are a built-in chart choice in Excel.

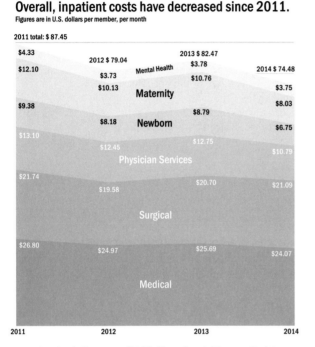

Overall, inpatient costs have decreased since 2011.
Figures are in U.S. dollars per member, per month

SOURCE: Stephanie Evergreen (2015). "Area Graph." Oregon Health Authority Office of Health Analytics. Used with permission.

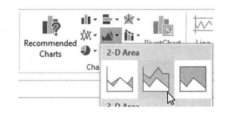

of that segment. The other segments are harder to interpret. But, hey, who am I to say? Maybe the attribution question isn't a big deal for you. In that case, area graphs can be your pal.

The tweaks and variations we've discussed so far can make the line graph more interpretable, but line graphs still have downfalls and other graph types can elevate the story in better ways. Let's explore.

DOES THE Y-AXIS HAVE TO START AT ZERO?

On bar graphs, absolutely yes, 100%, always and forever. On line graphs? Previously, I was comfortable pushing the "Start at Zero" movement simply because it's a common mistake most novice graphers make.

So, there I was the other day, giving a dataviz workshop inside a supergiant corporation, preaching the Start at Zero gospel. And this person in the audience says "Whoa wait. I mean, come on. We have so many instances in our review meetings where the data really don't fluctuate very much, but a rise of 0.4% is a big deal to us. With a graph that starts at zero, we won't be able to detect these changes."

(Continued)

(Continued)

PEOPLE. HE'S RIGHT.

If you are working to detect tiny changes, adjust your scale so that you can see them. Data visualization has to be useful.

If zero doesn't naturally fall in your dataset, such as when graphing the graduation rates at your local high school, it doesn't make sense to include it in scale of the visualization.

Yes, adjusting the scale changes the slope of the line. But, that actually translates to real significant change in many situations!

If it's really a concern, you can always add a little mark at the base of the y-axis to bring more attention to the fact that it doesn't start at zero.

STACKED COLUMN

I say: Trend over time?

You say: Line graph!

I know, that's how it goes, right?

But, sometimes it helps to have other options that better fit your data.

Let's say you are graphing the number of male and female CEOs of Fortune 500 companies over time. Here it is our reliable line graph shown in Figure 9.10.

FIGURE 9.10   The traditional line graph doesn't give much visual weight to each quantity.

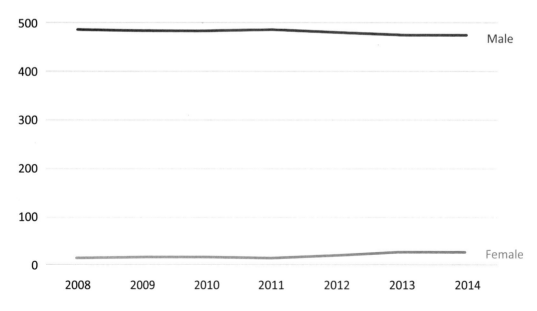

While increasing slightly over the years, female CEOs for Fortune 500s are still few in unmber.

The number of female CEOs is so small that the line is barely distinguishable from the x-axis. Not good (for several reasons—and every year the finance magazines are all like "Yay, we increased our female Fortune 500 CEOS by 300%," but what that really means is that we just went from 3 to 9). Whenever my categories are parts of a whole AND one of my categories is really tiny, I prefer stacked columns (Figure 9.11).

FIGURE 9.11   Stacked columns visualize the data in chunks, which are easier to see.

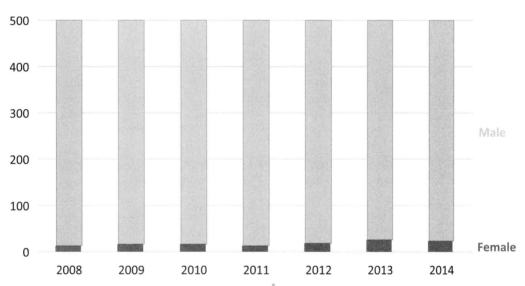

While increasing slightly over the years, female CEOs for Fortune 500s are still few in number.

Stacked columns create a visual chunk that is easier for the eye to detect, in my opinion, and this is helpful for those tiny trends. It is as if the area under the line in the line graph is filled in, creating more of a visual (and yes, an area graph would be an alternative).

FIGURE 9.12   The regular, not 100%, stacked column is sufficient because we are visualizing actual numbers and not percentages.

This graph is made using the Stacked Column graph type in Excel. Highlight all of your data and, in the *Insert* tab and inside the *Chart* family, click the column icon and then choose a *Stacked Column* (Figure 9.12, the second option in the top row).

EXCEL NINJA LEVEL: 2

This will cast your data into the stacked columns. The data will be even easier to interpret if your category of interest (female, in this case) is on the bottom of the stack. If it isn't, right-click on the graph and click *Select Data*. In the *Select Data* box, click the Female series in the window on the left and use the arrows to move the order. Changing the order here will adjust where each stack is located in the graph (Figure 9.13).

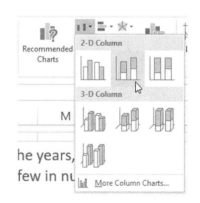

FIGURE 9.13   Click the arrow buttons to rearrange each series so that it is presented in the order you desire.

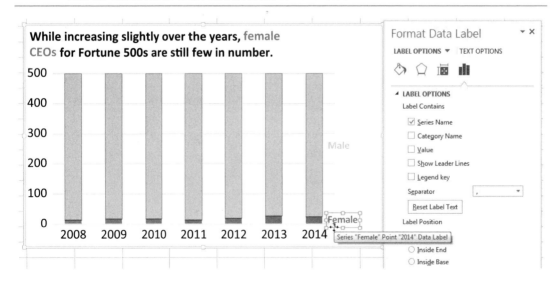

You'll also notice that I changed the colors of each segment so that the Male segments are all light gray, with a dark gray border and the Female segments are a more saturated blue. My labels are color-coded and out to the right of each series. You could insert these labels with textboxes if you'd like. I had Excel do the labeling for me by using the last stacked bar on the right (Figure 9.14).

FIGURE 9.14   Add the Series Name to the data label and remove Value.

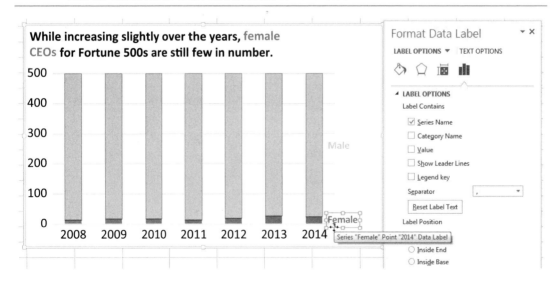

Click on one series (this will highlight all the segments for that series in each stack) and then click again on just the rightmost segment so that it is the only one highlighted. Then right-click on it and select *Add Data Label*. It will probably add the number instead of the word Female. So right-click on it again and choose *Format Data Label*.

In the *Format Data Label* menu, you can probably see that the only content currently checked is *Value*. First, check *Series Name* and then uncheck *Value* (Figure 9.15). This will populate the label with the word Female. If you look in *Label Position*, you'll see we don't get an automatic choice to pitch the label out to the right. So just hover over the label until your cursor turns into a pointy plus sign and then drag the label from the stack out to the right. If your label stays tied to your stack with a line, goodness please get rid of the line by unchecking *Show Leader Lines* in the *Format Data Label* menu.

Add stacked columns to your suite of choices for graphing trends over time. They are a great alternative to show small categories, such as college students who are homeowners vs. renters, days of sunshine vs. snowfall in Texas, or times you thought about sending me beer in the mail vs. times you actually did.

HOW CAN I SHOW THAT DOWN IS GOOD?

People from western cultures tend to see lines that trend upward as positive and lines that trend downward as bad. But, what if bad is good? And, not like my college boyfriend . . . but in the sense that a decrease is a good thing. Let's use the example of weight loss.

If you made a line graph of your weight while in an exercise program (Figure 9.10), it

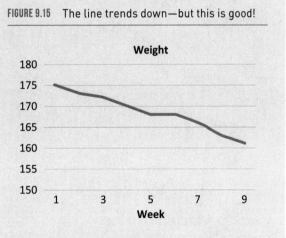

FIGURE 9.15   The line trends down—but this is good!

would (hopefully) trend downward, but down is usually interpreted as bad, especially when presented in the context of other metrics where down really is bad. Here are three possible ways to handle this scenario.

(Continued)

(Continued)

FIGURE 9.16   The line trends up—and this is good!

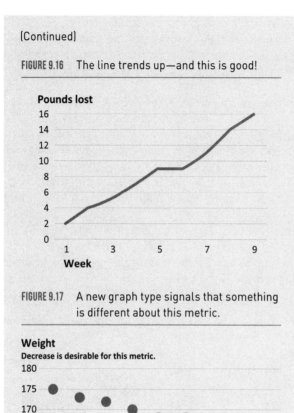

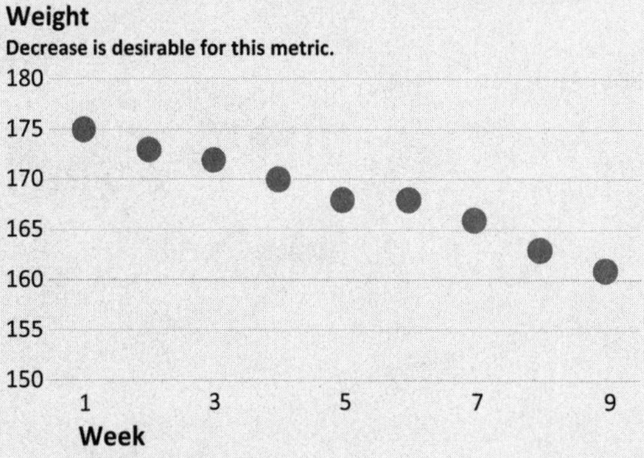

**Possibility 1:
Reverse the Variable**

This is my favorite suggestion because it's so simple. Rather than track weight, track cumulative pounds lost (Figure 9.16). This number will (hopefully) increase over time and it fits with our existing sense that up is good.

Such a very easy fix. That said, I've suggested this remedy to clients in the past who have literally cringed and/or laughed. Many times folks are not in a position where they can just transform variables.

FIGURE 9.17   A new graph type signals that something is different about this metric.

Weight
Decrease is desirable for this metric.

**Possibility 2:
Use a New Graph Type**

This suggestion is best when presenting this metric with several others that trend upward. To make it visually really clear that there is something different about this metric, change the graph type.

While line graphs are normally used to depict trends, a dot plot can work here because it's purpose is to say Hey this metric is not like the others—and the subtitle tells the story (see Figure 9.17).

Possibility 3: Shade under the Line

This is the most Excel ninja suggestion of them all, and this works best when down is good—to a point. Let's say your weight goal was 165. Figure 9.18 shows that down was good until week 7 and then down became bad. We have a benchmark target weight for comparison and we can shade the areas between the trend line and the benchmark to help show the difference.

The ninja skills required for this one are beyond the scope of this book, I'm sorry to say. Mainly because I don't fully understand the formulas required, myself! Check the exercises at the end of the chapter for access to the original spreadsheet that this viz was based on, and see what you can work out.

What about changing the order of the y-axis so that the trend is essentially reversed? Then the

FIGURE 9.18   Changing the shading of the area between the actual and benchmark lines indicates that down was good and then bad for a period.

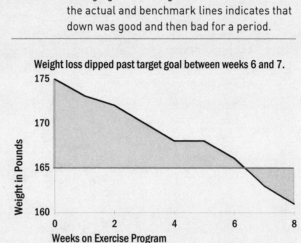

same data would be on a line going up. Muscatello, Searles, Macdonald, and Jorm (2006) ran a randomized controlled trial on graph types and compared a typical line graph where decrease is actually supposed to be good to a line graph with a reversed y-axis so that up was good. They found that accurate interpretation of the trend nearly tripled. Yowza! But, I have to wonder how closely respondents looked at the y-axis labels when making their judgements because the reversal of the axis is an unusual sight. It violates some of our graphing traditions and has led to at least one recent visualization that was targeted as misleading by national news sources. Take your chances?

DEVIATION BAR

Here's what typically happens when I'm helping an organization figure out whether its interventions are making a difference in the world: We devise instruments to measure impact, start measuring, and keep measuring every six months or so for several years. Why measure so often? Well, as you likely know, we are monitoring the outcomes, looking for any signs that we may need to make a midcourse correction. Good! That's what should happen! And we would show those changes as a line graph. But, usually the only data we ultimately care about at the end of the project is how much change has happened since the beginning. So let's just show the change; and the way to show that is with a deviation bar graph.

Thankfully, there's nothing really complicated about making a deviation bar graph. The magic happens in the data table.

In this example (Figure 9.19), I'm seeking to display U.S. Census projections for proportion of population by race from the collection in 2012 to 2060. Races are in Column A

EXCEL NINJA LEVEL: 3

FIGURE 9.19   Add a new column and calculate the difference.

▲	A	B	C	D
1		2012	2060	Growth
2	2 or More Races	2.4%	6.4%	4.0%
3	Asian Americans	5.1%	8.2%	3.1%
4	African Americans	13.0%	15.0%	2.0%
5	American Indian & Alaska Native	1.2%	1.5%	0.3%
6	Native Hawaiian & Other PI	0.2%	0.3%	0.1%
7	White	78.0%	69.0%	-9.0%
8	Hispanic (of any race)	17.0%	31.0%	14.0%
9	Non-Hispanic	63.0%	43.0%	=C9-B9

and the Census data are in Columns B and C. If we were to just graph that data, it would look very much like the Census's own visualization (Figure 9.20).

Not only does this kind of display minimize growth in smaller groups, it also puts a lot of burden on the reader. For many, the real question will be, "How much change has

FIGURE 9.20   A side by side column chart dwarfs smaller racial groups.

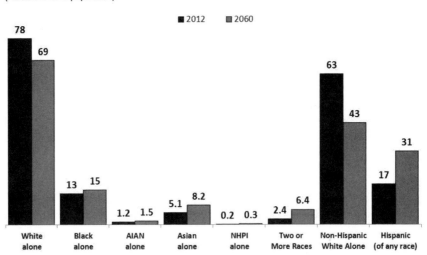

Population by Race and Hispanic Origin: 2012 and 2060
(Percent of total population)

■ 2012   ■ 2060

AIAN=American Indian and Alaska Native; NHPI=Native Hawaiian and Other Pacific Islander

United States™ Census Bureau
U.S. Department of Commerce
Economics and Statistics Administration
U.S. CENSUS BUREAU

SOURCE: United States Census Bureau

FIGURE 9.21   This map is a great example of incredibly misleading data visualization.

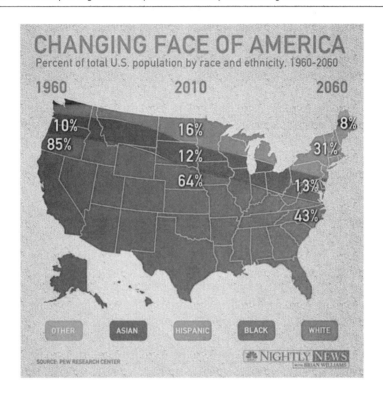

occurred?" And to figure that out, the reader has to subtract the tops of each column, a bunch of math that most people don't want to take on.

In fact, it could be even worse.

The display of the data in Figure 9.21 is from the Nightly News with Brian Williams and was likely an area graph that some well-intentioned designer masked with a map of the United States, but the unexpected consequence is that the visualization makes it appear as if all the white people live in the south and that all the Asians moved to Canada in 2020. Moreover, imagine actually trying to figure out how much change has occurred from a visualization like this! Yikes!

The better option in this case is to just graph the change. You can see I added Column D, where I simply subtracted the 2012 figures from the 2060 figures to calculate the change. Also—importantly—I reordered the original categories so that they run from largest to smallest growth. And in this case, I did so twice. First, I highlighted rows two through seven. Then I clicked on the drop-down arrow by the *Sort* button, which is all the way over on the right in the *Home* tab. Click on *Custom Sort* from the drop-down menu (see Figure 9.22).

This action opens a new window.

FIGURE 9.22   Sort the data before graphing so it will run greatest to least.

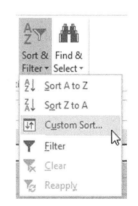

In the window I'm showing in Figure 9.23, I specified that I'd like Excel to sort on Column D and that the sort should be greatest to least. I repeated this process for rows eight and nine since those are technically a different set of variables, ethnicity, not race (and oh my, the Census is a bit confused on this).

Now that the table is all set, highlight that Growth column and insert a regular bar graph (Figure 9.24).

FIGURE 9.23   Tell Excel how you'd like it to resort your table.

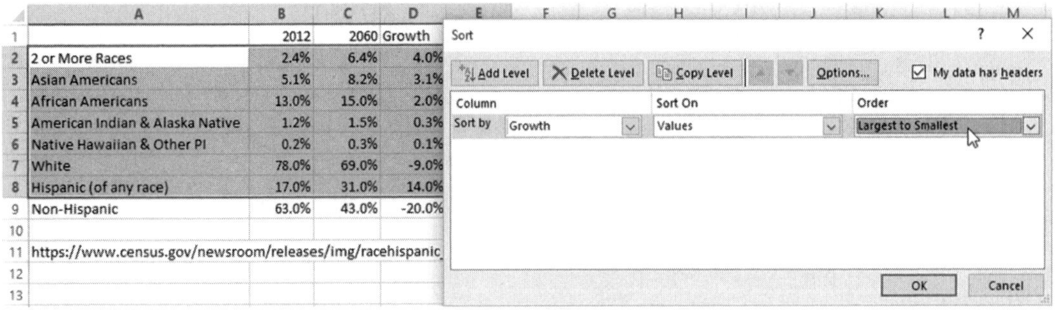

FIGURE 9.24   The very familiar bar graph will do the trick for a deviation bar.

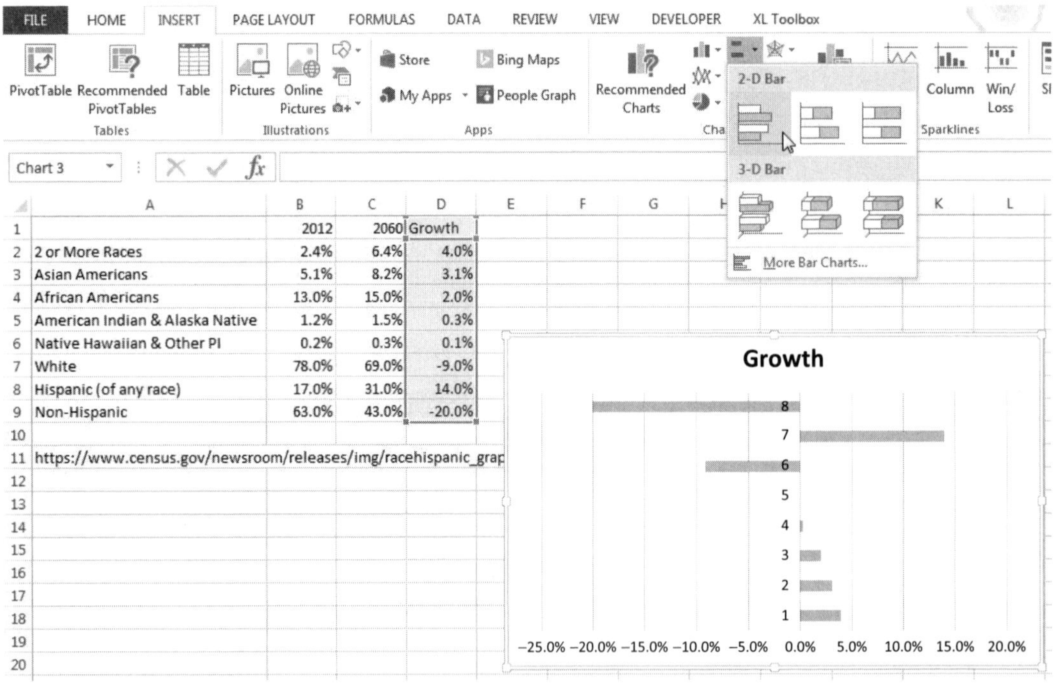

If you compare the graph (Figure 9.24) to the table (Figure 9.20), it's pretty clear that the graph is in the reverse order (yet another sign that perhaps Excel really hates me). Right-click on the y-axis (in the center of the graph) and select *Format Axis*. We are going to adjust several things in this new window.

To get the categories running from greatest to least within each grouping, check the box in the middle of the window that says *Categories in Reverse Order* (Figure 9.25).

You'll notice when you check that box that the bars rearrange, but Excel also pulls your x-axis to the top of the graph and that's terrible. Push it back down to the bottom of the graph. Look at the set of options here called *Horizontal axis crosses* and click the radio button by *At maximum category*. Boom.

Soon, we will add the actual category names—the races and ethnicities—instead of the numbers 1 through 8 running down the middle. But, won't that be annoying? Some bars are going to cover the labels and make it hard to read them. We can fix that by sending the labels all the way out to the left. In this same menu (Figure 9.25), open the section called *Labels* and then in the *Label Position* menu, select *Low*.

FIGURE 9.25   Sort categories in reverse order and make the x-axis cross at the maximum category.

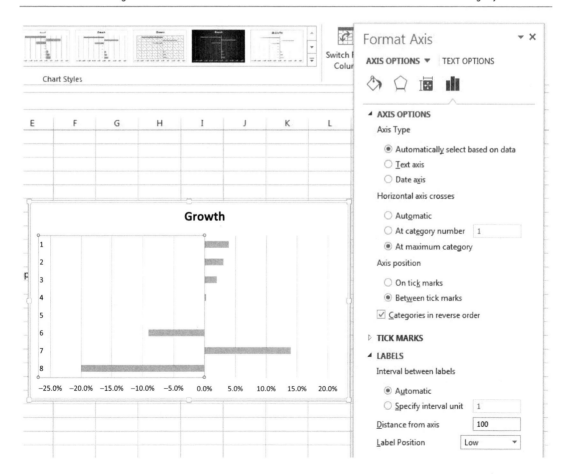

FIGURE 9.26   Add the names of the races and ethnicities.

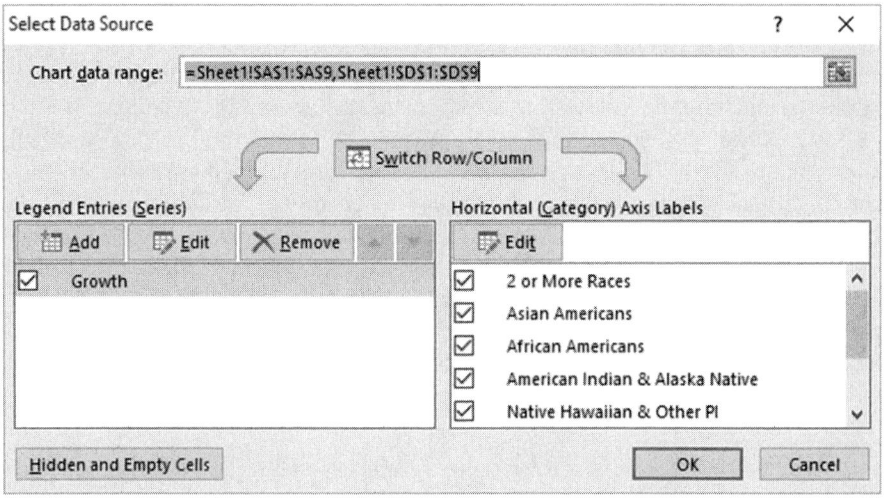

Great! Now that the labels are in the right spot, let's add the proper names. Right-click on the graph and choose *Select Data*.

In this window, you'll see the label names one through seven listed over on the right under *Horizontal (Category) Axis Labels*. Click the *Edit* button and then use your mouse to select the cells with your labels. Click OK a couple times.

The y-axis is now rocking, but the x-axis looks like a hot mess. Right-click on it and choose *Format Axis* (Figure 9.27).

In here, let's adjust the minimum and maximum values so that the axis runs from −0.2 to 0.15, closer to our data (Figure 9.27). We can also remove the extra decimal from the axis numbers by opening the *Values* window and changing the *Decimal places* number from 1 to 0. Or, once you have the axis range all set, you could delete the axis and the gridlines and add data labels to the deviation bars (right-click on the bars and pick *Add data labels*).

We are almost done. The bars themselves are looking really wimpy. Bulk them up by reducing the gap width between the bars. Such Excel geek speak! Right-click on any bar and select *Format Data Series*. In that window, move the slider next to Gap Width way to the left (Figure 9.28).

For my final touches, I'll change the colors of the bars and the data labels. I'll drag some of the labels outside of the bars (the ones that are overlapping the end of the bar). And I'll add a title (see Figure 9.29).

Visualizing the data in this manner means we have lost the actual figures in terms of the percentages in 2012 and 2060 for each race, but the story it captures is the amount of change that is expected to take place.

If you wanted to show the actual values in both years as well as the growth, you could simply insert Data Bars within the spreadsheet using Conditional Formatting, just as we showed in Chapter 4 (see Figure 9.30).

FIGURE 9.27   Change the minimum and maximum values of the axis.

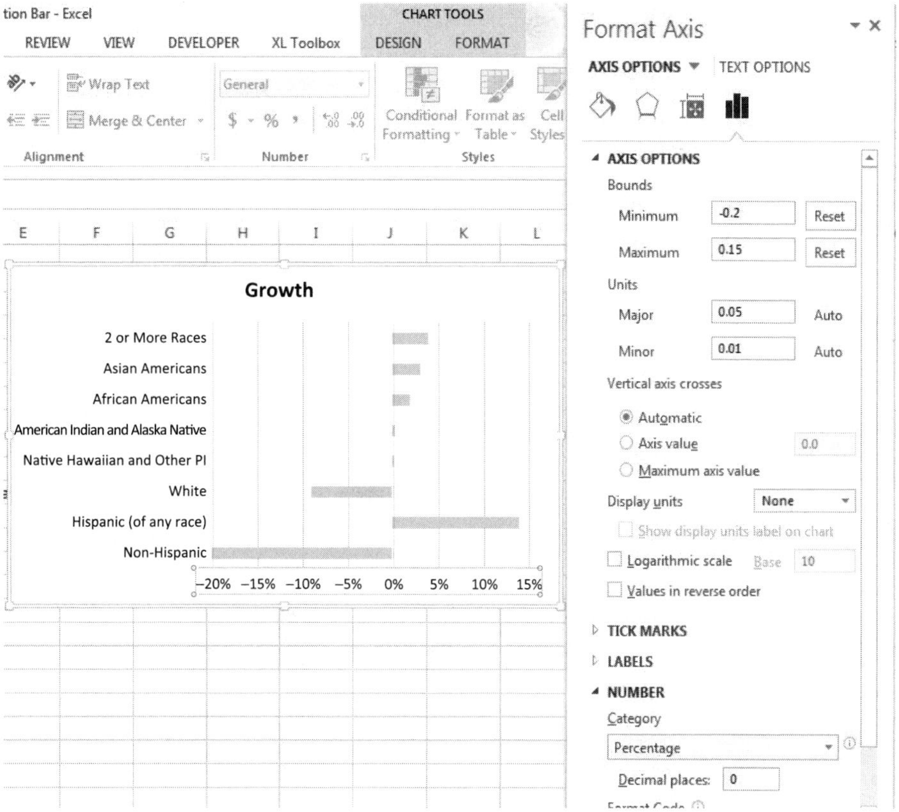

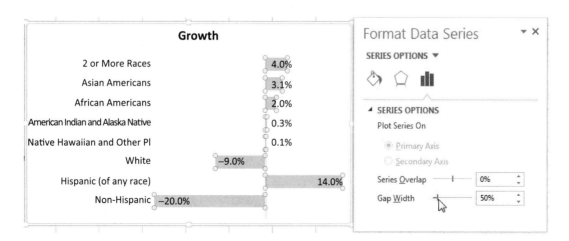

FIGURE 9.28   Reduce the gap width to make the bars taller.

FIGURE 9.29   The final deviation bar just shows how much change will occur.

From 2012 to 2060, the US Census predicts increases for all races except White.

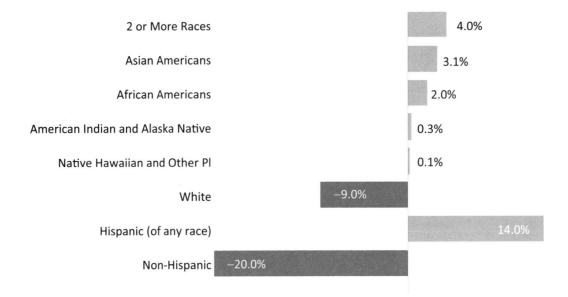

FIGURE 9.30   With data bars we can recreate the same deviation bar graph within the data table.

	A	B	C	D	E
1		2012	2060	Growth	
2	2 or More Races	2.4%	6.4%	4.0%	
3	Asian Americans	5.1%	8.2%	3.1%	
4	African Americans	13.0%	15.0%	2.0%	
5	American Indian & Alaska Native	1.2%	1.5%	0.3%	
6	Native Hawaiian & Other PI	0.2%	0.3%	0.1%	
7	White	78.0%	69.0%	-9.0%	
8	Hispanic (of any race)	17.0%	31.0%	14.0%	
9	Non-Hispanic	63.0%	43.0%	-20.0%	

SLOPEGRAPH (AS A MACRO)

We covered slopegraphs in Chapter 3, when we were comparing two things. What makes slopegraphs such stunners these days is that we can also use them to show change over time. If you want to make a slopegraph, just go back to Chapter 3 and follow the directions there. And if you want to make a second slopegraph, start back in Chapter 3 and follow the directions again. Getting tedious? I know. This is where we need to introduce macros. Macros score maximum ninja points.

A macro is a set of instructions or code that tells Excel what to do (i.e., make a slopegraph). We actually create the macro ourselves by recording our movements the first time we make a slopegraph (and the second and the third time since this takes some practice). While Excel is recording our movements, it is behind the scenes, writing code. The next time we need to make a slopegraph, we just tell Excel to run the code. If you are scared of code, rest slightly assured because this process is surprisingly easy, but it will require some trial and error.

First things first, make sure you have the macro capabilities in your Excel ribbon. It is in the *Developer* tab. If you do not see a tab called *Developer,* click the *File* tab and then click on *Options.* You'll see the window in Figure 9.31.

EXCEL NINJA LEVEL: 10

FIGURE 9.31   Add the Developer tab to the ribbon.

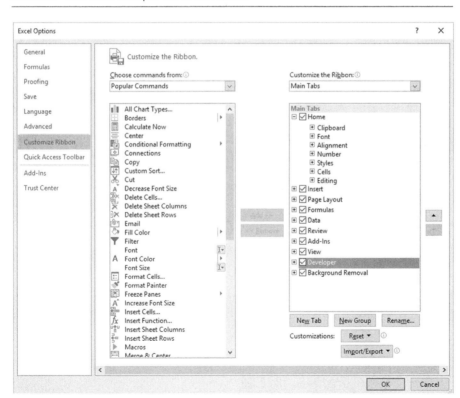

In the menu on the far left, click *Customize Ribbon*. You'll see a set of options to add to the ribbon. Locate *Developer* in this list and click the *Add* button in the middle of the screen. Then *Developer* will appear in the list on the right. Click OK. You may need to close and reopen Excel.

Now you'll see a new tab called *Developer* (see Figure 9.32).

FIGURE 9.32   The Developer tab is where you can work with macros.

The important button at this point is the one that says *Record Macro* (I told you this was easy!).

As soon as you click OK, Excel is recording your movements. You can tell this because the *Record Macro* button changes to a *Stop Recording Macro* button. So you go about making your graph.

The thing is, there's only so much the macro will be able to do for you. Some ninja moves break it. You'll get a lovely error box, and if you're like me, you'll have no clue what went wrong.

When I recorded the macro for the slopegraph, I was able to get only so far (see Figure 9.34).

Things I could record as a macro

FIGURE 9.33   Name and describe your macro so you can locate it easily in the future.

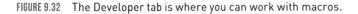

- Selecting all data (Hint: Make sure cell A1 has a label in it. Put your cursor there and then hold down Control + Shift and then arrow down and over to capture all data in the table.)
- Inserting a line graph
- Switching row/column to get six lines between two points
- Adding and formatting data labels
- Deleting the legend
- Deleting the y-axis

Things that broke the macro

- Deleting gridlines
- Changing plot size
- Changing graph aspect ratio
- Changing colors

FIGURE 9.34   The macro can take me about 85% of the way to a finished slopegraph.

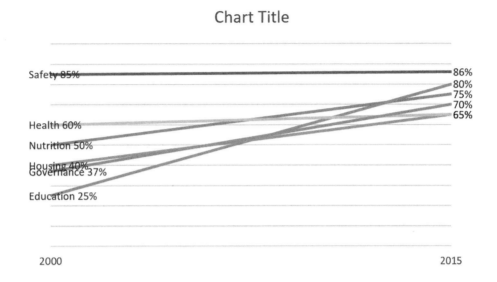

You will have to manually make these changes after the macro has run. And some of that manual work is just as it should be. For example, the colors should be leveraged to highlight key patterns, which is going to be different from graph to graph and will require your human brain to interpret and apply.

When you want to run the macro again, you'll want to start by placing your cursor in the A1 cell (or the equivalent for your table).

If you keep getting errors, try to build the macro one step at a time, basically testing what ninja moves give the macro a headache. If you know something about code, you can also attempt to debug the code and modify the piece that is causing the error.

Even though macros leave a little cleaning up to do, those of us generating graphs en masse will save approximately a billion hours of our lives by automating graph development to the extent possible.

DOT PLOT (AS A MACRO)

Oh yes, baby. We can use macros to speed up the generation of other graph types too.

Dot plots are such a blast because they can be used to show change over time as well. But, the process is just ever so slightly different because macros are a bit finicky. The main difference is in how the data table is set up.

Remember when we made dot plots back in Chapter 3? We had one secret y-axis column called DOT SPACING that helped us move each set of dots onto its own line. Macros don't like using the same column of data repeatedly. So, we need to create a secret DOT SPACING column for each series we want in the graph.

EXCEL NINJA LEVEL: 10

FIGURE 9.35   Each data series needs it's very own secret dot spacing column to love and cherish.

	A	B	C	D	E
1		Fall	FALL DOT SPACING	Spring	SPRING DOT SPACING
2	Literacy	34	5	69	5
3	Language	63	4	77	4
4	Mathematics	67	3	75	3
5	Science	92	2	98	2
6	Creative Arts	96	1	100	1

Then you'll hit that *Record Macro* button and move through the same steps we outlined in Chapter 3, just choosing each series and it's very own DOT SPACING column when adding the data to the graph. This means that if you want to use the Excel ninja method of adding the subject areas to each dot pair via a third set of dots (see Chapter 3), those data points will need a DOT SPACING column, too.

Excel let me use the macro to achieve an almost complete dot plot (Figure 9.36).

Things that broke the macro

- Changing the color of the dots
- Removing the vertical gridlines

FIGURE 9.36   The macro saved me dozens of clicks.

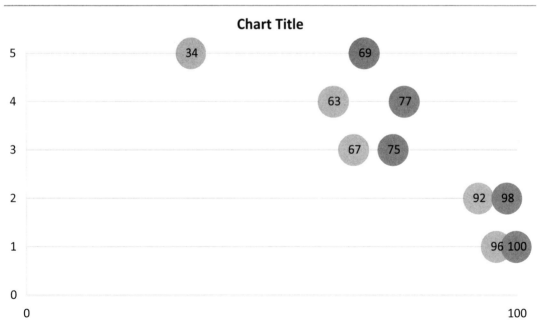

- Linking the labels (one through five) to the subject areas
- Moving the labels (one through five) out to the left
- Shrinking the plot area to make room for the subject area labels that would have been out to the left

So, you'll still have some clicking to do to finish, but the macro will take care of about 75% of the clicks it takes to make a dot plot.

Just remember, you'll need to save your file as a Macro-Enabled Workbook (Figure 9.37).

FIGURE 9.37   Choose *Macro-Enabled Workbook* from your file type menu.

File name:	Macros	⌄
Save as type:	Excel Macro-Enabled Workbook	⌄

And when you open the file again to use it, you'll likely see a yellow banner across the top of your spreadsheet that prompts you to enable the macros in order to use them (Figure 9.38). (Yes, *that's* what that notice has always been about.)

We are really only dipping our toes into the macro water here—macros are very powerful tools. Heading down this road might mean you learn a bit about coding (which earns you nerd cool points) because it can be handy to know how to debug the code when something's gone wrong—and it will. But, even if you just run through basic functions like we've done here, you'll move up several Excel ninja levels.

FIGURE 9.38   Click the Enable Macros button to make them functional.

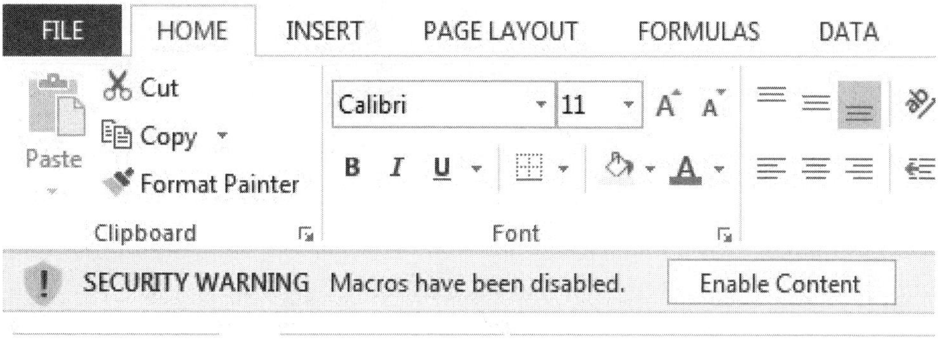

| FILE | HOME | INSERT | PAGE LAYOUT | FORMULAS | DATA |

Calibri 11

Cut, Copy, Format Painter, Paste — Clipboard, Font

SECURITY WARNING Macros have been disabled.   Enable Content

SANKEY

Funny name, right? I always think it's a typo for "snakey" because that's what this diagram looks like. It's a way to depict flow (usually over time) between lots of different stations. In fact . . . that super famous Minard visualization of Napoleon's march over

Moscow . . . you know the one . . . would be considered a Sankey. The width of each section communicates quantity from one station to the next.

These diagrams in Figure 9.39 tend to be pretty intuitive to read, but let's walk through one anyhow. Essentially, the diagram shows money flowing in and out of a household. On the left are the four roommates, who each contribute a certain amount of money each month. Each roommate is responsible for paying a share of the major expenses, which are listed on the right (except for Rose and her undying love for St. Olaf—she's the only one responsible for that expense). Not everyone pays an equal share, as you can see, because Dorothy's flow to Rent is thicker than the others. And not everyone is buying into Netflix. When you hover, you can see a somewhat crude popup that reveals the details of that segment of the flow. Cool, right?

FIGURE 9.39   Sankey diagrams capture flow from one point to another, where the line thickness indicates quantity.

Stephanie's Sankey Diagram stephanieevergreen.com

Drag to rearrange nodes. acknowlegement for d3.js and sankey diagram to Mike Bostok

EXCEL NINJA LEVEL: 5

I've never seen a better visualization for flow that has many inputs and many outputs. Can you make it in Excel? It certainly isn't a default graph type. But, some really awesome people out there (namely, Mike Bostock and Bruce McPherson) have written the code (similar to the macros we recorded earlier in this chapter) that generate Sankey diagrams. Figure 9.40 shows what the table looks like.

FIGURE 9.40   You populate the table with your inputs, outputs, and quantities and—boom—sankey diagram.

	A	B	C	D	E	F	G	H
1	SourceID	TargetID	SourceLabel	TargetLabel	Value			
2	1-Rose	2-Rent	Rose	Rent	100			
3	1-Dorothy	2-Rent	Dorothy	Rent	150			
4	1-Blanche	2-Rent	Blanche	Rent	100			
5	1-Sophia	2-Rent	Sophia	Rent	75			
6	1-Rose	2-Groceries	Rose	Groceries	40			
7	1-Dorothy	2-Groceries	Dorothy	Groceries	40		create	
8	1-Blanche	2-Groceries	Blanche	Groceries	60		sankey	
9	1-Sophia	2-Groceries	Sophia	Groceries	25			
10	1-Rose	2-Netflix	Rose	Netflix	0			
11	1-Dorothy	2-Netflix	Dorothy	Netflix	0			
12	1-Blanche	2-Netflix	Blanche	Netflix	5			
13	1-Sophia	2-Netflix	Sophia	Netflix	5			
14	1-Rose	2-Utilities	Rose	Utilities	50			
15	1-Dorothy	2-Utilities	Dorothy	Utilities	50			
16	1-Blanche	2-Utilities	Blanche	Utilities	50			
17	1-Sophia	2-Utilities	Sophia	Utilities	30			
18	1-Rose	2-Housekeeping	Rose	Housekeeping	25			
19	1-Dorothy	2-Housekeeping	Dorothy	Housekeeping	25			
20	1-Blanche	2-Housekeeping	Blanche	Housekeeping	25			
21	1-Sophia	2-Housekeeping	Sophia	Housekeeping	15			
22	1-Rose	2-St Olaf Children's Choir	Rose	St Olaf Children's Choir	100			
23								

You'll never enter text into Columns A or B. You'll insert your inputs into Column C. Output data goes in Column D. Those two feed into Columns A and B automatically. Each section of the flow needs its own line. So, Rose's rent payment of $100 means that Rose (input) goes in Column C, Rent (output) goes into Column D, and 100 (the quantity, in raw number) goes into Column E.

You'll notice that Columns A and B have 1's and 2's in front of each cell. This tells the diagram where to put the data. One designations are things that go all the way to the left in the Sankey—all the inputs. Two designations comprise the next set of stations—which means that, yes, you could add a third or fourth or fifth set of stations, you crazy monster.

You can also color code the stations by changing the fill color of the cells in the first two columns. These will carry over to the live diagram. Then you click the *Create Sankey* button and it publishes a live diagram in your browser window. Aren't Mike and Bruce amazing? Check the Resources at the end of this chapter to see where to download the file so you can try it out for yourself.

Line graphs are never going away (nor should they), but other graph types can help us emphasize different stories about how things changed over time. Try something new. Set aside a half hour, grab your favorite beverage, and plunge methodically into the world of macros. The near-term effort has long-term benefits for your longitudinal data.

EXERCISES

Head over to http://davidmerlemontgomery.blogspot.com/2009/09/two-color-xy-area-combo-chart.html where David Merle Montgomery has done some magic to create the intersecting line chart with the different colored fill areas. Read his instructions carefully and try to mess with the graph to make it fit your own data. You'll see it breaks. David told me that one big deal is that the formula in Column D has an error. Instead of dividing by 15, the formula needs to divide by the maximum value in Column A. So replace "15" with "MAX(A7:A14)" and it should work. Create your own graph.

Try a macro. Just do it. Download the sample data file from http://study.sagepub.com/evergreen edv and choose either a slopegraph or dot plot. Be patient and brave. It's easier than it looks, and will leave you feeling like a rock star.

The Sankey Excel file is located at http://ramblings.mcpher.com/Home/excelquirks/d3/sankey where you'll also find instructions for what code to change and what not to touch, along with acknowledgements to Mike Bostock and his work in other programs that have made it possible to hack a Sankey out of Excel. Bless these people. I made that whole example look easy, but the spreadsheet in the website will take a second to figure out. Set aside a little time and have fun! Develop a Sankey diagram that shows your household's expense flow for a month.

RESOURCES

I know you are curious about which recent graph came under fire (hint, hint) for using a reversed y-axis to change the perception of the trend over time. PS Mag is one source that discussed the issue, so go find out the culprit at http://www.psmag.com/politics-and-law/mislead-charts-stand-ground-laws-gun-deaths-79726

Run a quick Google search on Sankey diagrams and you'll also find several software packages that you can purchase which may have more features to them. Sankey visuals are growing in popularity.

Wondering if it's possible to create a break in the y-axis to show that it isn't starting at zero? Check out this step by step guide by Alesandra Blakeston on how to hack the axis at https://alesandrab.wordpress.com/2014/03/17/broken-column-and-bar-charts/

We've reached into the depths of what Excel can do and wrestled out some pretty amazing and compelling graphics. But, there's so much more than can be done with code. Learn more about coding and macros by searching "Excel VBA tutorial," or "Excel macros tutorial" and you'll launch into a path of coding. I'll come tap you on the shoulder to remind you to take breaks every 45 minutes. Seriously, it's a worm hole and you'll learn a ton of cool stuff on the way. Tell me all about it. ♥

REFERENCES

American Psychological Association. (2010). *Publication manual of the American Psychological Association* (6th ed.). Washington, DC: Author.

Javed, W., McDonnel, B., & Elmqvist, N. (2010). Graphical perception of multiple time series. *Visualization and Computer Graphics, IEEE Transactions on Visualizations and Computer Graphics, 16*(6), 927–934.

Muscatello, D. J., Searles, A., Macdonald, R., & Jorm, L. (2006). Communicating population health statistics through graphs: A randomized controlled trial of graph design interventions. *BMC medicine, 4*(1), 33.

Zacks, J., & Tversky, B. (1999). Bars and lines: A study of graphic communication. *Memory & Cognition, 27*(6), 1073–1079.

10

IT'S ABOUT MORE THAN THE BUTTONS

n this chapter you'll learn that while it's awesome to ninja Excel, it's really about something much bigger. There's nothing better than leading a class through an Excel training course because all throughout people exclaim "Yes!" and toss each other high fives and all sorts of wonderfully geeky outcries of elation and joy. Mastering the tools is a rad feeling, but the real riches are in what happens afterward.

Visualizing data effectively changes the conversation. It shapes organizational culture and grows leadership. It streamlines decision making and generates action. Remember the philanthropic foundation I discussed in Chapter 4? The simple revision of their dashboard led to a wholesale communication overhaul for everything internal and external because they realized the value they get by having clear conversations. Here are a few more examples.

DOT PLOTS GENERATE HEALTHCARE PIONEERS

Longtime clients, Oregon Health Authority (OHA), asked me to make a template for their report on health indicators. Every health indicator was going to have the same two-page spread, based on the template I was creating. They were seeking to communicate how much growth had occurred in the past couple of years and they wanted to compare growth across several categories like race (see Figure 10.1).

I created dot plots as part of the template and then I emailed the file to the team at OHA, a department of researchers. They cringed and said uh. . . . what's that thing? See, researchers who work with data in Excel for a long time can get a little uncomfortable with new graph types. But, I explained that position on a common scale is the easiest thing for people to interpret. I encouraged them to show the template to some members of their target population. They selected a few doctors, nurses, journalists, and members of the public who loved it so much, they asked the OHA researchers for the Excel template so they could make their own dot plots.

FIGURE 10.1   Dot plots in action! They show growth in the percentage of youngsters who had developmental screenings, by race/ethnicity, for three years.

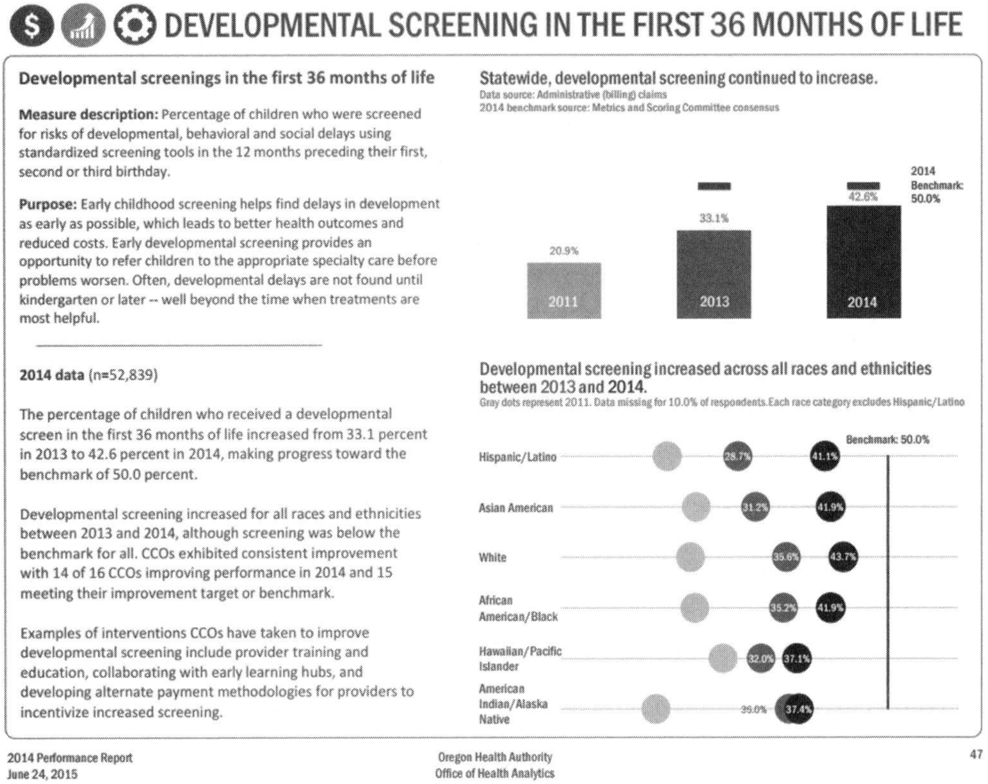

DEVELOPMENTAL SCREENING IN THE FIRST 36 MONTHS OF LIFE

Developmental screenings in the first 36 months of life

Measure description: Percentage of children who were screened for risks of developmental, behavioral and social delays using standardized screening tools in the 12 months preceding their first, second or third birthday.

Purpose: Early childhood screening helps find delays in development as early as possible, which leads to better health outcomes and reduced costs. Early developmental screening provides an opportunity to refer children to the appropriate specialty care before problems worsen. Often, developmental delays are not found until kindergarten or later -- well beyond the time when treatments are most helpful.

2014 data (n=52,839)

The percentage of children who received a developmental screen in the first 36 months of life increased from 33.1 percent in 2013 to 42.6 percent in 2014, making progress toward the benchmark of 50.0 percent.

Developmental screening increased for all races and ethnicities between 2013 and 2014, although screening was below the benchmark for all. CCOs exhibited consistent improvement with 14 of 16 CCOs improving performance in 2014 and 15 meeting their improvement target or benchmark.

Examples of interventions CCOs have taken to improve developmental screening include provider training and education, collaborating with early learning hubs, and developing alternate payment methodologies for providers to incentivize increased screening.

Statewide, developmental screening continued to increase.
Data source: Administrative (billing) claims
2014 benchmark source: Metrics and Scoring Committee consensus

2014 Benchmark: 50.0%

42.6%
33.1%
20.9%
2011   2013   2014

Developmental screening increased across all races and ethnicities between 2013 and 2014.
Gray dots represent 2011. Data missing for 10.0% of respondents. Each race category excludes Hispanic/Latino

Benchmark: 50.0%

Hispanic/Latino	28.7%	41.1%
Asian American	31.2%	41.9%
White	35.6%	43.7%
African American/Black	35.2%	41.9%
Hawaiian/Pacific Islander	32.0%	37.1%
American Indian/Alaska Native	35.0%	37.4%

2014 Performance Report   Oregon Health Authority   47
June 24, 2015   Office of Health Analytics

SOURCE: Stephanie Evergreen (2015). "CCO Graph." Oregon Health Authority Office of Health Analytics. Used with permission.

A few more reports down the road, my friends at OHA passed along an email of kudos that reads, in part, "I just wanted to send you a quick note to let you know that I just read through the 2014 Performance Report, and I was exceptionally impressed by its readability and the visualizations throughout. It wasn't just attractive, but also very easy to understand—bringing those together is exceptionally difficult to do with complex health data like this. Anyhow, I just wanted to make sure you knew that someone out in CCO-land appreciates the work you and your team do to help us understand how we can work to improve the health of our communities."

The impact for Oregon Health Authority is clear communication, a greater understanding of health status in Oregon, more support for healthcare workers and most of all, community leadership on important topics—way more important than the steps it takes to create an amazing graph.

CLEARLY LABELED LINE GRAPHS STREAMLINE DECISIONS AT A FORTUNE 500

Like many organizations, Verizon Telecommunications Company was in the rush to be data driven. They were collecting every bit of data they could accumulate, but it was almost like they had too much data. They didn't know how to make sense of all the information they had collected. So, they ended up with slides full of tables with text so tiny it wasn't legible. They were producing slides like this (Figure 10.2), which is totally not real data at all.

Believe it or not, there are three stories embedded in this chaotic slide.

FIGURE 10.2   Existing slide designs were confusing, requiring a lot of explanation and discussion.

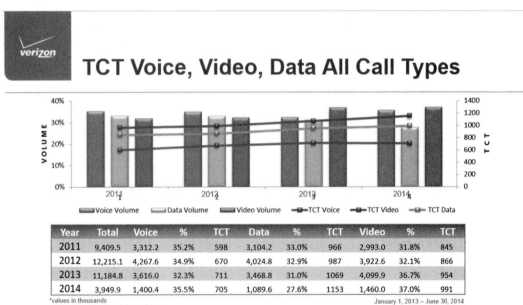

SOURCE: Courtesy of Verizon. Used with permission.

Geoff Walls, vice president of product marketing and communications at Verizon, put it this way: "Our challenge at Verizon is that we've got more data and more information on what's going on, or investments we're making, or customer purchase patterns. Ultimately, we have to take all that data and synthesize it into something that we can make decisions on."

Everyone who looked at the slides, including those who made them, had trouble distinguishing the important stuff—the signal from the noise. And as a result, Verizon was wasting time and money.

"It was a struggle and always required rounds and rounds of interaction in the business with the folks that have the data in hands, to come to conclusions via the data they were sharing," Geoff disclosed.

They lacked intentional reporting. Clear data visualization supports truth telling. It helps decision makers connect dots, engage in precise discussion, and make straightforward decisions. And that's where organizational culture is sculpted.

My colleague Gavin McMahon and I didn't radically overhaul anything for Verizon. We added simple visualizations to their tables of numbers. Things like sparklines to visualize their quarterly reporting. Bullet graphs to show how close they are to their target. And, where possible, we encouraged them to ditch tables in favor of line graphs and bar graphs. Nothing too radical—see Figure 10.3.

FIGURE 10.3   Grouping the items that belong together and using more straightforward data visualization clarified the story.

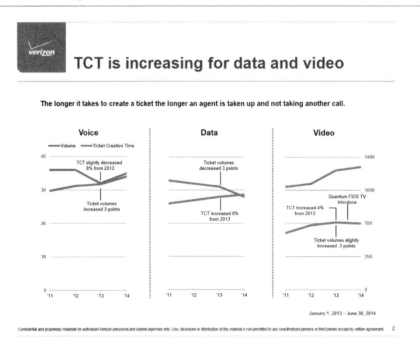

SOURCE: Courtesy of Verizon

In this particular case, we just rearranged all the chunks of the slide that belonged together so they told a complete story. The right line associated with the right columns (which we turned into a line) associated with the right parts of the table associated with the right bullet points (which we embedded into the graph as extra notes). Three stories, chunked together, on one slide. Clarity!

What happened? After a workshop delivered by me and Gavin, these baby steps toward better visualization were tested. It was good news and bad news.

One of the managers told us, "Our feedback on the weekly call was [Geoff, the boss] liked the new charts. He didn't like what they said (because we are going down), but he liked that they identified the issue clearly."

In other words, he was excited, not that the data pointed in the wrong direction, but that the graphs clearly showed performance. Geoff could anticipate results and take immediate action.

Geoff reports, "We're starting to see better decisions, more clarity, less top down, more true interaction between the levels of the organization, which is critical for our team culture."

Data visualization and intentional reporting are two of the most important tools to shape organizational culture.

DIVERGING STACKED BARS MAKE FOR COMMUNITY LEADERS IN THE MIDWEST

The Welborn Baptist Foundation works out of the very southern part of Indiana and tries to fix literally one of the hugest problems that part of the U. S. Midwest could face—obesity. By and large, the Foundation monitors health indicators throughout this cluster of geographic space where the bottom of Indiana, the bottom of Illinois, and the top of Kentucky all converge and where physical health is an uphill climb. Each year they publish a report on community health indicators, in an effort to lift awareness and provide data for the many nonprofits in the region focusing on the same work. Their report used to look like Figure 10.4.

And, it's worth noting that their "before" version still has more graphic enhancements to it than many reports I see—there's a photograph, a not too terrible table, some color highlighting on key words, and even a page number design. But, the graph . . . oh, the graph.

Then something pretty typical happened. The lead for this project, Liz Tharp, sat through one of my workshops and saw the possibilities. She started dreaming big about a total renovation. She understood that there were more graphing options than a simple clustered bar graph, but she caught the design bug and began rethinking everything—the photos, the layout, the whole package. How color can impact a graph is also how color can impact the full report (Evergreen, 2013).

Liz, her graphic designer, and I worked together on the next draft of the report. Total dream team—the program specialist, the designer, and the data viz expert. Together we produced Figures 10.5 and 10.6.

FIGURE 10.4   This page is a great start, but not quite as professional and on point as Welborn is in reality.

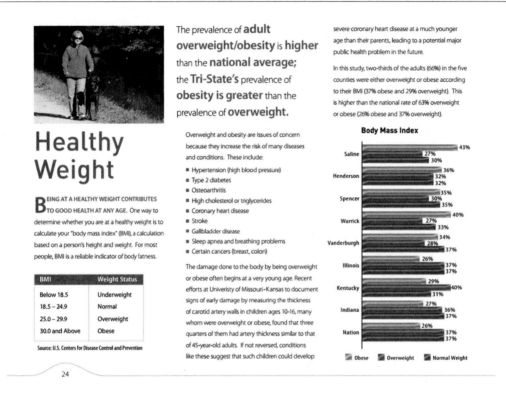

SOURCE: Liz Tharp (2014). "Welborn Before." Welborn Baptist Foundation. Used with permission.

Same page, revised. Into two pages. Usually people think it's a mortal sin to *add* pages to a report, but guess what? If the report is stunning to look at, and the content is educational and engaging, people don't care how long it is. In fact, they barely notice because they are so engrossed. It's only when each page is dull that people quickly flip through to see how many pages are left to have to read.

And we did keep a pretty basic chart style in the report. We added in a column graph of the state- and county-level data, color coded so that the darker shades represented the state and the lighter shades represented the counties. We also shook up that sad, beveled, clustered bar graph on weight categories. This kind of data is perfect for a diverging stacked bar, where it's much easier to see how the categories of concern add up for each county and compare across counties. In the upper right of Figure 10.6, you can also see that we added a variation on a thermometer graph, where the vertical line represents the ideal and the markers on either side show the U.S. average and the tri-state area average. That tiny graph packs in a ton of powerful data—and it's just a variation of the lollipop graphs we made in Chapter 5.

But, beyond that addition, the whole spread benefits from more white space, a better use of photography, cleaner fonts, and descriptive headings. Pow!

The real impact, though, is what happened afterwards. The report has been used by the Foundation as an entry point for conversations with the larger community about tackling health problems. They've shared the report during speaking engagements with specific nonprofit boards, county health officials, and collective impact groups to develop new programs aimed at increasing physical activity and nutrition. Liz said "The feedback we've received has been very positive. People say that the results of our survey have confirmed the top health issues for the Tri-State, and more importantly, have helped encourage conversations about strategies to improve those conditions."

FIGURES 10.5 AND 10.6   Interesting and revealing data visualizations help engage readers.

SOURCE: Liz Tharp (2015). "Welborn After 1." Welborn Baptist Foundation. Used with permission.

(Continued)

FIGURES 10.5 AND 10.6   (Continued)

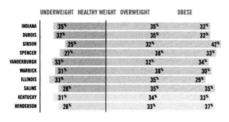

There tends to be **more obesity in the Tri-State region** compared to the U.S. as a whole. **One out of every three adults** in the Tri-State region is obese.

POOR

HEALTHY WEIGHT

TRI-STATE ▸ ◂ U.S.
34% | **29**%

TWO-THIRDS OF THE TRI-STATE ARE OVERWEIGHT OR OBESE.

	UNDERWEIGHT	HEALTHY WEIGHT	OVERWEIGHT	OBESE
INDIANA	35%	35%	32%	
DUBOIS	32%	35%	32%	
GIBSON	25%	32%	42%	
SPENCER	27%	38%	33%	
VANDERBURGH	33%	32%	34%	
WARRICK	31%	38%	30%	
ILLINOIS	33%	35%	29%	
SALINE	28%	35%	35%	
KENTUCKY	31%	34%	33%	
HENDERSON	28%	33%	37%	

For most adults, the BMI is a reliable indicator of whether one is underweight, normal/healthy weight, overweight or obese.

The Healthy People 2020 Initiative through the U.S. Department of Health and Human Services has set a national target for obese rates for adults age 20 and older to be no more than 30.5% by 2020. Currently, in the Tri-State region, just over 34% of all adults, (18 and older,) are obese.

BMI – ADULT BODY MASS INDEX

BMI	WEIGHT STATUS
Below 18.5	Underweight
18.5 – 24.9	Normal
25.0 – 29.9	Overweight
30.0 and above	Obese

OTHER LOCAL FINDINGS

MALES AND FEMALES HAVE SIMILAR RATES OF OBESITY

34% of males and 34% of females are obese. However, males are more likely to be overweight and females are more likely to be normal weight. Less than 2% of females and 1% of males are underweight

MIDDLE TO UPPER AGES REPORT MORE OBESITY

Between 35-74 years old obesity rates ranges from 34% to 41%. Younger than 35, rates are less than 33%. Rates of obesity are lowest among those 85 and older, only 11% report being in this weight category

BLACK ADULTS AND ADULTS IN "OTHER" RACIAL/ ETHNIC GROUPS REPORT HIGHEST OBESITY RATES

Respondents indicating an "Other" race/ ethnicity, e.g., Asian, Multi-racial adults, indicated the highest rates of obesity. 44%. Next highest are Black adults, 40%, then White adults, 34%, and Hispanic adults, 26%

OBESITY INCREASES WITH POVERTY

50% of individuals earning less than $10,000 are obese, compared to 29% of those earning $75,000 or more

OBESITY DECREASES WITH EDUCATION

Residents with a college degree are less likely to be obese than those with less education

OBESITY IS ASSOCIATED WITH POORER HEALTH OUTCOMES

Obese individuals in this survey are almost twice as likely to have arthritis, asthma, COPD, and high cholesterol, and twice as likely to have had a heart attack. They are also nearly three times as likely to have high blood pressure, about four times as likely to have coronary heart disease and five times likely to have diabetes compared to normal weight individuals

31

SOURCE: Liz Tharp (2015). "Welborn After 2." Welborn Baptist Foundation. Used with permission.

ICONS SUPPORT INFORMED POLICYMAKING

Rakesh Mohan works for the Idaho government, researching and evaluating topics that are coming up for legislation. He knew the politicians were having trouble engaging with his traditional long reports (Figure 10.7).

But, he hesitated to make them more visual with the concern that an opportunistic politico may accuse him of wasting taxpayer dollars. We held two workshops together and identified a perfect balance. Figure 10.8 illustrates our introduction of trim fonts and navigational icons and large well-constructed data visualizations.

It's truly some of the best reporting I've seen. Rakesh spelled out the impacts he has experienced since our work together.

"In less than a year since we first received training from Stephanie, I have clearly seen three benefits of embracing data visualization:

FIGURE 10.7   Rakesh's reports were conservative in design and lacked sustained interest.

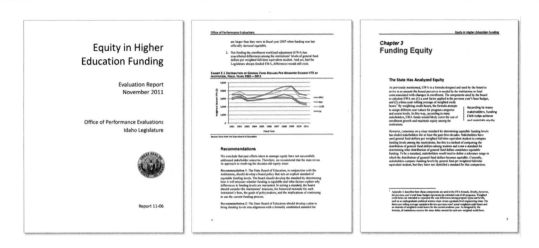

SOURCE: Rakesh Mohan (2012). "Rakesh Before." Idaho Office of Performance Evaluation. Used with permission.

FIGURE 10.8   The revised reports are magnets for attention and inspirations for action.

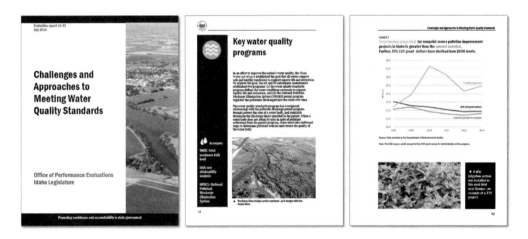

SOURCE: Rakesh Mohan (2015). "Rakesh After." Idaho Office of Performance Evaluation. Used with permission.

1. Collective Creativity. My staff love to work on data visualization and want to use their creative energy for producing evaluation reports that are used. They are eager to learn and help each other. As a result, the collective creativity of the office has increased tremendously. All staff, including consultants working on our projects, now feel that they have something special to contribute to the project. For example, on our water quality study, our consultant took the initiative to take aerial photographs from his

plane—all on his own time and dime. Because of our new emphasis on data visualization, he knew his pictures would have a place in the report and would be appreciated.

2. Clarity of Message. Increased emphasis on data visualization has forced us to be crystal clear about the main message of our reports and presentations. Because we are replacing the 1,000 words with a picture, we can no longer hide behind jargon and get away with a less clear message. Now we have to make sure that we have selected the 'right' picture so as to not give our readers and audiences a chance to find their own 1,000 words for interpreting the picture and derailing our intended message.

3. Flexibility. My personal favorite is the flexibility I have gained by using more pictures and fewer words for my slide presentations. Now, I can make last minute changes to my oral comments without worrying about making my spoken words exactly match with the written words on the slides. This helps me tailor my comments to meet the needs of my audiences."

A few months ago, I was back in Boise and had the privilege of attending a legislative session where Rakesh's team was presenting the results of their study to a committee. Slides included icon arrays and some other visuals from Chapter 1. After the hearing was over, Rakesh introduced me to the legislators, who thanked me for my work with his team because now it was so much easier for them to do their jobs well. They had clear, compelling, straightforward, easy-to-navigate answers to their hardest questions.

This kind of culture change happens consistently when we visualize data effectively. And it's the data nerds who lead the way!

The whole point of this chapter, and indeed this whole book, is that it is important to know which graph type is going to showcase your story the best—with the most accuracy and the most clarity. It is important to know how to create those graphs by mastering the tools you already own. This all makes us feel like rock stars. But, the real reason we devote our time and energy to the graph is because it is how people learn. It is how people come to understand information so that they can make decisions and take action. And this clear communication changes the game. Visualizing data effectively shows that we are credible, professional, and trustworthy. It makes data-driven decision making a true reality, transforming internal culture and external industry leadership. Our audiences are more informed, but also they are grateful and loyal because we have given them information they need in a format that is useful. We have cooperated with how their brains work.

Learning how to push the buttons is a critical skill, but it is just the means to a much greater end. I can't wait to see where you go.

EXERCISES

Save your "befores." When you embark on a redesign, you'll make such tremendous growth that you'll forget how far you've come. It's easy to lose sight of your progress. Don't forget to enact some version control so that you work in a new file. Because when it's time to make a pitch to your boss or team about overhauling the way you present data, the best argument will be your own development and you will need those "before" graphs as examples.

Save your "afters." Six months later, you'll look back on them with a slight twinge of shame and disgust. It happens to me all the time. The good news is that we are all evolving. You'll keep making progress. Track it.

Remake someone else's design, respectfully. Beginners in the data visualization world, especially, often find it a bit easier to hone their chops by revising a visualization in need of love somewhere out there in the world. Many well-known trustworthy visualization wizards and designers today got started by doing this very thing. It's tricky—you don't want to be rude—but try several revised visualizations and see if you can develop something clearer than the original. Then share it with the original designer—always in kindness and gratitude.

RESOURCES

For more on how to integrate a data visualization into a slide or a report page, check out my first book, *Presenting Data Effectively*.

We really killed it with our reports at Oregon Health Authority. The OHA reports are available here at **http://www.oregon.gov/oha/OHPR/RSCH/docs/OHPB/OHPB_030414_dashboard.pdf** and also at **http://www.oregon.gov/oha/Metrics/Documents/2014%20Final%20Report%20-%20 June%202015.pdf**

The Welborn report is wonderful and available by downloading the following website at **http://www .tristatecwi.org/sites/default/files/downloads/2015_TSHS.pdf**. Also check out their website at **http://www.tristatecwi.org/**, which goes into more detail and shows how the same data can be made a bit more interactive on the web.

Rakesh's work is all funded by taxpayers and thus is open to the public and can be retrieved from **https://legislature.idaho.gov/ope/publications/reports/ryear.htm**. Download anything he's published in the past two years for stellar examples of high quality reporting. Also snag his one-page handouts. For kicks, download something they published in 2012 and marvel at the growth that is possible in a short amount of time.

Check out an incredibly thoughtful post on how to gently critique data visualizations at **https:// medium.com/@hint_fm/design-and-redesign-4ab77206cf9**; This should be required reading for everyone.

REFERENCE

Evergreen, S. D. H. (2013). *Presenting data effectively*. Thousand Oaks, CA: SAGE.

• INDEX •